RACING'S
GREATEST
Characters

RACING'S
GREATEST
Characters

Fabulous Stories of
Winners and Losers,
Runners and Riders

GRAHAM SHARPE

BOOKS

First published in Great Britain in 2009 by
JR Books, 10 Greenland Street, London NW1 0ND
www.jrbooks.com

A catalogue record for this book is available from the British Library.

ISBN 978-1-906779-14-6

1 3 5 7 9 10 8 6 4 2

Printed by Thomson Litho Ltd, East Kilbride, Scotland

CONTENTS

INTRODUCTION

Racing abounds with great characters – well, with a history stretching back some five hundred years, the surprise would be if it didn't.

However, you need go no further than the closest racecourse to your front door to prove it for yourself. From the moment you reach the track and receive a cheerful welcome from some shady looking reprobate who invites you to part with several hard earned notes of currency in return for a piece of half dead, but allegedly 'lucky', heather, you'll see virtually nothing other than characters.

Characters keen to advise you on the next winner; characters anxious to ensure that you enjoy the experience of paying a vast amount of money for a very average repast; characters who appear from their mode of apparel to have come from an era already best part of a century gone – these are racehorse trainers, by the way – and other, colourfully clad, highly opinionated, quirkily shaped characters – these are either John McCririck – or, possibly – jockeys.

In this book, I have taken a purely arbitrary decision on who to include and who to omit and should you disagree with my selection and believe that I have left out certain candidates, then in the event of a follow-up volume I shall endeavour to correct the omission – just drop me a line care of the publisher or at gsharpe@williamhill.co.uk.

I have put in a number of obvious characters such as Frankie Dettori, Lester Piggott and John McCririck, but also delved back into the rich panoply of the past to emerge with characters whose names may not be immediately familiar but whose stories will fascinate and/or amuse you.

Graham Sharpe

LIVING LEGENDS

HENRY CECIL
Wonderful, what?

Everyone in racing loves Henry Cecil. Never has a trainer been so successful yet, apparently, so universally admired, respected and revered.

He is the urbane, elegant Englishman – born, ironically enough, in Aberdeen – who effortlessly bestrode the turf, sending out a lengthy string of Classic winners, all the while playing down his own importance in the scheme of things with a mixture of modesty and an slight air of bewilderment at his own proficiency and good fortune.

Cecil has a racing pedigree as illustrious as many of the thoroughbreds he has groomed for Classic success. Born on 11 January 1943, a few minutes before twin, David, Richard Henry Amherst Cecil is the stepson of former champion trainer Sir Cecil Boyd-Rochfort.

He never knew his real father, Henry senior, who was killed in North Africa, aged 28, whilst there serving with the Parachute Regiment, in circumstances which resulted in a posthumous recommendation for the VC, several weeks before the birth of his twin boys. His mother, Rohays, remarried to Sir Cecil.

Henry worked for his stepfather between 1964 and 1968, marrying Sir Noel Murless' daughter Julie in 1966, then took out a licence of his own in 1969, sending out his first winner, Celestial Cloud, a 5/1 shot, at Ripon on 17 May.

Lester Piggott related a wonderful story of the night in the early 1970s when Cecil dined with jockey Greville Starkey after he had won a big race at Deauville on Katie Cecil – named after Henry and Julie's daughter, Katrina. They flew back to London and celebrated in an up-market restaurant, where Starkey decided to give fellow diners the full benefit of his party piece – an imitation of a barking dog. 'The guests in the restaurant included some VIPs who seemed far from amused. But the "terrier" just wouldn't stop his barking and growling throughout the remainder of the meal. After they had settled their bill, Henry must have thought he couldn't be any more embarrassed, so he took hold of one of the napkins, rolled it into a loop and led Greville out of the place on all fours still barking like mad on the "lead".'

By 1975 he had registered his first English Classic win when Bolkonski landed the 2000 Guineas, having already two years earlier saddled Cloonagh to win the Irish 1000 Guineas.

In 1979 – the year in which he scored a then record 128 winners – and 1980 he sent out Le Moss to win all three Cup races at Ascot, Goodwood and Doncaster and in 1981 Ardross won the Ascot and Goodwood Cups before being withdrawn on the day of the Doncaster Cup.

In 1985, the year in which he first won the Derby, with Slip Anchor, he became the first British trainer to pass the £1m prize money mark, taking four of the five Classics in that year. Between 1974 and 2002 he sent out at least one Royal Ascot winner every year but one, and reigns supreme at the meeting, with 70 winners to his credit.

He was always destined to be successful at his chosen, some may say inbred, profession, but he still insists – with a kind of false modesty – on suggesting that it is all a fluke. 'I'm not qualified to do anything else. I failed my Common Entrance, the first person ever from my prep school to fail. I'm probably qualified to be a porter on a railway station if I wasn't a trainer' he told Clare Balding in an interview in 2005. He did put his finger on his popularity with the betting masses, though – 'I think the public have always followed our horses because they know they are trying and they'll get a run for their money.'

Unsurprisingly, Cecil was always far happier when they won, though. 'I'm not a good loser. I'm conscious of the fact that I ought to be more gracious in defeat. I should rush up and congratulate the winning trainer more than I do, but I can't put on an act because that's not my style. It's not resentment, I just prefer winning myself.'

In the hope of helping with his winning percentage, Cecil indulged in a number of superstitions. He refused to wear green, claiming 'most of my family have died in green. One ancestor fell down the stairs when wearing green and another died eating watercress'. He once told the *Sporting Life* that he always stopped to fill his car en route to the races as 'if I don't fill it up, I don't win.'

Particularly patient and talented with fillies ('They mustn't be rushed, they need confidence, time, understanding.'), Cecil, who at the time of writing could boast over 30 Classic winners at home and abroad – winning the Oaks eight times and the 1000 Guineas six. Mind you, he's no slouch with colts – as four Derby successes, a couple of 2000 Guineas winners and four (one with filly, Oh So Sharp, who also won the 1000 Guineas and Oaks) St Leger triumphs prove.

There was never much chance of Henry emulating Sir Michael Stoute and other dual purpose trainers by becoming involved with jumpers. 'The only tip I can give on jumpers is – where to buy them in London' he once told the *Racing Post,* and he was overheard at a mixed Newbury meeting commenting 'Hell! I thought they had done away with this game.'

His fortunes began to wane during the mid nineties, after he fell out with Sheikh Mohammed who had been sending horses to his Warren Place yard, close to Newmarket, but then withdrew them – reportedly because he believed that Henry's wife of the time, Natalie, was getting too involved.

Undaunted, Henry kept his feelings to himself – although he has since insisted 'We (he and the Sheikh) get on very well and we never had a row' – and battled on through a series of personal crises.

Independent writer, Richard Edmondson revealed his own take on the split in April 1996. 'Dubai's Crown Prince believes he knows as much about horses as many of his trainers, while (Henry) Cecil thinks the only words he should hear from his owners are "the money is in your bank account, O Great One".'

Later, a fallow spell set in as the big winners dried up at the turn of the century. Cecil and Natalie later split up and, subsequently, the services of his stable jockey Kieren Fallon were dispensed with. This must have been tough in the extreme for a man who, in his own autobiography asserted, 'I could never be content to be an also-ran.'

In June 2000 Cecil commented, 'I used to think if anyone wanted a horse trained by me they would ring up and ask, and that if I had to ask anyone to train their horse they probably weren't the people I wanted to have as owners. But I haven't had many people ringing me up recently.' Not that he would ever dream of begging for patrons, though – 'Trainers who spend time prostituting themselves at cocktail parties get the owners they deserve.'

He retained his sense of humour, nonetheless, and turned it against his own flamboyant dress sense in June 2004 when he remarked, 'If you have six runners and they all come last, you can't wear purple check trousers, can you? You'll just look like a clown.'

In February 2007 he announced that he had been undergoing treatment for stomach cancer for nine months (his twin David, an alcoholic, died of cancer in 2001). But he confounded those who had believed he was past it, by producing another Classic winner on 1 June 2007. The victory sparked an unprecedented on-course spontaneous outpouring of affection: Henry received a round of three cheers as Light Shift entered the winner's enclosure after battling to beat Peeping Fawn by half a length in the Oaks.

Visibly emotional himself, 10-time champion trainer Cecil gasped: 'That was fantastic. It's lovely to be back – a fairytale, a dream' while son Jake said, 'This means everything – he's back. He has worked so hard. He will never give up training – he just loves it too much.'

Light Shift was Cecil's eighth Oaks winner – but his first since 2000 when Love Divine won the race – and his first as a sixty-something almost-pensioner! He later reflected on the sober triumph – 'I thought I'd got the job done as long as I didn't put the wrong saddle on, which in the old days, I did when I'd had a drink.'

To his relief he was at last able to return to the stable tradition of hoisting the family crest up the flagpole. It's a tradition you'd believe he'd want his son, Jake, to succeed him in when either he decides to quit, or is carried out in a box. 'I would rather retire when I want to, rather than hand the decision over to anybody else. I would hate to retire on a down. I don't want to give up by being made to give up.'

Part of Cecil's public appeal lies in his ability to deflect how importantly he may regard his standing in the world. 'There's no point in taking anything too seriously, is there?' he told an interviewer in 2005, 'Never take anything seriously.'

He probably was being serious in 2006 when he gave a useful tip to anyone looking to acquire a decent horse. 'All my good horses have had good heads, their eyes wide apart. Do you trust a human when their eyes are too close together? I never had one good horse with small ears. The best horses had big ears like Arkle. Almost like a deer.'

Cecil once observed, 'You realise that God doesn't actually mind whether you win or not. You look at the children of the world who are deprived, abused, ill-treated, starving – you get much more realistic.'

Yet, Henry's demeanour when he returned to Classic winning form suggested strongly that there are some things in life worth taking very seriously indeed, particularly given that in a June 2008 interview with the *Guardian*, reporter Paul Kelso revealed: 'The business has been losing money, £180,000 a year by his (Cecil's) estimate.' However, the trainer believed, 'we've managed to pull things together . . . and the business is secure, rather than looking like it was going to go bankrupt.'

In July 2008 another incredible story about Henry Cecil broke, when the *Sunday Mirror* headlined: 'Cannabis factory in Cecil pad'. The story explained: 'A house owned by champion racehorse trainer Henry Cecil has been used as a secret cannabis factory.' A police search had apparently 'found evidence' that some 300 cannabis plants had been grown at the property 'on the racing legend's Newmarket estate – without his knowledge'. Phew, so Henry – who was a serious fag smoker until 2003 only to pack it in so that he wouldn't poison the environment for his young son, only to lapse back again a couple of years later– wasn't chillin' out, after all!

The house had, the story continued, been let out to 'a family from the Far East. But in reality it's believed to be one of the notorious Vietnamese gangs who make millions from selling the drug.'

Cecil does go in for plant growing – but only roses. He downplays his ability in that quarter, as he does with so much in his life – 'People think I'm a great authority on roses, but I'm not really. It's just a question of buying them and putting them in. If they die, you put another in.'

Cecil's illness has given him a new slant on life: 'Ever since I've been ill, my attitude has changed. I just take the good things out of every day now. There is always something positive to think about.' Discussing his inoperable cancer, Cecil told Paul Kelso, 'It hasn't spread and it is probably under control, but Rome wasn't built in a day. I've had lots of chemotherapy . . . 15 or 16 lots maybe.'

Shortly after giving that interview, Cecil married for the third time, to Jane McKeown, the couple choosing to honeymoon at . . . Royal Ascot.

Recently, still smoking, Cecil told the *Guardian*'s Greg Wood, 'I think I'm training much better now than for quite a few years.' Long may that continue.

FRANKIE DETTORI
Frankie speaking, we DO give a damn.

It is difficult to imagine that there could be a more charismatic jockey anywhere in the world than Frankie Dettori, who has endeared himself to the British nation despite being both an Italian *and* an Arsenal fan.

He has enriched most of the population of the British Isles at some time or other like no racing figure since Lester Piggott. Be that by his exploits on a racetrack, via his trademark flying leap from the back of big race winning mounts, or when they have watched him captaining a team on the popular *A Question of Sport* TV show.

Certainly he has changed lives. Like those of struggling builder Darren Yates from Morecambe, who won over half a million pounds because of Frankie – as did Somerset care-worker, Mary Bolton. Both of them collected half a million pounds when Frankie made racing and sporting history on 28 September 1996 at Ascot – riding all seven winners at accumulative odds of over 25,000/1. The feat was immediately dubbed the Magnificent Seven and, as it cost Britain's bookies the best part of £50 million, Dettori's place in the folklore of the nation was guaranteed.

Frankie's father, a 13-time champion jockey in Italy, Gianfranco Dettori was born, the son of a bricklayer, on 25 April 1941. He was known in England for riding successive 2000 Guineas winners for Henry Cecil – on Bolkonski in 1975 and Wollow in 1976. Gianfranco's son, Lanfranco, was born on 15 December 1970 in Milan. When he was just six months old Frankie's parents split up, and the young boy went to live with his mother, Iris Maria, once a circus trapeze artist, until he was five, before moving in with his father and stepmother.

Football was Frankie's early sporting passion, and he recalls being 'forced' to ride for the first time at the age of six. Within a couple of years his father bought him a pony called Sylvia, on which he would contest his first race at the age of nine – a Pony Derby at the San Siro racecourse. Frankie's career did not get off to a winning start – he was unseated into a water-jump. The flamboyant nature of his life was already taking shape.

At the age of 11 Frankie began betting. 'That's when I really got the love of horse racing' he said in the book *A Year in the Life of Frankie Dettori*, a comment which shows where his instinctive understanding of the relationship between racing and betting, and therefore with the hopes and aspirations of the punters, has evolved from.

Frankie became a stable lad at the highly regarded stables of Roman lawyer and owner, Carlo d'Alessio, where for 15 years his father had been first jockey to the late trainer, Sergio Cumani, father of Luca, himself a very successful trainer in England.

'Only one in a thousand makes it as a jockey' Gianfranco warned his son, before he arranged a six-month stint for him with Newmarket-based Luca, who believes, 'nobody is born a jockey.' Frankie was then to spend six months with Patrick Biancone in Chantilly before returning to Italy.

He arrived in England aged 14. 'When he (Gianfranco) sent me to England he gave me a million lire. At the time it was worth £366. He told me there was no more where that came from. I didn't learn English, I just picked it up as I went along (NO! – GS). I think the first word I ever learned was goodbye.' His charmingly mangled English also helped boost his popularity.

The Cumani experiment proved so successful that parts two and three of the masterplan would never need to be put into action. Having ridden 16 winners (according to his autobiography) in Turin and Naples in November 1986, he got off the mark in England on Lizzie Hare at Goodwood on 9 June 1987.

On his first English ride he had partnered Peter Walwyn-trained Mustakbil to finish second at Kempton, after which he told the veteran handler that his horse was 'fet', by which Walwyn soon realised he meant 'fat' rather than 'fit'. Walwyn promptly bawled Dettori out, calling him either a 'cheeky little blighter' or 'bugger', depending on which report you refer to, and banned him from his horses for a year. Mind you, Mustakbil never did win!

In 1989 Dettori became champion apprentice – already, punters were quickly cottoning on to the new kid's mounts, and liked his style on and off a horse. In 1990 Frankie became Cumani's first choice jockey, and during the season became the first teenager since Lester Piggott in 1955, to ride a century of winners. A year later he won his first Derby, the German version, on Temporal. He would wait almost 20 years to claim the real thing.

The first setback in the young Italian's rise to prominence came in 1993 when it was revealed that he had been cautioned by police, who had found drugs on him. This incident subsequently led to the Hong Kong authorities revoking the offer that had been made to him to ride there for a year, an intended career move which had not played well with his mentor. Cumani took some while to forgive and forget, and for the first time Dettori experienced public criticism, later confessing 'I was at my lowest ebb'. Advice from controversial trainer/owner/punter, Barney Curley, was to re-focus Frankie's mind and set him back on the right road; 'He made me understand that I had too much, too early in my life.'

On 17 April 1993 he rode his first four-timer, landing odds of 15,969/1 at Newbury and by 1994 he was riding regularly for Newmarket's John Gosden, having been appointed as retained jockey to Sheikh Mohammed Al Maktoum.

Having finished runner-up in the jockey title race in 1993 behind Pat Eddery, with 149 winners, Frankie hatched a cunning plan to 'steal' the title in 1994 by riding at the winter all-weather meetings, which were generally boycotted by the more established riders who took the opportunity of a holiday to prepare for the rigours of the season to come. So successful was this ploy that by the start of the section of the season Frankie had already chalked up over 50 winners – a virtually insuperable lead. These days those winners would have counted only towards the 'All Weather' title, but the youngster ended up as champion with 233 winners – satisfyingly four ahead of another great champion's record seasonal score – his dad's.

During the season Frankie went to America and won the Breeders' Cup Mile on Luca Cumani's Barathea – celebrating with his new trademark flying dismount – borrowed from his hero, showman South American rider, Angel Cordero.

On 12 June 1996, Frankie rode six winners in a day – three each at Yarmouth and Kempton – but a day later broke his elbow in a fall in the Newbury paddock when filly Shawwani reared up and went over on to her back with Frankie still on board. He was out until early August – and turned up at Royal Ascot resplendent in morning suit, top hat, multi-coloured tie, red rose buttonhole – with his arm in a sling.

Then came that miraculous day of days when Frankie broke all the rules and captured worldwide headlines by winning at Ascot on Wall Street, Diffident, Mark of Esteem, Decorated Hero, Fatefully, Lochangel and Fujiyama Crest.

After that, Frankie became ubiquitous – a few weeks later he presented TV show *Top of the Pops*; he appeared on Clive Anderson's chat show; and on *TFI* Friday with Chris Evans, where he caused quite a stir by performing a party-trick levitation stunt, which ended with him leaping out of a box, having appeared to hover in mid air. He was voted into third place in the BBC TV Sports Personality of the Year Award – unprecedented for a jockey – and a foreign one, at that.

In her insightful book about the turf, *The Racing Tribe*, anthropologist Kate Fox discussed him: 'Frankie has been officially declared Good for Racing, and has accordingly been granted a sort of diplomatic immunity from traditionalist censure . . . he represents racing not just as a spokesman, but as a tribal icon. To express disapproval of racing's lucky charm would be to invite divine retribution.'

He married Catherine on 20 July 1997 – and the pair soon set about populating the world with many small Dettoris! His son Leo, one of five children ('I'm not getting pregnant again – you can print that' – wife, Catherine, *Daily Mail*, 6 June 2008) was born on 4 October 1999. In 2001 his daughter Ella was born – Mia, Tallula and Rocco would follow.

He was runner up in the title race in both 1997 and 1998 but in the latter season found that no one can enjoy upward momentum for ever. Riding the Godolphin representative, Swain, in the Breeders' Cup Classic, the world's richest ever single race with a $5.12m purse, Dettori seemed to lose control, allowing Swain to swing out wide on the track, and uncharacteristically gave Swain a very hard ride under the whip, as they were beaten by Awesome Again and Silver Charm. Frankie was harshly criticised for the ride – 'his reputation was subsequently lynched in the American media' wrote Richard Edmondson in the *Independent*.

For some while Frankie seemed to be in a state of self-denial, refusing grimly to accept that he had done anything wrong. He did once say, 'In racing it helps to be a good bull-shitter – you must have the ability to make excuses.' Frankie then courted controversy by admitting to having taken diuretic drugs in the past to keep his weight down.

But he bounced back to form big-time by consigning his Swain debacle to the history books as he won the Breeders' Cup Turf the very next year, 1999, yelling at the crowd in triumph and leaping off the horse looking 'like a prisoner suddenly set free' observed *Sports Illustrated*'s William Nack. On the way to weigh in he stopped to drink a beer handed to him by a fan. He was unburdened at last. 'Revenge is a plate you eat cold and mine was freezing. Everybody tried to kill me last year. OK I made a mistake, but don't judge me on one ride.'

Then came the traumatic incident which cemented his place in the affections of the entire nation, and tinged his reputation with an almost mystical sense of indestructibility. On 1 June 2000, Frankie and fellow jockey Ray Cochrane set off to fly from Newmarket to Goodwood racecourse in a Piper Seneca light aircraft. Just after take off the plane nose-dived, crashed and caught fire. 'Before the impact I didn't scream, because I didn't think there was any point. I knew that I was going to die.' Cochrane rescued Frankie from the burning wreck, but was unable to free pilot Patrick Mackey, who perished. Cochrane was awarded a Silver Medal by the Royal Humane Society for his actions. Both jockeys were treated in hospital – Frankie for a broken ankle, damaged ribs and facial injuries, Cochrane for injuries to his back, arm and face.

Cochrane returned to the saddle after seven weeks but soon announced his retirement and Frankie appointed him as his riding agent in season 2001. Frankie had come back on 5 August 2000 at Newmarket – completing a 10/1 double on his first two rides.

The crash, he admitted, changed his perspective on life. 'Life for me was like being in an empty room looking for an exit that was never there' he said, starkly, in October 2008, looking back to that time. He was now no longer prepared to neglect his home and family life in favour of chasing the championship.

Frankie was awarded an honorary MBE, presented to him at Sandown in April 2001 by racing fan and Foreign Secretary, Robin Cook.

In that year, for the first time, he cocked up his flying dismount – falling over as he jumped off in Dubai.

Frankie earned 'around a third of a million pounds from three winners' on Dubai World Cup night 2003, but 'little did I know it would be pretty much downhill for the rest of the year . . . Godolphin was desperately short of contenders in England . . . It was the start of a summer of despair that left me feeling more depressed than at any other stage of my career'.

After Italy won the 2006 World Cup he turned up for racing at Newmarket with his country's flag painted on his cheeks.

Later that year his wife cost him a potential winner. He had to get off the Mick Channon-trained So Sweet at the Curragh when officials pointed out that as his wife owned a half share in another runner in the race he would be breaching a 2003 rule which states that jockeys cannot have a potential conflict of interest.

As the Godolphin set up started to lose ground on their great Irish rivals, Coolmore, Frankie became engulfed in controversy again when he cried 'foul play' after claiming his mount, Librettist, sixth in the Queen Elizabeth Stakes at Ascot, was 'deliberately' run wide by Coolmore second string jockey, Seamus Heffernan, as their first string, George Washington, went on to win. Aidan O'Brien hit back that Dettori 'threw the toys out of the pram like a spoilt child', although Heffernan was suspended for 14 days, and suggestions of the use of 'team tactics' by Coolmore increased subsequently, despite denials by O'Brien.

With the media beginning to focus on the surprising inability of the sport's two biggest jockey names – jumping's Tony McCoy and the flat's Frankie, to win their sport's main events – the Grand National and Derby, it was an ecstatic Dettori who steered favourite Authorised to a straightforward yet thrilling (your author had invested heavily!) Derby victory in 2007.

In a June 2008 interview with Alan Fraser of the *Daily Mail* Frankie's wife, Catherine, revealed one or two intimate details about her husband, like his sleeping habits – 'We have got the darkest curtains. It is like the blackout. He gets into bed. It is already pitch black and he puts patches on his eyes. Then he covers his winkie with his hand. It's a habit.' When he does fall asleep, 'He dreams in English'. He is also very tidy. 'It doesn't matter how wobbly he is, he always hangs up his clothes.' Frankie is also prone to panic attacks, like his mother. 'Suddenly he just overheats and says get me out of here. It happened on a ski lift, in a helicopter, in a jet during a dodgy landing and in a taxi.' However, she believes he has changed her: 'He taught me not to give a toss and have fun.'

Frankie vowed in October 2008 to carry on riding 'for 10 more years, perhaps. It's within reach'. But to get that far he has to learn to pace himself and focus more on his priorities: 'I'll be honest: it just doesn't make me tick any more going to the smaller courses for insignificant races.'

There seems to be little chance of Frankie ever deciding that, after all, he is an Italian and heading back to the land of his birth. As he commented in August 2008, 'I've been here so long, I'm part of the furniture, an honorary Brit. I'm as English as anybody in some ways, so I'm claiming dual nationality. My Arsenal shirt is my passport!'

Late in October 2008 I travelled to America for the Breeders' Cup at Santa Anita Park – a place where Frankie had worked early in his career. A year earlier at a deluged Monmouth Park, Frankie had endured a dismal Breeders' Cup, trailing in behind in race after race – carrying my money in all of the races and reducing me to shouting 'You useless git' at him after yet another defeat!

This time round, the rain was gone, the sun shone warmly, there were no clouds to be seen and the beautiful mountains behind the course framed the view like a wonderfully vibrant landscape painting. So I backed Frankie again on Sixties Icon in the opening race of the afternoon, the 'Marathon'. The horse, fully entitled to be hot favourite, was given a disappointing, not to say negligent, ride and was never going to win. Trainer Jeremy Noseda was reportedly not best pleased, suggesting that if jockeys listened to their trainer's instructions and carried them out to the letter they could expect to win more often than not.

In his next ride Frankie looked all over a winner only to be touched off on the line. His gloomy body language was obvious.

That was enough for me. No more money wasted on Frankie. I pinned all my hopes and remaining dollars on Curlin in the Breeders' Cup Classic, the biggest of the big races. Curlin flattered to deceive, dropping back after a short-lived surge to the front, to finish fourth, as English raider, Raven's Pass stormed past him and the rest of the field to win the race from Duke of Marmalade in spectacular fashion, at double figure odds – with Frankie Dettori on his back.

Frankie was ecstatic, beaming, waving his arms, hurling his whip ebulliently into the crowd – to the displeasure of the stewards – and milking the moment for all it was worth, apparently failing to notice that every American in the place, all of whom had been anticipating a Curlin-fest, was glowering moodily at his antics.

But all the Europeans and Brits in the place were up cheering and applauding the charismatic honorary Brit. They couldn't all have backed him. And I certainly hadn't. But that's Frankie for you – you gotta love the guy, no matter how he's just let you down.

JOHN FRANCOME
Greatest jockey?

Dubbed 'Greatest jockey' by his Channel 4 colleague and avowed fan, John McCririck, as a rider John Francome was a master tactician, great sportsman and free spirit whose irrepressible nature, intrinsic distrust of authority (he famously dubbed stewards 'cabbage patch dolls'), and ongoing appeal to the female sex has made him a genuine all time great racing character.

Born in 1952 to humble beginnings in a Mulberry Grove council house, Francome's first riding experiences were on seaside donkeys and a milkman's horse. He entered racing via the worlds of Pony Club and show-jumping. He was a member of a Pony Club team that reached the finals of the Prince Philip Cup in 1963 and of the winning British team at 1970's Junior European Championships in St Moritz.

An introduction to great former jump jockey turned trainer, Fred Winter, secured Francome a trial at the stable despite Winter's misgivings about the size of John's appendages – his small hands and feet! Mind you, Francome's Dad's advice to his son on applying for a job working for the great man did appear to make reference to a different appendage. 'He told me Fred had no sons, only daughters. Dad reasoned that I'd have no unfair competition from sons so all I had to do was shag the prettiest daughter and I'd be well in.'

On 2 December 1970, 17-year-old Francome won on his debut, partnering Multigrey at Worcester, commenting, 'the horse just carried me round.'

With the assistance of both Winter and his stable jockey, Richard Pitman, Francome began to develop his natural attributes and by 1974/75 he was challenging Tommy Stack for the jump jockey title, finishing runner-up with 70 winners to his credit. Pitman retired in 1975 and Francome succeeded him as Winter's number one – he took full advantage, clinching the championship with 96 winners.

The relationship between Winter and Francome seems to have been more of a business arrangement than a mutual admiration society, but Winter said of him in his 1991 authorised biography, 'I would say it is a toss-up between three, Bryan Marshall, Martin Molony and Johnny, as to who is the best jockey of my time. Johnny has been a marvellous stable jockey. At times he is absolutely brilliant, probably the best of the lot. He has got everything. But there have been occasions when he has upset me. . . . I have to bite my tongue then, because he is a sensitive bloke.'

Sensitive is not necessarily the first word used to describe the Francome character by those who know him. In 1978 Francome was embroiled in what became known as the 'John Banks affair' when he was banned from late April until early June and fined £750. He was riding high profile bookie Banks' horse, Stopped, in the Imperial Cup at Sandown, finishing third, after which there was a stewards inquiry, during which Francome told the stewards he had spoken to Banks about horses he rode – 'I had no idea it was contravening the rules of racing. Like 99 per cent of jockeys I had never bothered to read them.'

He was reported to the Jockey Club and before his hearing the media made much of the links between Banks and Francome and there were unspoken suggestions hanging in the air. Francome himself had told his guvnor, Fred Winter, 'I want you to know that I have never stopped a horse in my life.'

Before the hearing took place Francome won the Cheltenham Gold Cup on Midnight Court, receiving a great reception from the crowd.

The hearing lasted nine hours 'during which time the stewards and their solicitors asked John and me endless questions about races in which I had been beaten on favourites' remembered Francome. He was eventually found in breach of the rules 'because they said I had given confidential information concerning horses in training to John at his request.' Banks himself was fined £2,500 and banned from racecourses for three years. The incident had no long-term effect on Francome's success.

Francome won the Champion Hurdle on Sea Pigeon in 1981, but the Grand National eluded him in nine attempts.

In 1982 Francome was trailing Peter Scudamore in the race to become champion jockey when Scu was injured and out for the rest of the season. Francome caught him up by riding his 120th winner of the campaign on Buckmaster on 1 June – whereupon, in an extraordinary gesture of sportsmanship, he announced that he would cease riding for the remainder of the season, to share the title with Scudamore. Ten years later Francome did admit a little ruefully, 'I now regret that decision' – possibly because Scu went on to win several more titles.

There was another brush with controversy in July 1982 when Francome, Scudamore and Steve Smith Eccles were suspended after Francome was said to have given the others £200 each by mutual agreement after riding Donegal Prince to victory in the Schweppes.

Francome's final – and 1,138th – winner before retirement in April 1985 was Gambler's Cup at Huntingdon. His last mount came on the next day, 9 April, when, after falling on The Reject at Chepstow, he decided he'd had enough and quit, many believed prematurely, having been champion jockey seven times.

His record shows that he one was one of the most effective jockeys in the game, but perhaps he was never the most stylish. He says deprecatingly of himself, 'Someone once said to me they would rather finish second than look like me in a finish.'

He was back in action on 18 May of the same year when he took on Lester Piggott in a match race on the flat at Warwick. With the great flat jockey partnering Liquidator and Francome on Shangoseer, John went out on a limb, predicting accurately, 'Whatever beats me will win.' Lester won.

By September 1985, and in the same year which Lester also did it, Francome became a trainer – his first stable representative Crimson Knight, ridden by Steve Smith Eccles, capsizing at the third last at Worcester. His first winner was a shock 25/1 triumph when That's Your Lot won at Sandown on 30 November, again partnered by Smith Eccles, who remains a good friend of 'Greatest' – 'John's attitude to life is that there is always a tomorrow, so why worry.'

He soon tired of being a trainer, though. 'It's the hardest job in the world – you wouldn't wish it on your worst enemy. I had the best set of owners, great staff and nice horses – but you have to be able to tell somebody to spend 200,000gns on a horse and then tell them that it's useless, now let's go and do it again.'

Widely regarded as a very good judge of horses, Francome was offered a free £500 bet for charity on the 1987 Grand National by William Hill – he plonked it on winner Maori Venture at 50/1, landing the charity a £25,000 windfall – but then put his own cash on a loser!

However, the Francome fortunes have been sustained and enhanced over the years, via his career as a writer of racing thrillers which have rivalled Dick Francis' efforts in the best seller charts. He has now penned more than 20.

Even though he still rates his original source of income the best – 'a more thrilling, uplifting, glorious way of living has yet to be invented – it's even better than shagging' – he makes money in other ways, too. In the late seventies he became the joint owner of a fish and chip shop in Swindon, later acquiring another. In 2006 they were both sold. 'If I was 16 again I'd buy more of them. I made more from fish and chips than being a jockey.' Francome has bought land and built 10 houses, still owning most of them and says, 'I'm more interested in building than riding.'

Francome split up with his wife of 15 years, Miriam, in 1990. They were racing's golden couple – once turning up at a Lambourn fancy dress party with the theme of 'couples' as Adam and Eve, stark naked but for four fig leaves between them. Francome was said to be devastated at the break up of their marriage and when she moved in with trainer Charlie Brooks, he reportedly burned many of her clothes and dumped what was left in Brooks' yard. It is unclear whether they ever officially divorced.

A confirmed teetotaller, ('I've never had a drink. I've seen enough drunk people to know that I can get through life without it') Francome was awarded the MBE in 1986 for services to racing.

He is something of a home buff and told the *Racing Post* in October 2008 'There is nowhere in the UK that I don't like (he had earlier nominated Cheltenham and Lingfield as his favourite racecourses), saying there are none he dislikes, 'just those that are a long way from home. As for abroad, I look forward to going to the departure lounge for wherever I am going!'

Stepping up to announce that the winner of the Jockey of the Year Award at the 2008 Horse Race Writers' And Photographers' Association was Johnny Murtagh, Francome told the audience of hundreds of racing personalities that he had spoken to Murtagh in Japan, where he had been riding and was therefore unable to attend that afternoon. 'He told me he had a bad flight out there. He had to sit next to a priest. When the stewardess came round and asked Johnny whether he would like a drink, he told her he would. She then asked the priest who said "I'd rather be raped by a whore than take alcohol." Murtagh called the stewardess back and said, "Hold the drink, I didn't realise there was a choice . . . ".'

Chatting on Channel 4, making guest appearances at dinners and the like, golf, reading, building – they are all ways in which Francome enjoys his current life. He also enjoys thinking up new ideas for his favourite sport – like parading horses for sale before racing; letting schoolkids sit on horses at the races; introducing green coloured artificial surfaces and inviting racegoers to ride around courses following a race, in open topped vehicles.

Always the first to tell a risque or risky story whenever the opportunity arises, Francome says that the strangest thing he has ever seen on a racecourse occurred at Chepstow 'where I was riding on a very foggy day. John Williams, who was riding against me, missed all the fences up the back straight before popping over the last and doing me for third place prize money. He couldn't believe he got away with it'. And that's a phrase which might well sum up the modest 'Greatest Jockey''s thoughts on his own life in racing.

JULIE KRONE
The one and Krone-ly

She was the girl who really made the boys sit up and take notice. Julie Krone – born Julieanne Louise in Michigan on 24 July 1963 – was destined to become involved with horses as her mother, Judi, was an accomplished equestrian. Her father, Don, was an art teacher and photographer.

Julie was already riding, aged two. She was winning rosettes at horse shows from the age of five, and grew up to become the first American woman to prove conclusively that she was more than a match for the male jockeys.

Hers was an unconventional childhood. Raised on a farm, she and older brother Donnie, were reportedly allowed to run wild. Julie often dined with the farm dogs, apparently, enjoying their dog food ('I could count on one hand the times my parents made a meal for me – and it wasn't because we were poor') and, aged five, she would often lead her horse into the family home for her mother to saddle. She once harnessed a Great Dane to a sled when it snowed. She learned how to do circus tricks on horseback, 'like standing up, and back flips. But my circus adventure didn't work out.'

Her mother added a year to Julie's age to help her get work at Churchill Downs as a groom and exercise rider when she was just 15 and she was desperate to get into racing, having been inspired by watching Steve Cauthen in action.

She stood up for herself, taking no nonsense whatsoever – even when it came to a physical altercation. And her physique was modest – even by jockey standards. She stood 4ft 10ins (1.47) tall and weighed just over 7 stones (44kg). This certainly worked against her and trainer John Forbes, for whom she often rode, commented: 'The notion that a rider has to be very strong and powerful so he can control a 1000lb (453kg) animal and hit it really hard with a whip is something that has been ingrained. The resistance we had was unbelievable.' Krone's attitude was: 'I approached the sport like there wasn't a gender issue, and I wouldn't participate in the mindset of "she is just a girl".'

She rode her first winner, Lord Farkle, at Tampa Bay Downs in February 1981.

Controversy followed. Julie shoved jockey Yves Turcotte off the scales as he weighed-in after a bad tempered race in 1982. In 1986, by which time she had ridden over 1,200 winners, she became involved in a contretemps with fellow rider, Miguel Rujano, during a race at Monmouth. Afterwards, waiting to weigh in, Julie hit Rujano with a right hook to the jaw, then battered him over the head with a chair when they later met up near a local swimming pool. Both were fined $100. In September 1989 she was again involved in a dust-up – during and after a race at Meadowlands in New Jersey. She whacked jockey Joe Bravo with her whip after he crowded her. She was later suspended for 15 days and fined $500 while he got 5 days and $250.

In 1987 she not only became only the third female jockey to pass 1000 career wins, but also won the track titles at Monmouth Park with 130 victories, and Meadowlands with 124. On 19 August she rode six winners in one afternoon at Monmouth Park. In March 1988 she became the most successful female jockey with 1,205 winners to her credit.

On 24 November 24 1990 she became the first female rider to win in Japan. She finished second on 30/1 shot Quilma at Gulfstream Park, Florida in January 1991 – but might have gone one better had she not suddenly and unexpectedly had to persuade her mount to jump a fox sunning himself on the back straight. With a 46/1 winner and 31/1 third, the trifecta paid an amazing 96,751/1. In June of that year she became the first woman jockey to ride in the Belmont Stakes, finishing 9th of 11 on Subordinated Debt as 4/1 chance Hansel won. Two months later she booted home five winners in one day at Saratoga, but 10 days later at the same track she fractured an ankle.

When Julie came to Europe, she won at Taby, Sweden, then rode in England for the first time, at Redcar, in July 1992, where she landed a 46/1 treble – which reportedly did not go down that well with the local riders. During the same year Krone enjoyed a hot streak at Gulfstream Park where, during a 59-day spell she rode 72 winners, taking the top jock honours there – the first female to do so at a major Florida track. She also landed a meeting title at Belmont Park, the first woman so to do, with 73 winners from 370 mounts.

She won the 1993 Belmont Stakes on 13/1 chance, Colonial Affair, but an accident in August that year almost killed her – she broke her right ankle and suffered a cardiac bruise, but credited her protective vest with saving her life.

Her 1995 wedding to TV reporter, Matt Muzikar, saw her riding six horses on the day, and back on course, riding six more the next day.

She suffered a potentially career-ending injury in the mid nineties at Gulfstream Park, breaking both hands. She temporarily lost her nerve. Back after a six-week lay-off, 'Horses felt my anxiety, they got weird, they reared up.' She was later diagnosed as suffering post-traumatic stress disorder and utilised anti-depressants as she fought back; however she was never quite the same, despite continuing to boot home plenty of winners.

In April 1999, Julie announced her retirement, winning three times in five races at Lone Star Park. Her fellow jocks laid on a huge cake to mark the occasion – and one of them pushed her face into the icing. 'Even being put into the cake was special' she insisted. She retired partly to spare her mother further stress. 'It was really good to stop racing successfully and that she could see me retire on top. She was so happy that she didn't have to worry about me on the horses anymore.' Her mother died shortly before Christmas 1999.

Julie returned to racing – albeit of the harness variety – when she piloted Moni Maker to a world record time in a 'trotters under saddle' race in Lexington, Kentucky. Julie joined the racing media for a while but was lured out of retirement in November 2002 when she rode at Santa Anita Park.

Making a decent start to the 2003 season, she suffered the fracture of two bones in her lower back and was out for four months, but she bounced back to become that year's leading jockey for prize money at Del Mar – capping the year by becoming the first woman to ride a Breeders' Cup winner, partnering Halfbridled to victory in the Juvenile Fillies.

But the year had a kick in its tail and on 12 December she fell at

Hollywood Park, breaking several ribs in the process. Clearly not fully healed, Julie bravely came back on Valentine's Day 2004 at Santa Anita, but despite the nature of the day, she must have felt that the game was falling out of love with her as she failed to win in three attempts. On 8 July of that year she made a statement suggesting that she would not ride, albeit stopping short of confirming her retirement. This time, though, she would not return on any kind of permanent basis. She did broadcasting work, became a motivational speaker, and an 'instructor in the discipline of natural horsemanship.'

She retired with more than 3,700 winners to her credit, worth over $90m in prize money. *Sports Illustrated* writer Gary Smith said of her style, 'She rode in a tight little ball that a horse hardly seemed to notice on its back. Other riders had to yank back on a colt that was chomping to run too soon in a race; she barely had to move her hands. Other riders had to slash the whip 15 times down the stretch; she might get the same acceleration with two.'

By now married to *Daily Racing Form* columnist Jay Hovdey, Julie became a mother on 27 September 2005 when she gave birth to Lorelei Judith.

She was the first female jockey inducted into the National Museum of Racing and Hall of Fame in 2000. During her acceptance speech, she said, 'I want this to be a lesson to all kids everywhere. If the stable gate is closed, climb the fence.'

Perhaps the greatest tribute paid to Krone came from another great jockey and Hall of Famer, Gary Stevens: 'She's not just a great woman jockey, she's a great jockey in general.'

A.P. McCOY
Initially, the best

Widely known as 'A.P.' (which stands for Anthony Peter), Tony McCoy MBE may well be the greatest jump jockey the world has known.

An Ulsterman, born in Moneyglass, County Antrim in May 1974, and whose father Peadar ('I never thought he'd be a jockey. There were no jockeys about here, ever.') was a racing fan who built stables at the family home. It is certain that there have been few more driven characters in a game notable for attracting driven characters. 'I don't want to be a gracious loser' he told racing writer Richard Edmondson in December 2002, 'I can't be. It's not in my head. I'd rather not ride at all if I thought I was going to lose all the time. I wouldn't do it. I'd have to give up.' He had also mused, 'Finishing second in a horse race is the worst feeling in the world. Bar none.'

He is aware that the pursuit of winners can sometimes over-ride an appreciation of his own achievements: 'I'll probably look back when I finish and wonder why I didn't appear to be enjoying it.'

Quite how anyone could enjoy riding a winner within an hour of being kicked in the face by a horse, losing teeth and still having blood trickling down his chin, is difficult for mere mortals to comprehend. But that's what happened at Cheltenham in December 2005 when McCoy and Risk Accessor parted company, leaving the rider to take a hefty whack to the face as he lay on the ground, costing him four teeth. McCoy picked himself up, cleaned himself up, missed the next race, then rode Black Jack Ketchum to victory, to the astonishment of trainer Jonjo O'Neill, who observed, 'He must have no pain barrier'.

McCoy told Derek Thompson as he came back in, 'I've got a nasty bang at the top of my mouth and they think I might have a small fracture of the gum, but you forget pain when you ride winners. My face could have been broken to bits and I would have come out to ride this lad.' And you have to believe him, because, actually, his face had been pretty much broken to bits – 'I have no feeling down the left side of my face' he admitted in a 2006 interview, 'From the top of my nose down to my upper lip is totally numb.'

In January 2008 he suffered a crashing fall at Warwick from Arnold Layne: 'I flipped over the horse and broke both sides of my T12 vertebrae and crushed the T9 and T11. I couldn't move anything – not even my feet.' He had to be taught to walk again. 'They held me up on this Zimmer frame so that they could teach me how to walk again. That's not a great feeling.'

As befits his image, McCoy is always prepared to go a little further than the next jockey in his effort to bounce back from injury. In February 2008, clad only in skimpy underwear, he endured a temperature of -135°C (-211°F) as he took advantage of cutting edge cryotherapy treatment, introduced to these shores by former jockey and trainer Charlie Brooks, which helped get him back in action for Cheltenham after the potentially career-threatening back injury. The treatment is supposed to accelerate the healing process and is especially good for muscle recovery. It supplies a 'dry' cold and looks like a freezing version of a steam room. 'I have no idea exactly how much of the improvement has been brought about by cryotherapy, but my circulation has never been better' declared the fit again McCoy.

This is a man so committed to winning, that if he doesn't he won't even go out that night – he told interviewer Lee Honeyball, 'If I go out to the pub and look miserable all I get is people telling me not to be such a miserable f****r. I don't want to give people that pleasure.' So committed that, according to his predecessor as champion jockey, Richard Dunwoody, a man who was pretty keen to ride winners himself, 'People say they would get off their death bed to ride the Gold Cup favourite, AP would get off his death bed to ride in a Taunton seller.'

The Arsenal fan – he named his boxer puppy Henry in honour of Thierry of that ilk – has been champion jump jockey since first claiming the honour in 1995, setting records on a regular basis, and riding his 2,000th winner in January 2004, courtesy of Magical Bailiwick at Wincanton. Later that year he suffered a bad injury to his hand – 'I thought when I took my glove off, my thumb might be left inside' – which was expected to keep him out for six weeks. He was back in the saddle in nine days.

The only major gap in his collection of top races at time of writing remained the Grand National, in which he had finished third on both Blowing Wind in 2001 and Clan Royal the next year. But, like Frankie Dettori and Sir Gordon Richards, who were made to wait what seemed like an eternity to them before winning the Derby, the day will surely arrive when McCoy manages to win the National.

The Cheltenham Gold Cup and the Champion Hurdle (he won both in 1997 on Mr Mulligan and Make A Stand respectively) are already in the bag, but in the Gold Cup of 2000 he experienced his worst moment in racing when the brilliant young Gloria Victis was put down after falling: 'Gloria Victis getting killed will always be the worst thing that ever happens to me in racing – and that includes whatever injuries I might have. On paper Best Mate is the best I've ridden, but Gloria Victis was exceptional.'

A keen amateur footballer and golfer, McCoy has regularly hosted an annual charity golf day to raise cash for charity, and has said that if he could choose to be anyone else in the sporting world it would be Tiger Woods.

His height – 5ft 10ins (1.78m) means that a 'natural weight' for him should probably be closer to 12 stone (76kg) than the 10 (63kg) at which he can ride on occasion – hot baths and cups of tea containing several spoonsful of sugar are often involved in the process of maintaining the lower level of weight, rather than the chips he once adored as 'food of the gods.' 'Once or twice I've put my head in my hands and wept because I didn't want to do it. I do it because I ride good horses and get plenty of winners. Other guys do the same just to earn a living.'

He accepts a little assistance from the fates by wearing a holy medal on his back protector for luck.

Writer Paul Hayward said of McCoy, 'You look at him and see only strength. His stomach is like his spirit, eternally hungry.' *Daily Telegraph* columnist Mick Hume declared McCoy 'the Roy Keane of racing, an Irish jump jockey so single-minded in pursuit of winners it is a wonder some educated eejit has not referred him for addiction therapy.'

The partnership between prolific trainer Martin Pipe and McCoy, ('Too many people forget that he re-invented how to train a racehorse.') which lasted into 2004 when he accepted a retainer to ride for owner J.P. McManus for whom Jonjo O'Neill, a marvellous jockey in his own right, trained most of his runners, propelled the jockey into the superstar league. He had initially learned his trade with the late trainer, Billy Rock, who first put him on a horse as a youngster. McCoy later dedicated his autobiography to the man 'who treated me like a man when I was a boy and who saw more in the boy than any other man'. Rock died of cancer in 2003.

McCoy then joined the strict Jim Bolger, who insisted on no smoking, no drinking and compulsory church-going, and for whom he partnered his first hurdles winner at Leopardstown in March 1994. His first flat winner, 20/1 shot, Legal Steps, was at Thurles on 26 March 1992, when he was 17. Bolger spotted the star potential of the lad early on – 'I must have thought a fair bit of him because, when he had his first ride on Nordic Touch at Phoenix Park on 1 September 1990, I made sure he was photographed.'

McCoy had already decided by 1994 that his future was over jumps when 'I knew the flat dream was over when the needle on the bathroom scales was stuck at 8st 10lbs (55kg).' He came to England later that year, at the behest of Toby Balding, getting off the mark on Chickabiddy at Exeter on 7 September, and going on to win the conditional jockey championship with a record 74 winners.

In 2001/02 he broke Sir Gordon Richards' record of 269 winners in a single season by 20, a record which had stood since 1947. In the process he earned what is still a jumping record total of £2,753,453 in prize money. Incredibly, though, (and summing up the massive financial disparity between the two branches of the same sport) that entire total was exceeded by US jockey Jerry Bailey in just one race that year – the 2002 Dubai World Cup won by Street Cry.

McCoy endured a terrible experience in the 2002 Champion Hurdle when Valiramix suffered a fatal injury. McCoy wept over the incident, as he had two years earlier when Gloria Victis was killed at the penultimate fence.

On 27 August 2002 at Uttoxeter McCoy recorded his 1,700th victory on Mighty Montefalco, exceeding Richard Dunwoody's career record in the process. By the age of 28 he had published two autobiographies in an effort to quench the insatiable thirst of punters for details of the man who was such a reliable ally in the battle with the bookies.

When he split with Pipe it was not entirely good natured, with owner Howard Johnson, who had most of his horses in the Pipe yard, commenting, 'There was all this crap in the papers about furthering his career. That's bollocks. He went to further his bank balance.' He is rumoured to earn a seven-figure sum annually from his employer, J.P. McManus.

In late 2008 McCoy made a rare foray into racing politics, when he announced that he was resigning as joint president of the Professional Jockeys' Association, citing 'false communication' from the Association's chief executive, Josh Apiafi – who he had endorsed when he acquired that position in September 2007 – over the issue of the appointment of the Association's £150,000 a year medical adviser. 'Something must be seriously wrong when McCoy, a man of impeccable integrity cannot stomach it any more. What's rotten in the PJA?' asked John McCririck.

A fan of rock bands Snow Patrol and Kings of Leon, McCoy,

married to Chanelle, who he first met at the 1996 Punchestown Festival, is a father to young Eve, 'the only person who ever invariably smiles when I come into a room'. That may be because McCoy doesn't exactly court popularity – and admires that trait in others. 'One thing I admire about Lester Piggott is the way he always got on the best horse. It didn't matter who was riding him, who trained him, or owned him, if he wanted to ride it that was it. He wasn't a popular person for that, but I think I could cope with that.'

Chanelle understands her husband – 'My view is that he is driven by the fear of not being champion' – and knows the sacrifices he makes to maintain that position. Recently he had asked to have chicken for dinner as he hadn't eaten anything for over a day and a half, but 'a while later he rang back and told me not to bother with the chicken.' He'd picked up a spare ride but needed to ride at his lowest weight: 'That night he made do with a cup of tea before spending two hours in the bath.'

He was present while Eve came into the world in 2007, watching and encouraging Chanelle's activities – 'It's not as hard as they say' he told writer Donald McRae, 'If labour was that hard God wouldn't have had women having babies.' Calm down – McRae said he was 'smiling broadly' when he made the comment.

Tony will continue to ride as long as the desire for winners remains – 'You've got to want success every day, and when you get it that makes you greedy for some more.' But he will surely not miss the permanent concern about wasting, which he admitted has been with him even in sleep – 'The thing I dream about is waking up lighter than I was.'

He even capped a highly successful 2008 by making a New Year's resolution: 'To be a little more successful next year than I've been in previous years' – much to the frustration of perennial jockey title runner-up Richard Johnson, whose own resolution was 'to get the better of AP in the championship.'

McCoy has insisted that he has no interest in training when he quits ('I just wouldn't have the patience'), but in December 2008 received planning consent for a 60 box training complex and separate house for a trainer on his Lambourn estate.

And when will he pack it all in? The McCoy mantra used to be 'I would like to reach 3,000 winners by the time I retire.' Then on 18 January 2009, it was pointed out to him when he dismounted from winner, Kilbeggan Blade, that he had now officially ridden 3,000 winners – albeit a dozen of these were flat winners, six each in Ireland and on British tracks. He had 2,905 British jumps winners and 88 Irish. However, the real celebrations were saved for the 'official' 3000th jumps winner – which eventually arrived in the shape of Restless D'Artaix at Plumpton on 9 February 2009 in the Tyser and Co Beginners' Chase (Class 4).

It all left John Francome recalling that when he had seen Stan Mellor become the first to clock up 1,000 jumps winners he had never believed anyone would ever double, let alone treble that total.

Don't be remotely surprised if, having reached that milestone, the incomparable horseman who collected his 13th consecutive title in 2008 is determined to set his sights on 4000!

Another failure to end his Grand National drought, on Butler's Cabin in 2009, left him lamenting: 'If, like me, you are stupid enough to believe you are going to win it, the anticipation of winning makes it that much more exciting.' Some may even have believed that he had resigned himself to the ever lengthening wait!

McCoy has always accepted that he may not be the greatest natural riding talent ever – 'There are people who have more talent than I have, but what is a more natural sportsman than someone who wins all the time?' he asked *The Times'* racing writer Andrew Longmore somewhat rhetorically in early 2009. 'If I was a footballer would I be looking at Cristiano Ronaldo? No, I'd be looking at Ryan Giggs and Paul Scholes.' John Francome concurred – 'Where Ruby Walsh is like Bobby Moore, McCoy is Roy Keane'.

Not everyone agrees with *Racing Post* statistician John Randall, who rates McCoy 'clearly the greatest of all time' and former champion jump jockey Terry Biddlecombe who calls him 'the greatest jump jockey of all time'. Ace *Post* tipster Tom Segal called McCoy 'the best jockey from Monday to Friday and brilliant on bad horses in bad races. But in terms of aesthetics I don't think McCoy is even in the top four. For me he doesn't win enough big races anymore.'

Yet his triumph on the ill fated Wichita Lineman, who was killed in his next race, which McCoy nudged, pushed, cajoled, kidded and drove to win at the 2009 Cheltenham Festival demonstrated that he was still at the height of his powers and to be ignored at punters' peril in those 'big races'. He did the same again on Hennessy in the Bet365 Gold Cup a couple of weeks later.

When he does give up a life in the saddle, wife Chanelle, a successful businesswoman in her own right, thinks he might wish to pursue a new career – as a secret agent! 'He idolises Jason Bourne (fictitious trained assassin) and reckons he'd be very good at his job.'

AIDAN O'BRIEN
Phone a friend

Few people would claim really to know much about the character of one of the most self-effacing, quietly spoken, yet universally respected and admired men on the racing scene worldwide.

The prevailing image of Aidan O'Brien is of a man celebrating his latest Group One success by receiving or making a call on his mobile phone – usually, it is suggested, to or from supportive wife, Anne-Marie. He met the part time model at Galway races in 1989, where he won a maiden race in which she finished down the field, and became involved with her and her father Joe Crowley's training set-up. They now have four children.

The bespectacled, softly spoken, baby-faced, teetotal handler, who has re-written the record books is no relation whatsoever to his legendary predecessor as top Irish trainer, Dr Vincent O'Brien, yet has dominated the flat racing world in Britain and Ireland to an even greater extent than that worthy achieved. (He was, though, also a champion amateur jump jockey, and champion National Hunt trainer in Ireland and has admitted, 'I suppose my roots are in jump racing'.)

O'Brien took over the massive Coolmore operation, a 285-acre farm ringed by mountains in County Tipperary, on behalf of the mega-wealthy triumvirate of John Magnier, Michael Tabor and Derrick Smith, aged just 23 from Vincent, who retired in October 1994. During 2008 all the talk was that the Ballydoyle-based trainer, would beat the record number of Group/Grade One victories worldwide, which was held by American, Bobby Frankel, who sent out 25 in 2003.

In the event, O'Brien came up just short with a nonetheless superb total of 23, matching his own personal best, first achieved in 2001.

The bid foundered, ironically enough, in the States, when he failed to manage a winner during the two days of the Breeders' Cup meeting; then his tilt at the Melbourne Cup ended in ignominy when he was called back from his hotel by the stewards – who took no action after a lengthy inquiry – to discuss his race tactics which saw three of his horses, well fancied Septimus, Alessandro Volta and Honolulu, set off to blaze a trail, only to run out of steam and subside to the rear of the field at the business end of the race.

The Aussie press laid into O'Brien – 'costly display of arrogance' shouted the *Melbourne Herald*; 'one of the most baffling Cup misreads of all time'; 'they had one game plan – a stupid one'; 'an Irish joke' jibed the *Morning Herald* in Sydney; even the *Sydney Daily Telegraph*, 'Septimus turned out to be a lot of blarney'. Even James Willoughby wondered in the *Racing Post* – 'Isn't he (O'Brien) in danger of getting a bit carried away with pacemakers? If you have the best horse, don't go and beat it yourself.'

'We got it completely wrong' said O'Brien – but it would be a brave man who would bet against his getting it right, sooner rather than later – 'We will have a long, hard look at how we will approach the race next time.'

It was also a season during which O'Brien's alleged 'team-tactics' during certain races, proved controversial with some observers indicating disquiet when they believed that not all of his horses were running individually to win, as much as to ensure that their stable won. This was an allegation levelled at them previously by Frankie Dettori, who O'Brien, in an uncharacteristic outburst after the 2006 Queen Elizabeth II Stakes accused of 'throwing his toys out of the pram like a spoilt child' when he spoke out, complaining that his mount had been carried wide by O'Brien's Ivan Denisovich, ridden by Seamus Heffernan, who got a 14 day suspension – reduced on appeal to 6 – for careless riding. This might suggest that Frankie had a point. Aidan did not agree – 'When things didn't work out, he (Dettori) had to blame someone.'

O'Brien attended an inquiry (clutching his phone en route) at the British Horseracing Authority in September 2008 and was far from happy when he was fined £5,000 after being found in breach of the rules following the Juddmonte International Stakes the previous month when Johnny Murtagh on winner Duke of Marmalade appeared to have been assisted by a manoeuvre from stable-mate

Colm O'Donoghue on Red Rock Canyon. Both jockeys were suspended for seven days. Betting expert Greg Wood, of the *Guardian*, summed up what the hearing had achieved: 'This looks like an ill-judged inquiry founded on a poorly-framed rule. Team Ballydoyle is now in no doubt about the BHA's attitude to pacemakers, but at what cost? Europe's top trainer is left feeling persecuted and the most successful jockey (Johnny Murtagh) may well decide that talking to the media is no longer worth it.'

O'Brien contented himself by saying 'We were very disappointed with the outcome but it's time to move on.' The *Racing Post* blasted the hearing as 'a shambles from late beginning to sorry end.'

The season was nonetheless record-breaking for O'Brien, who became the first trainer since 1935 when Jack Rogers achieved the feat, to win all five Irish Classics in one season.

There is little doubt that O'Brien is as close as racing has ever come to a perfectionist – seeking such a level of performance from his entire stable is unattainable. 'He devotes such obsessive energy to the job that the undoubted strains of training for men whose expectations match their wealth once seemed likely to crush him' wrote *The Times'* racing journalist, Alan Lee, also suggesting that 'if anecdotal evidence is to be believed, O'Brien used to be physically sick on the gallops, such were his anxiety excesses.'

Perhaps one of the ways he has dealt with the pressure was revealed when he was asked by writer Paul Haigh about the stresses of being a celebrity. He described himself as being 'delighted to be part of a team like this.' He has also said, 'It's really a 24/7 job and teamwork is the key.' He did admit during 2008 that the pressure could still get to him. Discussing Septimus' Irish St Leger win with Tony O'Hehir, O'Brien conceded, 'While I underplayed it at the time there was big pressure. Going to the Curragh that day we were in a situation that we might never be in again.' That team ethic is backed up by an inherent modesty – his entry in the *2008 Directory of the Turf* consisted of just three lines, listing name, address and contact details, plus date of first trainer's licence. Other entries by far lesser lights of the profession ran to some 40 lines.

Born in October 1969, in Clonroche, County Wexford, the third of six children, (father Denis – who died in December 2008, on the eve of Aidan's latest Flat Trainer of the Year accolade from the Horse Race Writers' and Photographers' Association – rode 140 point-to-point winners) Aidan Patrick O'Brien had a great grounding in racing. From the age of 17, shortly after leaving college – where the principal had the closing stages of Dawn Run's Gold Cup triumph broadcast over the tannoy system – he decided the first two paid jobs he had, picking strawberries and driving a fork-lift, were not for him. He decided he wanted to be in racing, and after a brief stint with P.J. Finn, learned his trade for over three years under Irish master trainer, Jim Bolger – 'I did just about everything there'.

On 11 January 1989, he contested a bumper (a race for jumps horses run on the flat) at Punchestown, landing his first win on Bolger's 7/2 chance Galacto Boy – 'Riding my first winner was special and it felt very good at the time.'

He eventually left Bolger to work with Anne-Marie, who by now had a full training licence of her own. Bolger was a little reluctant to lose him, but admitted, 'I would have done anything to keep Aidan, bar marry him!' The partnership flourished and she became Ireland's first female champion jumps trainer in 1992/93. When they began a family, Aidan took over the licence and by 1993/94 he was champion jumps trainer. He had already decided that a central plank of his technique would be to keep his horses fit and busy – 'Horses are happier kept on the go.' Unlike many trainers, he also believes, 'I don't think it does any horse any harm to get beaten.'

When the call came to move to Ballydoyle, 'I met with Paul Shanahan who works for the boss (John Magnier, who was well aware of O'Brien's impact on Irish racing), and he asked me if I would be interested.' He needed no second bidding.

He was soon on the road to greatness, sending out the first three in the 1995 Galway Plate, winning at Cheltenham with Urubande in 1996, winning for the first time at Royal Ascot in 1997. King of Kings won him the 1998 2000 Guineas, the year Istabraq won his first Champion Hurdle. O'Brien became Ireland's champion flat race trainer for the first time in 1999 and Istabraq completed his Champion Hurdle hat trick in 2000. He had 23 Group One wins in 2001, a record tally – with Johannesburg netting him a first Breeders' Cup victory – followed by 19 more in 2002.

He was involved in a cause celebre involving record breaking Rock of Gibraltar. During his two seasons in racing (2001/02), the colt was trained by O'Brien who also bred him in partnership with his wife

Anne-Marie and father-in-law Joe Crowley. Over the course of two seasons, the horse set a world record of seven consecutive Group One wins and was voted the 2002 European Horse of the Year.

For much of his racing career, Rock of Gibraltar ran in the colours of Manchester United manager Sir Alex Ferguson, who was named as a part-owner along with Susan Magnier, wife of Coolmore owner John Magnier.

Upon Rock of Gibraltar's retirement, though, Ferguson and John Magnier were involved in a dispute over the exact nature of the ownership of the horse which threatened to get a little, er, untidy, and was eventually settled out of court.

In 2003 O'Brien dipped to nine Group One wins, although High Chaparral completed a Breeders' Cup double in the Turf race.

In 2004, with Jamie Spencer now stable jockey, the stable managed a mere three Group Ones – and many pundits were blaming Spencer who, in 2005, quit the job – but then proved he was indeed a fine jockey by winning the British jockey title. Kieren Fallon succeeded Spencer and quickly established himself as Ballydoyle once more became the stable to beat, winning three English Classics in 2005, two more plus the Ascot Gold Cup in 2006, and the Gold Cup again 2007 along with the French 2000 Guineas, Irish Derby and Oaks.

In 2006 punters were not best pleased after George Washington was backed down to 5/6 to win at Goodwood on his comeback from injury, only to finish third with O'Brien declaring, 'I couldn't be happier. It was not about winning today, it was about coming here and doing things right'. Punters might have appreciated being told that a little earlier.

There was also tragedy in 2007 when the same George Washington, brought back to race from stud where he had reportedly not enjoyed himself that much, was killed, far from home, at Monmouth Park racecourse in New Jersey on the second day of a Breeders' Cup meeting staged in what often seemed like a monsoon. I was there and, as the accident happened – he suffered a fracture of the ankle – the place went silent. Celebrations by connections of the winner were muted as a pall of gloom fell over the racecourse.

The one question which remains about O'Brien's place in the pantheon of greatness is whether he could do it on his own without the patronage and resources to which he currently has access. But his own level of success heaps pressure on his shoulders to exceed it each year. Although recognised as a master trainer, he is not the top man at Ballydoyle and maybe part of him still wonders what heights he might reach if every decision were his own. Perhaps he would even like to get back to training jumpers. I for one would not bet against him maintaining his reputation and success should he ever strike out on a solo flight.

PETER O'SULLEVAN
For Pete's sake

'Reaching ninety has to be a long shot in any lifetime, but, considering the health troubles I had when I was young, you couldn't have invented a price about my chances of making it. A million to one might have been about right'. Which makes it all the more baffling that Sir Peter O'Sullevan did not collect a huge bet when he reached that particular milestone in his life on 3 March 2008. To mark the occasion Cheltenham Festival's National Hunt Chase was renamed in his honour.

When I had spoken to him a matter of weeks earlier – he had been kind enough to take the trouble to call me when I contacted him to say I was researching a book about Dorothy Paget – he had sounded as sharp and on the ball as someone half of his great age.

In 2008, a number of his best known commentaries – dating from Arkle winning the Gold Cup in the 1960s – were made available as ringtones, sold for £3 a time to raise money for charity. Those commentaries, as much as his long-surviving *Daily Express* racing column, were what made O'Sullevan a household name and no one has ever described his style more accurately than Hugh McIlvanney, when the great writer paid him the tribute of saying of him, 'had he been on the rails at Balaclava he would have kept pace with the Charge of the Light Brigade, listing the fallers in precise order and describing the riders' injuries before they hit the ground.'

At this point O'Sullevan was in his 11th year of retirement, having quit after calling his 50th Grand National in 1997, using his trusty binoculars, which allegedly came from a German submarine. It was also the year of his knighthood, and the instantly recognisable vocal tones remained pretty much intact and still instantly recognisable.

No one has captured the appeal of the O'Sullevan voice better than the *Daily Telegraph*'s Sue Mott, who described it as 'accompanied by a magnificent authority, mellifluous beauty, grammatical proficiency and a hint of drollery.'

His last race commentary was the 1997 Hennessy Cognac Gold Cup at Newbury – the next race on the card was won by O'Sullevan's appropriately named Sounds Fyne in the Fulke Walwyn Chase.

He was by this time devoting his considerable energies to the charity bearing his name, the Sir Peter O'Sullevan Charitable Trust, which works for the protection of animals – appropriately enough for someone who as a child raised fears that he had been kidnapped when he disappeared for hours, only to be discovered sheltering a poor pony left out in the pouring rain by holding an umbrella over him. His Annual Award Trust Luncheon has raised over £2 million, which has been distributed to six equine beneficiaries – the Thoroughbred Rehabilitation Centre; Racing Welfare; Blue Cross; Compassion in World Farming; the Brooke Hospital for Animals; and World Horse Welfare. Explaining once why he and wife Pat remained childless, he said, 'I have a warmer leaning towards all types of animals than humans and Pat said that doubtless I would rather have a horse.'

Enlarging on his interest in the welfare of animals, O'Sullevan said: 'One of my obsessions is the way we abuse and exploit animals. I have this simplistic view that harmony is unlikely to break out among us until we accept our responsibility for the lesser creatures.'

He has never tolerated over zealous use of the whip – 'In the course of my career as a commentator, one practice which developed, in both flat and jumping, which I found disturbing was the habitual misuse of the whip. I considered it unnecessary, unproductive and offensive.'

Mind you, perhaps he has been ever so slightly guilty of neglecting one of his own animals, as the dedication in his very successful *Horse Racing Heroes* was to 'Pat, my wife whose forbearance has been matched only by that of our understanding, under-exercised poodle, Topo'!

He was born in County Kerry, Ireland – but you would struggle to detect that from his polished vocal chords – the son of Colonel Joseph O'Sullevan, DSO, resident magistrate at Killarney, and his wife Vera. He was brought up by his maternal grandparents in Surrey, when his parents divorced. Peter was educated at Hawtreys, Charterhouse School and at college in Switzerland, the latter to help combat his chronic asthma.

It was not always believed likely that he would make it to an advanced age. 'I was so sick and feeble as a youngster. I had double pneumonia four times – and you're not supposed to have it more than once, really.' He also suffered from a severe skin complaint which confined him for months before and after his 17th birthday, to the Middlesex Hospital where he had to wear a medicated mask – he now refers to the ordeal as his 'Phantom of the Opera time.'

He always wanted to get into racing and in early 1925 he became the owner of a pony – 'When Fairy and I galloped round Tattenham Corner some three months before the 1925 Derby winner, Manna, I had the sure conviction of a seven-year-old that I would be a jockey.' He nearly achieved his aim but, looking back, now regards 'contracting pneumonia on eve of intended association with equally unskilled partner in wartime novice chase at Plumpton' as his 'most fortuitous racing experience.'

In 1928 he struck punting gold at the age of 10 when he invested a large proportion of the O'Sullevan coffers – 1/- (5p) – on a gamble in the Grand National. 'I had sixpence each-way. Only two finished that year and one had to be remounted. That was Tipperary Tim who won at 100/1.'

The 'voice of racing' as he would become known, (by everyone except Richard Pitman who once dubbed him 'the race of voicing') was in the vanguard of TV commentaries towards the end of the 1940s. He also wrote as racing correspondent for the *Daily Express* for 36 years. His early TV appearances did not impress his mother, who told him, 'Darling, I saw you on television yesterday and you looked absolutely ghastly. I do hope you're never going to do that again.'

During the War, unfit for service, he joined the Chelsea Civil Defence Rescue Service, for which he dodged bombs and rescued many civilians. It was at this stage that a slow beast named Wild Thyme became his first runner. In his first 15 years as an owner, he took on 16 animals, all of which had something in common – none of them ever finished in the first three. Of owning in general, O'Sullevan has said, 'Though success provides emotional compensation for countless reverses, it has to be admitted that racehorse ownership in general represents the purest form of economic suicide.'

It was inevitable that at some point he would have to call a winner for himself – and it happened in the 1974 Triumph Hurdle at Cheltenham. As they came to the winning post, O'Sullevan declared deadpan 'And it's first Attivo . . . trained by Cyril Mitchell . . . ridden by Robert Hughes . . . owned by Peter O'Sullevan.' He always tried to remain detached from the punting implications of runners in races on which he was commentating – 'People used to say to me, "I can tell what you've backed". And I'm glad to say 90 per cent of the time they were wrong. Which pleased me. I tried to keep my bias to myself. Even when I was haemorrhaging fiscally they couldn't spot it.'

On another occasion O'Sullevan was commentating on the 1956 Royal Hunt Cup, won narrowly by the Queen, whose Alexander just pipped Rae Johnstone-ridden Jasp, on which 'I had had quite a serious ante-post bet.' Confessed Sir Peter, 'Jasp and Alexander finished on the opposite sides of the course. It was very difficult to tell. That was the one time when I think I announced the Queen's winner with possibly just a faint tinge of regret.'

O'Sullevan also bred the versatile Attivo – twice a winner on the flat under Lester Piggott – and first impressions had not been promising: 'He was as narrow as a plank, with his feet turned out like Charlie Chaplin and the trainer said, "You'll be lucky enough to run this one at White City"!'

O'Sullevan has an enduring relationship with Piggott and recalls a time in the earlier days when he fixed the jockey up with a winning ride. 'At Newbury races he slipped into my hand a neatly folded square of white paper which, in those days, was a £5 note. When I politely rejected the gift on the grounds that, as a journalist, I was fully recompensed by being first with the news he clearly regarded my reaction as indicative of possibly dangerous imbalance.' Piggott said of his commentating career: 'Compared with him, the rest are all amateurs.'

Attivo wasn't his only high profile winner, by any means – his Be Friendly won the King's Stand Stakes at Ascot and Longchamp's Prix de l'Abbaye. The horse also twice won the Haydock Sprint Cup in 1966 and 1967 and was denied the chance of a hat trick when the 1968 meeting was abandoned due to waterlogging.

Another bugbear for commentators is their pronunciation of various names – no one seems sure, for example whether it is SouthWELL or Suthll – and Sir Peter alluded to this once – 'Sometimes, where an Irish horse is concerned you can ring up half a dozen of its connections and they'll all pronounce it differently themselves.'

A keen and regular punter, Sir Peter's advice to others of this type is worth hearing, 'I believe that punters who impose restrictions on themselves – never betting odds-on, for example – act against their own interest. The only limitation should be, never bet beyond capacity to pay.' He also pointed out, 'There's a big difference between a punter and a gambler. I've been backing horses all my life – but I'm not a gambler.'

Maybe Sue Mott was being only a little fanciful when she suggested that in order to cement his immortality, 'The sound of Peter calling the horses should be one of our exports into outer space to signify the depth of our civilisation.'

LESTER PIGGOTT
Action not words

'An iconoclast who became an icon' wrote Peter O'Sullevan of the incomparable Lester Piggott – and those words were inscribed on The Piggott Gates at Epsom in a unique tribute to the 'Long fellow' in 1996.

Although a slight speech impediment and deafness have contributed to a paucity of words from Lester over the years, he summed up his glittering career succinctly when he returned in June 2005 to the scene of his first ever public ride on 17 April 1948, to open Salisbury's new stand. 'You just knew that you worked very hard, a lot harder than people do now, and you turned up to do a job.

You didn't think about where it might lead, to the Derby or races like that, you just got on with what you had to do.' He also pointed out, 'that's one thing about not wanting to talk very much – I get time to read about racing, and to listen and to think.'

This winner of winners – a record 30 domestic Classic winners to his credit – said that 'winning isn't all that important, it's the wanting to win that matters.'

As single minded as any sportsman who ever lived, Piggott shrugged off the deprivations integral to his trade, telling writer Hugh McIlvanney in 1967 that 'wasting's not much fun but maybe it's just as bad being a big fat man'. In the same year he showed off his mastery of his profession when his bridle broke just after the start when he was riding Chestergate at Newmarket, yet still finished second, using the horse's mane to steer with. Jump jockey Graham Bradley, for whom Piggott was a childhood hero believes that 'he could even think like a horse'.

Lester came from a family steeped in racing. His great-great-great-great-grandfather John Day was a trainer in 1775. His grandfather was a top jump jockey, who married Margaret, the daughter of champion jockey Thomas Cannon. His mother, Iris, a lady rider, was daughter of Classic winning jockey, Frederick Rickaby – whose son, also Frederick, was a Classic winning jockey too, whose middle name was Lester. He was killed in action during the First World War. As former BBC racing correspondent Julian Wilson observed: 'Lester Keith Piggott was born and bred to ride; there was no alternative. His pedigree is the human equivalent to that of the finest thoroughbred.'

Born on 5 November 1935, Lester Piggott was apprenticed to his three times champion jump jockey/trainer father Keith. There is a marvellous tale concerning Piggott Snr dating from his victory in the 1925 Welsh Grand National on Vaulx. Keith recalled: 'On pulling up, Jack Anthony – who had ridden Old Tay Bridge – asked me where I'd finished. "I won" I replied. "Don't talk rubbish, I won" said Jack. He hadn't seen me, probably because he'd drunk a ginger-beer bottle full of port before he went out to ride.'

Lester won his first race at Haydock Park on The Chase on 18 August 1948, aged 12 and weighing out at 6st 9lbs (42kg). There would be 4,492 more domestic winners.

He grew to 5ft 8ins (1.72m) and rode at around 8 stone (50kg), but had to waste to remain at that weight. It was said of Lester that he survived on a diet of half a glass of Champagne, coffee and a cigar a day and that the only thing he ever digested was the *Sporting Life*.

His first Derby win came in 1954 on 33/1 shot, Never Say Die. To say he was underwhelmed might be an under-statement. 'I was driven home by my parents, spent an hour mowing the lawn and, as usual, was in bed soon after 9pm.'

This was followed just a fortnight later by a major setback when he was accused of 'dangerous and erratic' riding by the stewards after the King Edward VII Stakes at Ascot. His licence was withdrawn for six months – later commuted to just over three – and he was forced to serve time with a trainer other than his father. He was allowed back in 1955 when he became first jockey to Sir Noel Murless, a 12-year association which produced glorious success. February 1959 saw Lester win on Jive at Sandown – the last of his 20 winners over hurdles. He became champion jockey in 1960 and won both the Derby and St Leger of that year on St Paddy.

In 1962 Lester was in trouble again when he had his licence withdrawn once more, this time for making no effort to win on a horse called Ione in a selling race at Lingfield – won by that horse's stablemate, Polly Macaw. Trainer R Ward had his licence withdrawn too.

Lester and controversy would be frequent partners: 'In one race at Deauville he snatched a whip from Alain Lequeux when his own had gone flying; in another at Sha Tin, he pushed away the head of a persistent challenger with his hand. The inevitable penalties were shrugged off as inconsequential' wrote the late racing journalist Graham Rock. Fellow jockey Bryn Crossley once neatly summed up Lester's attitude to racing's powers-that-be: 'One of the grandest sights in racing has always been to see Lester hauled before the stewards. He goes in there like Clint Eastwood and he comes out like Clint Eastwood. Lester doesn't give a monkey's.'

The winners were soon flowing again, and in 1964, Lester regained the jockey championship, and held on to it for a further seven years. In 1967 Lester became a freelance rider. He won the 2000 Guineas and Derby on Vincent O'Brien's Sir Ivor in 1968, then completed the Triple Crown on Nijinsky in 1970, also winning the 1000 Guineas on Humble Duty.

In 1972 he controversially 'jocked off' Bill Williamson ('It is part of a jockey's job to get on to the best horses, and if that involves ruffling a few feathers, so be it.') to take his Derby mount on Roberto and in one of the hardest fought of all finishes, Piggott forced Roberto home ahead of the battling Rheingold. 'I had to win, you know, and he wasn't doing much for me. I felt he could go faster if only he would' was how Lester later justified the stern examination of Roberto's character, some of which was administered via the whip.

Lester was awarded the OBE in 1975, the year in which he rode eight Royal Ascot winners for the second time. Piggott's record seventh Derby win was on Empery in 1976 – then he did it again a year later on The Minstrel. Finally, he landed his ninth Derby win on Teenoso in 1983.

'Lester Piggott was the greatest of contemporary jockeys' declared 1978's prestigious *Biographical Encyclopaedia of British Flat Racing* – and few argued with that description.

The majority of punters loved Lester – particularly the once a year Derby punters, for whom he booted home a string of winners. Some were a little less enthusiastic, believing that he would pick and choose the mounts he really gave the full 'Lester treatment'.

Retiring in 1985 he took up an almost forgotten training career which produced 34 winners from his Eve Lodge stables which boasted 97 inmates at its peak.

In October 1987 Lester was sensationally jailed for what the *Daily Mail* called 'tax fraud' involving £3.25m. He was handed a three year sentence, serving 366 days and, reportedly earning money inside by tipping winners to inmates. Later, he was stripped of his OBE, about which Peter O'Sullevan commented: 'He considered that an unacceptable and unwarrantably hurtful act. So do I'. There has since been a movement formed with the aim of getting the honour restored to Lester who, as far as I know, has not backed the objective.

He returned to the saddle in 1990 aged 55 (asked how he would find the game on his return, Lester suggested 'It's still the same. One leg each side.') and within a fortnight had landed his most valuable winner ever, riding a sublime race to win the Breeders' Cup Mile (worth $450,000 to the winner) in the States on Vincent O'Brien-trained Royal Academy: 'the most dramatic comeback in sporting history' according to Peter O'Sullevan. In that year the annual Jockey Awards known as the Lesters were inaugurated.

Rodrigo de Triano gave him his 30th and final Classic winner in the 1992 2000 Guineas. Later that year he was rushed to hospital after taking a terrible fall at Gulfstream, which his mount, Mr Brooks, failed to survive. 'A tragic loss of a fine horse' said Lester, who played down his own injuries, (broken collarbone, two broken ribs) declaring he had suffered worse falling out of bed.

Lester narrowly avoided death when he, Michael Hills, Philip Robinson and George Duffield were all aboard a plane to York which narrowly missed colliding with an RAF jet in August 1992.

Lester's comeback apparently did little to alter his appreciation of money, and when he was offered a nice keepsake by grateful owner Robert Ellis after winning on 100/8 shot Pirate Victory at Nottingham in May 1994, the jockey admitted, 'I'd rather have a cheque.'

He rode his last winner (possibly) in October 1994 and retired once more in 1995, although he did return to the saddle for a veterans' race in November in 2000 at the age of 65. Always a fundamentally modest man, when, in August 2008, Lester thought back on the 60th anniversary of his first ever winner, he commented, 'It was just the start of the job, really, wasn't it? That's all.'

Bookies of a certain age who have yet to forget the ritual poundings they would take from Lester fans must have felt a twinge of apprehension when they read the *Sunday Telegraph* story of 10 August 2008. It revealed 'in a move that will send a chill down the spine of bookmakers, Lester Piggott's child, Jamie (14-year-old son of long term mistress, Anna Ludlow), is poised to follow in the footsteps of his celebrated father and become a professional jockey.'

MARTIN PIPE
Pipe dream

A man who would only eat straight bananas and whose only vegetable of choice is processed marrowfat peas was always likely to bring a different approach to whatever area of work he opted to take up. So, when Martin Pipe, born on 29 May 1945, the son of a Somerset bookmaker, and with no grounding in the racing world, decided to begin training racehorses he was initially greeted with a mixture of scepticism and condescension.

At least he was, until winners began to flow from the former pig farm at Pond House, Nicholashayne, Wellington, stables in record numbers, at which point others in the game were obliged to take him seriously and begin to reconsider their own approach to a business in which Pipe was not only re-writing the record books but also changing the way in which horses were prepared for their races.

His first winner as a trainer was unremarkable enough, and few paid much attention to Hit Parade's victory under Len Lungo in a selling hurdle at Taunton in May 1975 – but it sent Pipe on his way to the top of the training charts. Pipe's tough task-master father David, who had predicted that his son would never train winners, told him that the credit for Hit Parade's win belonged with Gay Kindersley, the trainer responsible for him until shortly before the race.

Pipe believes there was method in his father's tough love – 'Maybe he did that to make me more determined.' Or perhaps he was miffed that Martin's efforts to follow in his father's footsteps did not last much longer than his bookie apprenticeship in the family's Taunton office. Whatever, he didn't really hold it against his son. 'The best advice I ever received was from Dad – he said "there's no such word as can't".' He later ran a betting shop at Minehead Butlin's. Perhaps because he was a bookie's son, Pipe was quoted in 1988 as saying: 'Nowadays the bookies don't give you a chance. And, anyway, I'm far too busy to bet. The bookmaker always wins in the end you know.'

In 1981 he broke through to the big time when his outsider Baron Blakeney was his first Cheltenham Festival winner, landing the Triumph Hurdle at odds of 66/1. And the success flowed. An incredibly successful partnership was cemented on 2 March 1985 at Haydock, when Hieronymous was jockey Peter Scudamore's first ride – and first winner – for Pipe. Two years later he sent out seven consecutive winners at Devon and Exeter in August 1987. Beau Ranger made history for Pipe on 1 March 1989, giving the trainer a previously unachieved 150th winner in a single jumps season. Three days later his rivals must have believed that Pipe could be in more than one place at the same time – as he sent out two runners at Hereford; two at Newbury and two at Haydock – and all six won.

On 22 April he became the most successful trainer over one season when High Bid at Uttoxeter was his 181st winner of the campaign, passing the record formerly held by Henry Cecil, who set it in 1987. He duly crashed through the 200 barrier, winning his first title in 1989, surrendering it only twice during the nineties and early part of the 21st century.

On 28 May 1990 Pipe produced nine winners at six different meetings. On 27 December of the same year he became the youngest trainer ever to send out 1,000 winners when his Catch the Cross won at Kempton.

Pipe made an odd choice of assistant when former table tennis great, Chester Barnes joined his set up – his Three of Diamonds, unplaced at 100/1 in 1981 was Pipe's first Grand National runner. Barnes, who divulged details of the straight banana fetish, also once revealed a hitherto unexpected side to Pipe, when he spoke of visiting 'one of the roughest pubs in Brixham – you can see him there singing along with all these hairy trawlermen!'

He became the first trainer in history to win £1 million prize money in a jump season when Colour Scheme won at Southwell on 15 April 1991. Four months later on 23 August he and Peter Scudamore had the first five winners at Devon & Exeter – finishing agonisingly in second place with 5/6 favourite Ever Smile in the last.

His total of winners in 1991/92 was 224. During 1991 Pipe was badly affected by the experience of an episode of the investigative programme, *The Cook Report*, which endeavoured to cast aspersions on his training methods and pointed to what it regarded as an unacceptable attrition rate amongst the stable's inmates. He later called it 'the lowest moment – a very spiteful programme without foundation.'

It was no mean feat for Pipe to saddle the first *four* home in the 1992 Coral Welsh National as Run For Free, 11/4 joint favourite, beat Riverside Boy, 50/1, with Miinehoma, 11/4, third and Bonanza Boy fourth. He had also won the race for the previous three years.

Pipe was never averse to borrowing ideas from different sources and revealed that in his early days as a trainer he would visit top handlers and 'borrow' a little of the feed they were giving their charges – 'I've still got packets of samples at home from Henry Cecil, Michael Stoute, Geoff Wragg, Clive Brittain and a dozen other stables.' Blood tests and relentless fitness training made up an integral part of his training technique.

He was so commited to his profession that on the rare occasions he took holidays he and wife Carol would travel to Barbados – where he rapidly discovered a betting shop where he could watch British racing. 'They know me well and they even let me watch in the back room.'

In January 1993 Pipe completed his seventh consecutive century of winners in a season. On 20 February of that year Milford Quay won at Chepstow for stable jockey Peter Scudamore to bring up Pipe's 1,500th winner over jumps in Britain. Pipe revealed one of the secrets of his success: 'We have Radio One playing in every box – it keeps the horses relaxed.'

Scudamore was clearly okay with Pipe – but not all riders – 'It can be very hard to get through to jockeys. Some are deaf, some can't count, and some are brilliant.' What of his own exploits in the saddle? He'd dabbled at being a jockey, but retired with a career total of one winner. 'I think my saving grace as a jockey was determination, backed up by bravery, bordering on stupidity – I fell off more times than I stayed on, yet doggedly refused to let go of the reins. As for race riding, I admit I lacked the basic skills, although I got quite good at falling.' One of those falls, resulting in a smashed thigh, was at Taunton in December 1972, from a horse called Lorac – his wife's Christian name in reverse.

Martin Pipe has nominated chaser Carvill's Hill as 'the best I'll ever train', but that horse was the subject of a great falling out with Jenny Pitman after the 1992 Gold Cup, for which he was well fancied. Controversy surrounded the running of Pitman's Golden Freeze which stayed very close to the market leader, whose jumping seemed to suffer as a result. She was later cleared of any offence in the race which Cool Ground won.

With his reputation for innovation, an unorthodox ploy at Taunton in January 1993 saw Martin's wife Carol called into action when Elite Reg's tongue strap was found to be missing pre-race – Mrs Pipe promptly dashed to the ladies, where she removed her tights, which were then used to hold down the horse's tongue. The horse was pulled up.

The remaining valid criticism of Pipe – that he did not train the winners of top quality championship races went flying out of the window on 16 March 1993 when Granville Again and Peter Scudamore were the 13/2 winners of the Champion Hurdle. The following month Scudamore retired with 1,678 winners to his credit. In 1988/89 he rode a then record 221 winners.

Scudamore would say of Pipe, 'He broke all the boundaries. Martin has never accepted boundaries, never.' He thrived on the way in which other stables regarded them with suspicion – 'We would get down to the post and set off from the front and would already have the race half-won because the rest thought we were doing this or that, cheating, all those rumours. We had them psychologically.'

Pipe had a somewhat difficult relationship with most of the media – a racing writer friend of mine, Gary Nutting, told me that he had apparently been literally black-listed by Pipe who would refuse point blank, rather in the style of Sir Alex Ferguson, to respond to any questions he asked. Perhaps, when you read the answer he did give when asked for a reason to explain the recent improvement in behaviour of one of his hurdlers, Pridwell, you'll sympathise with the members of the fourth estate, as he deadpanned, 'It could be something to do with the fact that Donna, who looks after him at home, has got married since last season.'

Respected racing writer J.A. McGrath of the *Daily Telegraph* believes that his 'natural tendency to be suspicious of, and less than open with, the Press' was 'a legacy of his time in bookmaking' but 'eventually led his critics to believe he had something to hide.'

He received a kind of Royal approval later in 1994 when he and other racing figures were invited to a lunch organised by the Queen Mother. 'Maybe she wanted some tips for the last days of the jumps season' speculated Chester Barnes, who later suffered a heart attack and whose first question to Pipe when he recovered was 'How did the runners at Taunton perform?'

Owned by comedian Freddie Starr, who had bid for it at auction by sticking his tongue out, Miinnehoma won the 1994 Grand National for Pipe, completing a full set of Nationals, as he had won the Welsh five times, the Irish in 1991 and Scottish in 1993.

In January 1997 Pipe showed he could laugh at himself – when he sponsored a race at Taunton, he called it the 'Am I That Difficult? Handicap Hurdle.'

Make A Stand won the 1997 Champion Hurdle for Pipe – causing mixed feelings for TV and radio commentator John Inverdale, who had been a part-owner of the horse, only to leave the syndicate.

1999/2000 was his most successful season in numerical terms, as he sent out 243 winners in all. In December 1999 he was awarded the CBE for his contribution to horse racing.

He was asked in 2001 how he could spot prospective winners amongst untried horses which could be anything: 'Look at people pushing wheelbarrows. You can tell those whose hearts aren't in it, and you can tell the triers. It's the same with horses. I don't always get it right, but it's lovely when I do.' He was responsible for 10 Grand National runners that year – a quarter of the entire field – only one of which completed the course, Blowing Wind, third of the four who got round.

Those who believe that Pipe never really warmed to the horses in his stables should note his response to the loss of excellent hurdler Valiramix, who was fancied for the 2002 Champion Hurdle. 'Valiramix was an especially lovely horse and we kept his box empty for about six weeks. Whenever you walked past you felt his death all over again.' Pipe's father, David, died early in 2002, aged 78.

Tony McCoy, champion jockey nine times in a row when stable jockey for Pipe, departed in April 2004 to team up with trainer Jonjo O'Neill, riding wealthy owner J.P. McManus' runners. He said, 'Martin and his family have been my family for the past eight years. I owe him everything I've achieved and hope to continue to ride for him whenever possible. He's a genius. Too many people forget that he re-invented how to train a racehorse'.

An incident in December 2004 suggested to some that maybe Martin Pipe was not averse to putting one over on the industry from which his father had profited. A horse called There Is No Doubt, trained by Helen Bridges won an obscure National Hunt flat race at Exeter. So far, so unremarkable. However, someone fancied the horse, which was backed from 28/1 to 5/2 favourite. It later emerged that the horse had previously been called Le Saadien, and it had recently been sold by one Martin Pipe to Mrs Bridges, whose jockey daughter Lucy was very close to David Pipe junior, and who later commented: 'It was an incredible win [at Exeter] and I'll never ever forget being accosted by reporters over what had happened. I hadn't a clue,' she said. 'Martin chose this horse for me, but I could have sent him back if I'd wanted to.' Asked how the publicity had affected her, Mrs Bridges added: 'At one point I never wanted to see another horse or another racecourse. But life has to go on – it's a storm in a teacup.' The horse's name change was, quite properly, carried out via Weatherbys, who organise such things.

Then rumours about the extent of, and the involvement in, the gamble by certain people possibly connected with the Pipe set-up began to do the rounds. The Jockey Club took an interest, but after interviewing various people, decided to take no further action.

In December 2004, *Daily Mail* sports diarist Charles Sale pointed out an apparently illogical situation involving the trainer, asking readers, 'How can the Jockey Club have any jurisdiction on gambling by racing insiders when the country's leading jumps trainer, Martin Pipe, hands out cards promoting his Pipeline betting service?'

When Contraband won the 2005 Arkle Trophy, Pipe revealed that he had bought the horse when he became bored whilst watching the film *Seabiscuit* at the cinema, where he had been taken 'against my will', so slipped out to arrange to buy the horse, thinking 'I don't want to be here – I'd rather be at the sales buying Contraband.'

The 2004/05 season turned into a photo finish as Pipe sought to peg back his great rival for the trainers' championship, Paul Nicholls, who at one stage was well clear, only for Pipe to overtake him on the final day of the campaign, showing how obsessive was his desire to retain his top dog tag. 'Everything was planned down to the last £15,000 race at Uttoxeter. I lay in bed, night after night, working out how we could catch him.' Not everyone welcomed his victory. Nicholls' owner, David Jackson griped: 'His desperate tactics in trying to hang on to "his" championship bordered on the unprofessional, unsporting, underhand and uncaring' he protested in the *Racing Post*.

Controversy had loomed again during the season when he was fined £7,500 after refusing to allow beaten favourite, Tanterari, to enter the sampling unit at Haydock, maintaining that the unit could be a cause of the spread of infection.

Pipe admitted in late 2005 that he had always wanted to have a crack at the French equivalent of the Gold Cup but, in something of a Little Englander manner, he complained, 'That's a race I've always wanted to win, but it's in June, which just doesn't suit us.' Trust those dastardly Frenchies to run their races at the times which best suit them!

In February 2006 there was a hint of what lay just around the corner when Pipe told *The Times*, 'Owners all seem to want young trainers now. The same thing happened to Fred Winter and W.A. Stephenson but I can't understand why. You wouldn't pick a doctor just because he's young, would you?'

Approaching 61, Pipe announced his retirement to the world via a telephone call to Channel 4's *Morning Line* programme at the end of the 2005/06 season, after which he began to work alongside David, his son and successor. He had 4,180 winners (including 250 or so on the flat), 15 titles, 32 (some sources say 34) Cheltenham (his favourite course, together with Haydock) Festival winners and six at Royal Ascot, to his credit. 'It is one of the few times on television I actually felt like crying. It is one of the saddest things I have ever had to deal with in racing' was Tony McCoy's rather melodramatic response. Some felt the timing was deliberate – to take some of the limelight away from newly crowned champion, Paul Nicholls.

After his retirement, flat trainer Sir Mark Prescott paid a glowing and thoughtful tribute. 'Only three people have changed their side of how the business of racing is conducted. The first was Admiral Rous (dictator of the turf of his day, 1795–1877), who worked out weight-for-age and handicapping. The second was (controversial jockey) Tod Sloan, who came over and changed the way jockeys rode. The third is Martin Pipe, who completely changed the way the National Hunt horse is trained. All those who whined and spread appalling rumours ended up training like him – and never had the good grace to apologise or thank him.'

Poor health was one of the reasons he quit, and when he met up with *Guardian* writer Donald McRae in October 2006 he told him of the effects of the muscle wasting disease which has affected him. As he and the journalist shook hands he said, 'Don't squeeze too hard' and revealed that 'like a lame old horse the doctors have put me on steroids. I say I'm fine, but it's not going to get better.'

The University of Liverpool conferred an honorary doctorate on Pipe as 'one of the world's leading trainers.' The University's Professor Chris Gaskell, himself a vet and Principal of the Royal Agricultural College said, 'In honouring Martin Pipe this University, with its Faculty of Veterinary Science, recognises someone who has reached the pinnacle of their profession, and recognises also the immense contribution that he has made to horse racing, and through that to the enjoyment, and occasional enrichment, of very many members of the general public.'

In January 2009 came a strong indication that, if they ever did harbour any grudges against him, the racing establishment was inclined to consign them to history, when it was announced that the Cheltenham Festival would feature a new race, to be known as the Martin Pipe Conditional Jockeys' Handicap Hurdle on Gold Cup day. A delighted Pipe declared, 'This is a huge honour. To be celebrated at The Festival is an amazing accolade, not only for me, but for all of my family and the magnificent team of people who made Pond House tick for 32 years.'

JENNY PITMAN
Knicker elastic

Jennifer Susan Pitman was the first female trainer to win the Grand National when Corbiere – named after Jersey's lighthouse – triumphed in 1983. He ran in the race five times in all, finishing third twice, 12th and falling once. Jenny Pitman's patience in training horses is demonstrated by the fact that she took on Corbiere as a three-year-old.

A plain speaking character who rapidly became very popular with the public for her no-nonsense approach to racing and life, she once gave a *Sun* reporter a mounted toilet roll 'for writing so much crap about me'. Never one to keep her opinions to herself, Pitman was described by respected *Times* sportswriter, Simon Barnes, in 2005, as 'by a considerable margin, the rudest woman I have ever met.' Yet for all that she was thoroughly devoted to her trade, as *Daily Telegraph* writer, Sue Mott, summed up: 'The only reason she banks with Lloyds is because of the black horse on their logo.'

Born the fourth of seven children in 1946, nee Harvey, Ms Pitman kept her married name despite divorcing jockey husband Richard, who she wed in 1965. Richard once described the qualities he looked for in his ideal woman – 'Gentleness, firm contours and a sense of humour.' While his ex's comment that 'I've had the greatest romances in my life with my horses' might help to explain their split.

After they broke up for the first time, Jenny – dubbed 'the Cuddly One' by John McCririck – considered working in a shoe shop but instead opted for working on a shoestring by taking on the almost derelict Weathercock House stables in Upper Lambourn. She sent out her first winner in 1975 and the relationship with Richard ended for good when he walked out on her at Christmas 1977.

Corbiere's 1982 Welsh National win brought her to prominence. By 1984 she was also trainer of the Cheltenham Gold Cup winner with Burrough Hill Lad, of whom she said, 'He's had more operations than Joan Collins – and maybe more men working on him.'

In April 1990 she was fined £200 by stewards at Ayr after striking unfortunate jockey, Jamie Osborne, in the face after her horse Run to Form collided with the rails – for which she blamed Osborne, who was riding Dwadme. She admits that during their contretemps she asked the jockey, 'Why don't you f***ing grow up, Osborne. I told you at Aintree, this job's dangerous enough without you being an arsehole.' Osborne later predicted, 'I'm going to be remembered for two things: being hit by Jenny Pitman in the weighing room at Ayr, and arrested on fraud charges.' Another jockey who is apparently not Jenny's greastest fan is John Francome who said of her, 'She is about as cuddly as a dead hedgehog.'

The 1992 Cheltenham Gold Cup saw Pitman mired in controversy as her Golden Freeze stayed very close to market leader Carvills Hill, whose jumping seemed to suffer as a result. She was later cleared of any offence. BBC commentator Julian Wilson was outraged by this incident: 'It was a widely held view that Golden Freeze had only been run in the race as a "stalking horse", whose only purpose was to prevent Carvills Hill from winning.' Jenny took legal advice and threatened to sue Wilson. She did not do so, but declared, 'I would sooner kiss my horse Garrison Savannah's arse than speak to Julian Wilson.'

She hit out angrily after the fiasco of the 1993 Grand National, when her Esha Ness passed the post first, only for the race to be declared void following the shambles of the botched false start. Whilst the 'race' was proceeding she invaded the weighing room in an effort to force stewards to stop the race, telling them 'My bloody horse has already gone one circuit. I don't want to win the National like this.' She later contemptuously and memorably described the National's malfunctioning starting tapes as 'knicker elastic'.

She finally won the National again in 1995 with 40/1 chance Royal Athlete, to cement her nickname, the Queen of Aintree. After which triumph she literally kissed and made up with Wilson. She then landed the Scottish National with Willsford.

In 1997 her Mudahim won the Irish Grand National – the first time anyone other than Martin Pipe had won all four major Nationals.

Jenny married for the second time in 1997 – after an 18-year engagement to David Stait, whose pet name for her was 'waggle bum', and a year later she received the OBE. On Christmas Eve 1998 Jenny heard that she was clear of the thyroid cancer with which she had been diagnosed during the previous year.

Her last and 797th winner was Scarlet Emperor at Huntingdon in May 1999. Later in the year she was presented with the Helen Rollason Award for Inspiration, celebrating women who overcome great adversity, inspiring others in the process. However, she was far from becoming a back number and set about attacking the literary world, producing a best selling autobiography and a series of thrillers. She also made a return to training – this time of greyhounds.

A somewhat fractious relationship with the numerically dominant male side of her sport has been a feature of Jenny's working life, as she recalled in her autobiography. 'I was the only woman at a function, when one of my colleagues came up to me and said, "You're looking bloody good, Jenny. Tell me, has your sex life improved?" I was taken aback by his rudeness, but I wasn't going to let him see it. "Yes, it certainly has" I said, "But I can see yours hasn't".'

RACING ROYALS
King and Queen of the turf

Racing has had few finer and more loyal or genuinely committed friends than the current monarch and her mother.

Her Majesty the Queen was born 21 April 1926, and first visited the races on 21 May 1945, attending Ascot's Whit Monday meeting where she saw Sun Up become the first winner of an Ascot race to be trained by a woman, Florence Nagle – although for 'official' purposes at the time it was listed as being trained by her head lad, R. Brown.

Her first runner as an owner was Astrakhan (Willie Smyth-Tommy Burns) which finished second in Ascot's Sandwell Stakes on 7 October 1949. Her first winner, and the first for 235 years owned by a Queen of England since Queen Anne's Star, was Monave'en, owned jointly with her mother, which won at 3/10 favourite over fences at Fontwell on 10 October 1949, ridden by Tony Grantham, for trainer Peter Cazalet.

In 1954, the year in which she first became the country's leading owner by prize money, her Aureole won the King George VI and Queen Elizabeth Stakes, and finished runner up in the Derby.

She won her first Classic with Carrozza, ridden by Lester Piggott, in the 1957 Oaks and was again leading owner, with 16 horses winning 30 races, worth £62,211. During the season, on 17 May at Haydock, she had her first treble with Pall Mall, Atlas and Might and Main.

In 1977 her colours – purple, gold braid, scarlet sleeves, black velvet cap with gold fringe – were carried to victory in both the Oaks and the St Leger with Dunfermline.

In 1989 she had her first winner in America, when Unknown Quantity, her first runner there for 35 years, won the Grade 1 Arlington Handicap at 10/1, ridden by Jorge Velasquez, at Arlington International, Chicago.

The Queen's Abbey Strand won at Lingfield on the final day of

1992, crowning her most financially successful year as an owner, taking her final score for the year to 26. Earlier that year TV viewers were fascinated as they watched a documentary about the royal family in which footage of the Queen showed her winning the royal party's Derby sweepstake. Her Majesty had drawn favourite, Generous and duly collected winnings of £16. The film showed Her Majesty receiving three fivers and a pound coin and, deadpan, asking, 'What does one do with these?'

In 1993 Spanish racing officials delayed handing over £57,000 prize money due to the Queen after her Enharmonic won at San Sebastian's racecourse – claiming that, for tax purposes, they needed proof that Her Majesty was British! Of course it was coincidence, but on the 40th anniversary of her Coronation on 2 June 1993, the same horse won at Epsom, ridden by Frankie Dettori at 12/1.

She visited the Kentucky Derby for the first time in May 2007 – where she shared the balcony with Ivana Trump and the President of Latvia – to the delight of course spokeswoman Julie Koenig Loignon, who enthused, 'I don't know how you top the Queen of England when you throw a party.'

Many wonder just how keen is the Queen's knowledge of racing. Certainly it's often on her mind. Addressing parliament during the Queen's Speech in 2003, she inadvertently gave away where her attention really was, when she said, 'My Government will continue to reform the National Hunt' – before correcting herself immediately with the words, 'National Health Service'. In 1999 she left American jockey, Gary Stevens in no doubt of her knowledge. He won for her on Blue Print at Royal Ascot, revealing afterwards that she had given him his riding instructions: 'I expect you'll be no worse than fourth coming off the bend and try to be on the outside, at that point you'll make your move' she told him. 'It was like following a road map' he said.

In December 2007 a TV documentary about Her Majesty showed BA staff preparing to welcome her on board a flight to the Baltic and being told that the *Racing Post* must be provided as it was 'essential reading' for the royal party.

When her promising two-year-old, Free Agent, won the Chesham Stakes at Royal Ascot in 2008, TV pictures showed the Queen demonstrating considerable excitement and pleasure, and in August of that year another of her juveniles, Golden Stream, broke the track record for two-year-olds in winning at Newmarket.

The Queen's Barber Shop contested the 2009 Cheltenham Gold Cup finishing unplaced behind winner Kauto Star. If the horse – originally owned by the Queen Mother and foaled during the year she died – had won, the Princess Royal's daughter, Zara Phillips, would have presented her grandmother with the trophy. *The Times* reported that her Majesty had backed the horse, a 10/1 shot, but that it was 'not known' how much she had lost!

Her eldest son, Prince Charles, has had his moments on the racecourse. He raced in public for the first time, at Plumpton on 4 March 1980, riding Long Wharf to finish second behind Classified, partnered by ace jockey, er, TV's Derek 'Tommo' Thompson. Good Prospect at Chepstow, became Charles' first winner as an owner on 3 October 1981.

He has indicated that he may enjoy the odd flutter. On a visit to the 1985 Melbourne Cup, as he presented the trophy to winning jockey Pat Hyland, he told him 'I will excuse the fact that you beat the horse I put my money on.'

On 23 March 1989 Charles lost his first 'winner' as an owner-breeder, Devil's Elbow, which had finished first at Worcester in a hurdles race in December 1988, but was disqualified following a Jockey Club inquiry. A test revealed prohibited substances and trainer Nick Gaselee was fined £2,000 – although he was cleared of administering the substances intentionally.

Charles has said, 'I wish people could only understand the real thrill, the challenge of steeplechasing. It's part of the great British way of life, and none of the sports I've done bears any comparison'. These words echo strongly those of his racing mad grandmother, the Queen Mother, who said 'It's one of the real sports that's left to us; a bit of danger and excitement, and the horses, which are the best thing in the world.'

The Queen's daughter, Princess Anne, born on 15 August 1950; was stopped at the Sovereign's Gate entrance to the 1993 Royal Ascot meeting and told by gateman, Eric Petheridge, 'I'm sorry, love, you can't come in here.'

In 1982 Anne became the first lady Royal to ride a winner when Gulfland did the business at Redcar, and she made her jumps debut on 28 February 1987, finishing last of four at Kempton. In November 1988 she fell at the first on Cannon Class at Windsor. She won over sticks on Cnoc Na Cuille for the first time at Worcester on

3 September 1987 at 7/2 in the Droitwich Handicap Chase, for David Nicholson.

On 14 November 1973, Princess Anne wed Captain Mark Phillips – and bookies were almost cleaned out by coincidence backers as Windsor's Royal Wedding Handicap Chase on that very afternoon was won by Royal Mark. It also just happened to be Prince Charles' 25th birthday.

Although Princes Andrew and Edward seemed to remain immune to the appeal of racing, the rest of the family clearly inherited their love of the sport from the Queen Mother, an owner since 1949, when Monave'en made her the first reigning Queen to own a winner since Queen Anne, the founder of Ascot racecourse, in 1714. She would enjoy 449 winners in the next 50 years – the last, One Love, coming just 222 days before she died. But she would always be associated with a loser – Devon Loch, the horse ridden by Dick Francis, who had the 1956 Grand National at his mercy, only to collapse inexplicably on the run-in.

SIR MICHAEL STOUTE
Stout fellow

'**B**ritain's best trainer' was the verdict of veteran turf watcher Alastair Down in 2008 as Sir Michael (Ronald) Stoute duly filled one of the few gaps in his CV, the St Leger, after trying for 34 years, sending out 25 losers in that timeframe. Frankie Dettori rode Conduit to an 8/1 victory in the race, his fifth triumph for five different trainers. Flamboyant Dettori demanded a 'hug' from the undemonstrative trainer who responded 'I don't want to do it in public. I'm not Italian.'

And although he is undoubtedly one of the great characters of British racing, (he was, in fact, born in Barbados in 1945, where his father was Commissioner of Police, coming to England at the age of 19 to become pupil trainer to Pat Rohan) writer Alastair Down explained why, although he is also 'the most respected of British trainers' according to Alan Lee of *The Times*, he has never really been taken to the hearts of the public like, say, Henry Cecil. 'Stoute is strangely uncommunicative in the public forum of the racecourse. This is largely because he's temperamentally ill-at-ease with the role of actor on the stage as opposed to that of author and director in the wings.' Perhaps it is also explained by the fact that when he was knighted in 1998 it was for services to tourism – in his native Barbados.

Racing history may have taken a significantly different turn had Stoute been successful at a job interview he attended shortly after arriving in the country – he had made the final six of 800 applicants for the position of BBC TV racing presenter. Stoute narrowly missed out – to the successful candidate, Julian Wilson. Wilson and Stoute would later team up to take part in the other great sporting love of their lives – cricket – with the commentator remembering a game between Stoute's XI and his stable lads. 'We were 36 for 5 when he marched to the wicket, waving his bat, and told me at the other end: "Okay, let's stop the rot". Sadly he was bowled first ball by a full toss.' Stoute's other sporting passion is deep sea fishing.

This failure was to training's advantage, and Stoute struck out on his own in 1972, having picked up additional experience working with and for Doug Smith and Harry Thomson Jones. He had his first winner with his father's Sandal (ridden by Lester Piggott) on 28 April of that year. By the next year he was creating an impression as his Alphadamus won the Stewards Cup and Blue Cashmere the Ayr Gold Cup.

The upward curve continued when in 1976 Jeremy Tree sent him two horses he'd been unable to train on the prevailing hard ground at his stables. Stoute promptly won the Cambridgeshire with Intermission, and the Jockey Club Stakes with Bright Finish, cheerfully admitting: 'They gave me a real breakthrough in publicity.'

The Classics began to fall his way when Fair Salinia triumphed in the 1978 Oaks and two years later he was numerically the most prolific trainer with 101 winners to his name, topping that by being the biggest prize money winner in 1981, when Shergar won him the Derby.

Training from two sides of Newmarket's Bury Road at Freemason Lodge and Beech Hurst, Stoute's longevity is well established – he was champion trainer three times in the 1980s, twice in the 1990s and already four times in the new millennium. He was the only 20th century handler to win Classics in five successive campaigns. He has well and truly lived up to his opinion that 'there is only one place worth being and that is at the top.'

Racing writer Paul Haigh said of Stoute's stables: 'Places in his yard have been only slightly less difficult to come by than places at the best universities are for humans.'

He is also a versatile trainer – he won the 1990 Champion Hurdle with Kribensis. He has had no compunction about taking on the world, either – and has sent out big race winners in Canada, France, Germany, Hong Kong, Italy, Japan, United Arab Emirates and the USA.

He also has the respect of his peers. William Haggas said of him in 2004, 'He's the best at it. He's come from nowt to plenty. We all want to be that good.' When Kieren Fallon considered him and his great contemporary rival, he said 'Henry (Cecil) was like a God in racing. Stoutey was one of those guys that you could approach.' And Stoute has, in turn, stood by Fallon during some of the most troubled times of the jockey's turbulent career.

Stoute crossed swords with handicapper Richard Dangar in 1994 when he put up Dahyan by 18kg (39lb) after he landed an old fashioned gamble from 14/1 to 5/1, leading Dangar to comment, 'That is the sort of thing that makes handicappers sit up and take notice.' Stoute noticed, too, and snapped that it was 'an abuse of power.'

In 2006 Stoute figured in a rare run in with the racing authorities after his Florimund ran at Windsor in July, after which he was found in breach of Rule 155 (ii) and fined £6,500 while jockey Stephen Davies was found in breach of Rule 157 and suspended for 32 days – the horse was banned from running for 40 days. The stewards believed 'this was a case where the colt was deliberately not asked for sufficient effort.' Stoute, enraged, appealed, (although Davies did not) with the outcome centring on the instructions given to Davies. The appeal Panel were not inclined to agree with the reasons given. The Panel increased Stoute's fine to £8,500.

I was at the beautiful American track, Santa Anita, to see the 2008 Breeders' Cup meeting. Several members of our party were sitting with a couple of young (ish) ladies we know, and whose blushes I will spare by referring to them as the 'Chelsea Girls' as we have come to know them, courtesy of their attachment to that football team.

The Girls returned to our table in a state of high excitement, explaining that they had bumped into Sir Michael Stoute, who had tipped them up his Conduit as having a decent chance of breaking his Breeders' Cup duck. The horse was trading at around 6/1 and the Girls told anyone who would listen about the great man's comments and then rushed off to the betting windows.

The party re-assembled after the race, which Conduit duly won, excitedly calculating winnings. One member of the group had passed on the information to a third party who had bet a substantial amount on Conduit and rewarded his informant with a sizeable tip, none of which was seen to be passed the way of the Chelsea Girls who were bubbling away at the victory of Conduit and congratulating everyone on their winnings. Finally, we asked the Girls how much profit they had made from their hot info – surely enough to pay for the trip, at least.

'No' they confessed, 'We put the horse in all our combination forecast bets but got nothing to go with it and didn't actually back the horse to win.'

That didn't stop them toasting Conduit's triumph with a rather pleasant local sparkling wine, however. They also regaled us with another purported Stoute anecdote, in which the trainer had to explain to an owner convinced that the man to whom he was chatting was Royston Ffrench, who had ridden one of his horses to victory, and was insisting on congratulating the baffled looking 'jockey', that in actual fact he was addressing a certain . . . Lewis Hamilton!

Not everyone is fortunate enough to find Stoute so forthcoming – the media for example. The *Daily Mirror*'s 'Newsboy' complained in May 2009, contrasting how well, in general, the National Hunt trainers communicate compared to their flat counterparts, among them Stoute. Newsboy accused Stoute of being 'his usual noncommittal self' when asked about a horse with Derby aspirations. Newsboy declared that the BHA should 'spend some more money on educating our most successful flat trainers that they, too, have a responsibility to promote our sport instead of peddling this culture of secrecy.'

Stoute realises that at the end of the racing day a trainer's reputation stands or falls on the animals in his charge or, as he once memorably put it, 'What we do is very inexact, and horses can make an arse of you.'

Not many equines or humans have achieved that feat against the man placed ninth in the list of Champion Trainers of the 20th Century produced for the book, *A Century of Champions*. That achievement illustrated why his own belief that 'there is only one place worth being and that is at the top' is no idle boast, but in his case, a statement of fact.

OUTSIDERS: MAVERICKS OF THE TURF

JEFFREY BERNARD
Is now permanently unwell

'One night I woke up in a field outside Pontefract, and I still have no idea how I got there. And I once spent the night with a girl in the ditch of the celebrated Pond Fence at Sandown – perhaps I was pointing out to her that obstacle's peculiar hazards'.

On another occasion, said Jeffrey Bernard's biographer Graham Lord, 'after a meeting at Huntingdon he was baffled to surface the next morning in a hotel bed that also contained inexplicably the jockey Barry Brogan and a local charwoman.'

He also had a racehorse named after him, had five hundred lovers and reportedly threw up in front of – some say actually on – the Queen Mother. Lord wrote that in June 1971 Bernard drank heavily at Ascot, and that his companion, friend Bunny May remembered that they had been freeloading champagne off rich contacts all afternoon and were very drunk indeed when Bernard made the mistake of suddenly downing a large whisky. 'As we get to the door of the bar by the lift we're stopped by the security men' said May. 'The lift comes down, the doors open, the Queen Mother, all in the blue, with the hat, absolutely charming, nodding away, and out she comes, and at that precise moment Jeff's neck went back and up came the champagne, the scotch and the dried tomato skins all over the Queen Mother's feet.'

Sir Clement Freud addressed this particular story – or one very like it – in *The Times* in August 1992. 'His dismissal from *Sporting Life* was believed to have been for standing upon the top table and urinating into his soup plate while representing the paper at a racing dinner. He said this is apocryphal; he was sacked for vomiting into the geraniums at Ascot. They were the Queen's geraniums under the Royal Box.'

These were just some of the things which happened to Jeffrey (real names Jerry Joseph) Bernard, the then columnist of the *Sporting Life*, who was making a name for himself by writing about the art of losing, ('One way to stop a runaway horse is to bet on him' he said) describing the 'traps and pitfalls of punting' and taking 'the piss out of the racing Establishment.'

Bernard was a hugely entertaining writer, providing two columns per week for the *Life* for a year – until in October 1971, aged 39, he was sacked for arriving legless at the National Hunt dinner in London at which he was guest of honour and booked to present an award to the woman point-to-point rider of the year. Instead, 'two waiters had to carry me upstairs' and next morning he flew straight to France to go racing at Longchamp – where he met trainer Henry Cecil in the paddock, who broke the news to him – 'What a pity you've been sacked.' Nonetheless, while he was there, he staked a week's wages on the great Mill Reef and won 'a tidy sum'.

As a punter his successes were outnumbered by the losers – and he once recalled bookmaker Victor Chandler greeting him by pointing out to his tic-tac man, 'Here comes the lunch money.'

Pre-mobile phones, he was in Barcelona on Derby Day 1969, convinced that Blakeney would win, but with no way of contacting his bookie. Until he went to the British consulate and told them that he had to use their phone to call his 'dying grandmother'.

Jeffrey began writing for *Private Eye* in 1977, penning the scurrilous, gossipy 'Colonel Mad' column which was hugely critical and scathing about the great and good of the turf – often causing my then MD to demand 'Do you know who writes this Colonel Mad garbage – can't you get him to stop libelling me?' 'Even readers who knew nothing about racing became intrigued by the barmy people I was writing about' said Bernard.

It was at *Private Eye* where his drinking excesses often caused him to miss his deadline for filing copy, causing the magazine to appear with the legend, 'Jeffrey Bernard Is Unwell' in the space where his article should have appeared. That became the title of the West End show about him, starring at different times top thespians like Peter O'Toole; Tom Conti, Dennis Waterman and James Bolam, and penned by Keith Waterhouse. The play is set in the Coach and Horses, the Soho pub frequented by Bernard, whose columns made something of a celebrity out of the legendarily rude 'mine host', Norman Balon.

Bernard went on to write for the *Sunday Mirror* – where he was sacked for failing to mention that he was going away to Australia for two weeks, without leaving a column behind. Then he joined *The Spectator* in 1975 after they poached him from his home of the previous two years, the *New Statesman* where despite the relatively high-brow readership, his 'Low Life' column soon became the most read thing in it. 'A suicide note in weekly instalments' as it was dubbed by Jonathan Meades.

Bernard became a friend of many racing personalities – he once interviewed Lester Piggott then accepted his invitation of a trip to Newbury races where the 'Long Fellow' was riding. 'I said thank you very much and thought no more about it. A week later I got a bill for thirty five quid.'

On one occasion he stayed the weekend with Irish trainer, Mick O'Toole. 'They're two days I shall never forget, though I can't remember them'. They went to the pub for a quick one, prevailed upon by Mick's wife to arrive back speedily for the lunch she was preparing. 'We were still there seven hours later.' At the Cheltenham Festival meeting, 'I was knocked to the drink-sodden ground by the Elephant Man, actor John Hurt, and everyone immediately assumed I was drunk, which was only partially true.'

In 1985 the band, New Order, sampled Jeffrey saying 'I'm one of the few people who lives what's called the low life' for their *Low Life* album and the man who seemed to treat the law with disdain, threatened to sue!

When, towards the end of his life – he died on 4 September 1997 – Bernard was in court accused – and convicted – of taking bets illegally in the Coach and Horses, and when Channel 4 filmed him for a 'still living' obituary programme, there to support him on both occasions was the man who would pick up the baton from Bernard and run with it in the same spirited, wholehearted way, John McCririck.

FATHER BREEN
Racing's priest

U ntil the early 1960s bishops of the Irish catholic church prohibited priests from attending horse racing. 'The bishops thought it was wrong and evil for people to go racing, so they banned the priests from going' recalled Father Sean Breen, who was one of the first to take advantage when that stricture was relaxed. Father Breen went to the Cheltenham Festival and saw the immortal Arkle win the Gold Cup in 1964.

During the 1970s Breen, originally from Cavan, was parish priest in Glencullen near Leopardstown, where he rode out for local trainer Bill Durkan and became friendly with another handler, Seamus McGrath – at whose yard Joanna Morgan was apprenticed. He then moved to a parish at Templeogue, and thence to Eadestown. Trainer Arthur Moore named his winning hurdler, The Breener, after him in the 1980s.

By 1993 he had made enough of a name for himself to be invited to give tips for the Festival to *Daily Mail* readers – albeit, none of his nine selections won. Interviewed in 1994 by the *Guardian*, Breen told the paper, 'This is my 28th Cheltenham. A friend of mine once lost all his money at cards on the boat over and had to turn back for home without setting foot in England.' And he just kept on going, year after year, along the way creating a name for himself as racing's priest. Tragically, he was the victim of a vicious attack during 2004 and subsequently suffered chest problems – related to the TB from which he suffered as a child.

Father Breen not only went racing as an owner, tipster and gambler, he also became known for blessing race meetings, as befitted a man whose parish in County Kildare, contained both Punchestown and Naas racecourses, the former of which boasts a hillock just outside the track known as Priests' Hill – from where the excluded clergy would once watch the racing without entering the track.

In 2005 Breen celebrated mass pre-Festival for some 200 racegoers at the Thistle (formerly Golden Valley) Hotel prior to Cheltenham, telling them, 'We pray for winners, because they are so hard to get. We pray for Irish winners, no matter what part of the country they come from.' Behind Breen there were two glasses of red wine on the altar. He would also say mass on the final day of the Galway festival and at Cheltenham when the Festival included St Patrick's Day. Also in 2005 he blessed the horse Kicking King – which went on to win the Gold Cup for Tom Taaffe. 'The Breener', who had evidently poured his own strength into the blessing, collapsed after the race.

Breen wrote a tipping column for the *Kildare Post* – in which he nominated Grand National winners like Hedgehunter and Numbersixvalverde. He also had a tipster spot on radio station, Kildare FM.

He owned horses himself – one in conjunction with another priest, which they decided to call, because of the secrecy concerning their involvement, Nobody Knows. People would ask him what his horse was called, 'I'd just whisper Nobody Knows, to which the response was always, "Yes, yes, but what's his name?"'

That animal won six times, another, called One Won One – whose other owners were the members of the Heavenly Syndicate, was indeed a frequent winner, clocking up £300,000 in prize money, including a triumph in the Listed President Cup in Abu Dhabi. Yet another, Portant Fella, won 15 races, while Raise Your Heart scored over jumps and on the flat, and Show Blessed won five times for him.

Not unnaturally, Breen faced plenty of criticism over the years for his racing and betting connections, but pointed out: 'There is nothing in the Bible that says you can't gamble. We have to lighten up a bit. I'm not a big gambler. I can go to a race meeting and enjoy it without having a bet. I'm not anti-gambling or anti-drinking.'

He became well known in the wider world, once coming to the rescue of *The Sun*'s well known racing writer Claude Duval who found himself unable to convince the powers that be at Leopardstown of his bona-fides, until Breen identified him: 'I can vouch for him' he told the girl at the gate, 'It's the very devil himself.'

It's not only horses that Breen tipped. In April 2005 he told the BBC's Frank Keogh that he had urged people to back Cardinal Joseph Ratzinger to become Pope: 'A few of the lads got on at 13/2, but I did not back him myself out of reverence.'

Breen was featured in the book, *A Fine Place To Daydream* by Bill Barich, in which he told the author that he had first become interested in racing as a young priest in North County Dublin and that his favourite meeting was Galway's seven day July meeting. 'It's tremendous fun. Everybody's there, even the politicians have caught on. . . . The first three men I ran into one summer were the ministers for Justice, Finance and Agriculture.'

Breen regarded the Cheltenham Festival as an opportunity to catch up with friends and acquaintances from farflung parts of the world, and, sometimes, to discover that he would never catch up with them again: 'A lot of people die, you know. You don't see them there, and you say to yourself, he isn't at Cheltenham, he must be dead. The Festival's a sort of check on who's still alive.'

Breen himself, whose final parish was Ballymore Eustace, and was also a member of Horse Racing Ireland's Bookmaker Committee, became an absentee from the 2009 and all future Festivals, other than in spirit, when he died aged 72 in mid January 2009. He was buried in Glencullen cemetery, County Dublin. His lifelong friend, trainer Joanna Morgan, reflected, 'I knew him for 35 years. He was a great friend, and was so lucky you would almost give him a share in a horse.' One of Morgan's horses, Gorica, won in Dubai at 25/1, earlier on the night Father Breen passed on.

Morgan recalled 'one morning at Phoenix Park many years ago when Sean was riding out a half-bred I had stabled there. He was wearing a big black mac, and the horse took off with him and went full gallop, with Sean only a passenger and the mac flapping behind him. Unfortunately he got thrown off and broke his leg.' Arthur Moore's wife, Mary, said of him, 'He was everybody's friend, everybody's priest and he touched the lives of all who knew him.'

WINSTON CHURCHILL
Race rigger?

V for victory applied not only to the War for Winston Churchill
– his successes on the racecourse are less well documented than
his political triumphs.

Not that they cut much ice with his wife, Clementine, who in
1951 wrote to a friend – 'Have you seen about his horse, Colonist II
– I do think this is a queer new facet in Winston's variegated life.
Before he bought the horse – I can't think why – he had hardly been
on a racecourse in his life. I must say, I don't find it madly amusing.'
The letter is interesting almost inasmuch as it reveals how little
interest Clementine can have taken in Winston's life before he met
her – for he had not only been on racecourses – he had ridden on
them! And as Chancellor of the Exchequer he had been responsible
for a far reaching change in racecourse betting.

In fact, racing was ingrained in the family DNA – his maternal
grandfather was active on the turf in the States, even building his own
racecourse. Lord Randolph Churchill, Winston's father was a leading
owner and turf figure between 1889 and 1893, having bought black
filly, L'Abbesse de Jouarre (quickly corrupted by the public to 'Abcess
on the Jaw') after he quit politics in 1886. Randolph did not have
great faith in his filly, and although she was entered in the Oaks he
decided to go fishing instead. L'Abbesse promptly shocked everyone
by winning the 1889 renewal at 20/1. The filly won over £10,000
during her career – and the teenage Winston, born in 1874, took a
great interest in her exploits, writing from school at Harrow that 'I
have been congratulated on all quarters on account of the flukey filly.'
He celebrated one of her victories in a novel manner – 'I drank the
Abbesse's health in lemon squash, and we ate her luck in strawberry
mash.'

At school in Brighton, Winston first rode – and then took to
racing as a cavalry subaltern. 'Horses were the greatest of my pleasures
at Sandhurst' he wrote in *My Early Life*, 'The group in which I moved

spent all our money on hiring horses – we organised point-to-points and even a steeplechase in the park of a friendly grandee – and bucketed about the countryside.'

Winston finished second in the cavalry riding prize in which 15 of the 127 cadets took part. In March 1895 he raced in a steeplechase. 'The animal refused and swerved' he told his mother, 'Very nearly did he break my leg, but as it is I am only bruised and very stiff.' Mater was not best pleased – and Winston had to protest that 'you take rather an extreme view of steeplechasing when you call it "idiotic" and "fatal".'

Undeterred, Winston raced in the 4th Hussars Subalterns' Challenge Cup, finishing third. 'It was very exciting and there is no doubt about it being dangerous. I had never jumped a regulation fence before, and they are pretty big things.' The race had a fascinating postscript when it was declared void with allegations being made that the winner was, in fact, a ringer and that 'all those in the race must have been in on the plot'. The horse was an outsider in the betting. A publication called *Truth* said, 'The coup resulted in the defeat of a hot favourite by the last outsider in the betting.' Churchill was outraged at these allegations and urged his mother to take legal action – but the matter was allowed to drop.

When stationed in India, Winston was involved in pony racing via another filly, Lily. He also raced polo ponies, contesting one race with 'a ripping line of 49 fences' in which he was one of only five of thirteen starters to finish. He entered horses in other races, which took part with their jockeys wearing his father's racing colours of chocolate-pink sleeves and cap.

But it was not only via his father that Winston acquired a love of racing – his grandfather was the man who conceived and built the track on which America's oldest 'Triple Crown' race, the Belmont Stakes, was first run in 1867. Lawyer and financier, Leonard Jerome, 1818–1891, whose daughter Jenny Lind was Churchill's mother, built Jerome Park, New York, which opened in 1866, featuring a clubhouse, dining rooms, a ball room, facilities for sleighing (!), trap shooting, skating and, later, polo.

Once Churchill became an MP the racing colours were packed away for a considerable amount of time – the best part of half a century. It was in 1925 Churchill, then Chancellor, was confronted with the plan to introduce a tax on betting. The government wanted to register street bookmakers and set them up in offices, thus enabling regulation of the business – together with a tax income estimated at some £17 million per annum, which would obviously be paid by those doing the betting. Churchill was nervous that such a move would have the side effect of being seen to encourage gambling, and he wrote to Treasury advisers, warning that 'it would be essential to prohibit any notice, placard, list of betting odds, or other street sign which would flaunt itself before the passer-by.' The tax was duly imposed in spring 1926 – much to the aggravation of the racing industry as a whole, with bookmakers going on strike, and trainers even petitioning that it was discouraging racegoers. The opposition resulted in cuts to the rate of tax – but the objections remained and eventually the tax was repealed.

A couple of years later, Churchill introduced another brainwave – this one somewhat longer lasting – the Tote. Churchill supported this idea wholeheartedly – 'The rowdy rascal element so prominent on our racecourses is eliminated. The running of horses to suit the interests of the bookmakers disappears, and an altogether cleaner and healthier condition prevails. It would yield a revenue to the upkeep of bona fide racing sport, and the State contributions could be collected in the easiest manner.' Lord Hamilton of Dalzell, a Jockey Club steward complimented Churchill on the breakthrough – 'You have helped us to make racing a better and a straighter game than it has ever yet been; and you have helped to prevent its becoming a game that only millionaires and sharps can play.'

In 1949 Churchill, then Leader of the Opposition, and a mere spring chicken in his 75th year, was lured back into racing when his son in law, Christopher Soames, talked him into buying French three-year-old, Colonist II. Not only wife Clementine, but also secretary Jo Sturdee, did not believe that a return to racing would benefit Churchill, writing to tell him he might damage his reputation, as a result. The man who won the War and saved the country could have his reputation shattered because he owned a racehorse!

Winston paid no attention and his colours returned to the track in August 1949 at Salisbury when the grey Colonist II produced a fine display of front running. Despite his secretary's concerns that racing could cost him votes, 'There was a terrific cheer from the crowd when he won – and they all surged forward to see him come in and gave him a wonderful reception' remembered Soames. He ran 11 times in 1950, usually partnered by Tommy Gosling, and was never out of the first four. In 1951 they were the appropriate winners of the Winston Churchill Stakes.

As the horse went from strength to strength, winning race after race, including the Jockey Club Cup, and finishing second in the Ascot Gold Cup, the cry would go up 'Winnie wins!' Some wits noted that the horse was clearly of the same political leaning as his owner – running best on right handed courses!

Fellow political racing man, Sir Clement Freud recalled the occasion when he watched Colonist II winning, with 'a plump, elderly, possibly less than entirely sober, cigar-smoking Winston Churchill raising two fingers in the air long before the gesture was connected with anything but victory.'

The horse eventually won 13 races and some £120,000 in prize money, finding his way into *Hansard* when a Labour MP demanded that Churchill sell him. 'I could sell him for a great deal more than I bought him for, but I am trying to rise above the profit motive' responded the great man.

Winston certainly understood racing – American author Jane McIlvaine reported him in her book *The Will To Win* as interrupting Christopher Soames in the act of giving instructions to jockey Fred Winter – 'I shouldn't bother to tell Winter anything – you are talking to a master of his craft.' And, when Doug Smith once apologised to him for losing a race he felt he should have won, Churchill took the trouble to write to the apologetic rider – 'Dear Smith – I am sure you did your best. Yours, Churchill.'

When the end of the horse's racing days came round, Churchill pretended not to be interested in sending him to stud. 'And have it said that the Prime Minister of Great Britain is living on the immoral earnings of a horse?' But Colonist II was retired to the Royal stud at Sandringham. He died in 1973 and sired some good jumpers, including the grey, Stalbridge Colonist, who beat Arkle in a Hennessy Gold Cup.

Not only Colonist II ran in Churchill's colours, with his trainer Walter Nightingall handling 70 winners for him. He set up his own stud, initially at Chartwell, later, in 1955, at Newchapel in Surrey, where he kept around 10 mares at a time, and bred good horses like High Hat who beat Petite Etoile in the Aly Khan International Gold Cup at Kempton and Stewards Cup winner, Tudor Monarch. The half brother to Colonist II, Le Pretendant, won the aptly named Churchill Stakes and also contested the Washington International. Winston eventually managed a Classic victory when Dark Issue triumphed in the 1955 Irish 1000 Guineas – but the proud owner was absent – 'The General Election was my owner and I was already entered among the runners'!

Churchill's Vienna was reckoned not to be without a chance in the 1960 Derby but he missed the race in a bizarre manner when he was pricked by the blacksmith who was plating him, and had to be withdrawn. He was rated more highly than stablemate Auroy, who finished fourth at 33/1. Vienna went on to run third in the St Leger.

Becoming a member of the Jockey Club in 1950, although he played no part in racing's administration, Churchill's interest may even have become obsession, as he had pictures of his horses hung in his bedroom at the family home, Chartwell in Kent.

He finally severed his links to the turf in 1965, the year before his death when his health was deteriorating. He explained the decision to his trainer. 'It is very sad for me to have to end my racing activities, owing to the fact that my health does not allow me to attend race meetings any more. I know that this decision will cause sorrow to you, too, since we have had such a long association. My mind goes back to the spring of 1949 when Christopher persuaded me to buy Colonist. He gave us all great excitement and pleasure, and he was also the forerunner of many successes. It doesn't fall to many people to start a racing career at the age of 75 and to reap from it such pleasure.'

After Churchill died, the Newchapel Stud was purchased by Mr E.L. Knight who, with the permission of Lady Spencer-Churchill, renamed it the Churchill Stud.

In 1999 there was an exhibition entitled 'Racing to Victory' put together by Katharine Thompson, a member of the cataloguing team on the Churchill Papers at the Churchill Archives Centre in Cambridge, celebrating Winston's connections to the sport which was displayed at the National Museum of Horseracing in Newmarket.

BARNEY CURLEY
Human hat trick

'I know it's a popular belief that I'm a rogue, constantly stopping horses and fixing races.' Now, who in the racing world could possibly have exhibited the self-awareness to realise such a thing, the strength of character to admit it, and the sheer chutzpah to revel in the description? An enigma wrapped inside a riddle, looking like a moustachioed conundrum, generally seen in public under a trademark wide-brimmed hat, that's who. And that's Barney Curley.

The Irishman who trained to become a priest yet earned a reputation for pulling strokes left, right and centre in the racing world; who can't bear bookies but couldn't have been more helpful whenever I've had dealings with him.

Born in 1939, weighing a huge 12lbs (5.4kg), and originally named Bernard, he started betting at the age of six. Expelled from college at 14 for cheating at his exams, he went to study for the priesthood with the Christian Brothers at St Michael's in Enniskillen. However, the church's ultimate loss was the turf's gain as, having survived TB, and by then aged 22 he gave up thoughts of becoming a priest: 'I do believe in God, and I do believe we have to give an account of our stewardship in life and we will be judged on how we treat our fellow man.'

As if to break entirely with all thoughts of a holy profession, Barney became a smuggler of razor blades from his native North to Southern Ireland. Then he began to make a book on the dogs – 'Really, I had no idea what I was doing. I was ending up with an empty satchel 90 per cent of the time.' When another bookie told him, 'You're on the way to disaster. All you want to do is gamble' he gave up being a bookie – and started managing a pop group, The Claxton.

He married a girl named Maureen – Maureen Curley. No relation, though. Incest is one of the few things of which he hasn't been accused! He had, however, got involved in a dodgy car insurance scam.

By 1971 he had decided to become a serious gambler. He set off for the Cheltenham Festival in the company of one or two fellow Irishmen – with £700 in his pocket. He came back to Omagh and Maureen with £50,000, with which he promptly purchased a pub – oh, and he also acquired his own betting shop. He soon had a small chain of betting shops – the Barney Curley Organisation. After one or two problems, Barney sold off the shops to concentrate on his own gambling again.

'By the early 1970s my betting was becoming serious', he said. He was betting up to £2,000 a time at the major Irish tracks. Serious enough.

In 1972 he landed his first 'touch' when Little Tim won a bumper at Mallow, backed down from 20/1 to 8/1. 'It was the first time I laid out and won serious money.' But not the last. He sent out between 30 and 40 people to place bets of £100 each, and won £45,000.

The Yellow Sam affair in 1975 could be described as Barney's signature dish. He picked out 'one of the worst horses I've ever owned', Yellow Sam, for a handicap hurdle at Bellestown on 25 June 1975. The venue was selected for the plot 'because I knew that the rarely used, remote course had only one public telephone, which was the only means the on-course bookmakers had of receiving intelligence of market moves.'

So, as Curley's men began their task of unloading his thousands of pounds of stake money in 150 or so betting shops, Barney stationed his much trusted friend Benny O'Hanlon in that single telephone box with express instructions to prevent anyone else from using it and hence any calls from the outside world getting to the track. Benny rabbited away on the phone for hours, defying all efforts to budge him. Meanwhile, the cash was pouring on Yellow Sam until Curley had over £15,000 on the 20/1 outsider.

Nine lined up for the race with the on course bookies blissfully unaware of the off course gamble, and the off course bookies unable to get through to the course to put money on to cut the odds. Yellow Sam won by a comfortable two and a half lengths and Barney won £300,000. 'Never again was Barney Curley allowed to run a horse without the bookmakers treating it with the utmost caution' said Barney.

In 1982 he lost £150,000 by laying Golden Fleece when Vincent O'Brien's horse won the Derby, 'and exacerbated my plight by losing another £100,000 on other bets'. Even more serious.

He moved to the States for three months to recuperate and recover, becoming friendly there with renowned US trainer, Charlie Whittingham. Barney was warned off by the Irish Turf Club after a dispute over a bet. But he was able to get over £50,000 on Forgive 'N Forget to win the 1983 Coral Golden Hurdle at Cheltenham, which it did at 5/2.

More controversy erupted in 1984 when he put his Middleton House in Ireland up as a raffle prize – tickets were £175 and he flogged 9,000, leaving him with a million pound profit after a syndicate from Gloucestershire won the property. However, he was charged with running an illegal lottery – and sentenced to three months in jail – reduced on appeal to probation.

Barney began training in England – he bought the White House Stables in Stetchworth, near Newmarket, from fellow mega gambler Terry Ramsden. In 1985 Curley received a licence to train in the UK. He acquired his full jumps' licence in November 1985. No shrinking violet of the profession, Barney said: 'A good trainer knows when his horses are going to win. There aren't that many of us around. Most trainers wouldn't know if tomorrow was Wednesday or Thursday.'

In 1986 the defeat of Dancing Brave by Shahrastani in the Derby cost him £250,000. In 1987 he won £200,000 on Reference Point. Easy, come, equally easy, go.

Before he netted that two hundred grand, controversy had once again impinged on the Curley horizon, this time in the shape of the Robin Goodfellow affair. The horse of that name was 13/8 favourite to win a novice hurdle at Ascot in November 1986. Barney fancied it and slapped a couple of four figure bets on, only to notice that 'the more I put on, the bigger the price became.' The horse, ridden by Graham Bradley, was beaten – only to reappear 13 days later and win, beating the horse which beat him at Ascot in the process.

Barney reported Graham Bradley to the Jockey Club – just to make sure, he both wrote to them and rang them up. He rang Bradley, too, claiming that he told the jockey he was 'a disgrace'. The Jockey Club got the message(s), and two months later the charge of 'causing serious damage to the interests of British racing' was duly laid – at the feet of Mr Curley.

There was an inquiry in April 1987 – which banned Barney for two years. For a change the world seemed to be on Barney's side this time – the *Racing Post* even criticised the verdict and the Jockey Club permitted a re-hearing in August, at which his licence was restored. Bradley wasn't happy – 'I felt betrayed and had the distinct feeling I had been left holding the shi**y end of the stick'.

Once he was back in action – 1 October – Barney backed himself to train 10 winners in the remaining three months of the year. In all, he laid out £126,000 to win £275,000, having previously sent out nine winners in the previous two years. He got off the mark on day one when Above All Hope won a seller at Fontwell – then had a rant about his winner being subsequently bid up! With five weeks gone he had managed only three winners – but he then put on a spurt with five more in the next eighteen days. Number nine arrived on 21 December and the next day, Experimenting won at Folkestone to give him an early festive gift.

In 1992 Barney survived a plane crash – oddly, he didn't claim it was an attempt on his life. Bookie Pat Whelan, owed £13,000 by Barney, dropped him a line – 'Next time you owe me, travel by car.'

By now Barney had become very friendly with and influential to a slowly maturing Frankie Dettori, intervening once or twice to help keep the Italian on the straight and narrow when his career had threatened briefly to slide off course.

True tragedy hit Barney's family when his son Charlie was killed in a car accident in December 1995, aged just 18.

A visit to Gambia in 1997 saw Barney launch a charity, DAFA – Direct Aid For Africa – which has done great work to help the sick, orphaned and deprived, improving the lives of many on that continent.

There is no doubt that Barney has made the racing world a more interesting place over the years, but not everyone is a huge fan. Although long term observer of the turf, Marten Julian called him 'the all time master of bluff and counter-bluff' in August 2004, racing writer Graham Cunningham was moved to ask questions in August 2007:

> Mr Curley has mastered the art of priming a poor horse for a gamble. Yes, he has been a mentor for a string of top jockeys and adds colour to a profession that often tends toward the bland. And yes, his work for African charities speaks of a man who knows that racing, to borrow the

words of the late Phil Bull, is only 'a piddling little pond' really.

So why is it that so many things about the great man grate?

Most of all, it's the feeling that this is a man who trains half a dozen tin-pot winners a year yet still gives the impression that he feels he should be granted the same sort of status as Henry Cecil and Sir Michael Stoute rolled into one.

Not a fan, then.

For anyone wishing to discover more about Barney, a visit to his website www.dafa.co.uk is essential. Here you'll find information about the charity, along with a series of Curley articles in which he pontificates on 'the state of British racing'.

In December 2008 it appeared that Curley's involvement with the turf may have been coming to an end, as he announced that he had put his Cleveland House Stables and his 20 horses up for sale.

In the present climate we no longer feel it's justified to provide free entertainment for the big bookmakers.

If it wasn't for the Maktoum family, the sport would be a complete disaster. Some of these races are worth so little that you need to win 14 before you break even. There is no other country in the world I know of that would stand for this. I said 15 years ago that the sport had no future, except if there was a strike to bring people to their senses and I believe that more strongly today than I did then'.

But in February 2009 he appeared to be well and truly back on the scene. Firstly, when a horse called Tusculum, running in his colours and trained by Andrew Stringer, who had officially taken over his stables, landed a hefty gamble, at Kempton. Then it transpired that Curley himself planned to begin training again. Sure enough, come Easter Monday 2009, there was Curley sending out two winners at 7/1 and 4/1.

Blimey, we'll all miss the old buffer should he ever sustain his threat to walk away from racing!

EMILY DAVISON
Kingsize character

Emily Wilding Davison, born on 11 October 1872, was an obscure campaigner for women's votes, known to few outside of that movement, on the day she set out to protest at the Derby in 1913. She was completely unknown to the racing world. By the end of the day, the 40-year-old militant suffragette had brought down the King's horse, during the big race, when she ran on to the track and was hit by Anmer, ridden by Herbert Jones, causing rider and mount to fall. Davison was killed.

She did have something of a track record for causing public disturbances. She joined the Women's Social and Political Union in 1906 and rapidly acquired a lengthy prison record: seven separate convictions including obstruction, stone throwing, assault and pyromania. 'Emily Davison had already taken part in attacks on property as she became a leading member of the Suffragettes – and was imprisoned and force-fed. On one occasion she barricaded herself in a prison cell to escape force-feeding. Her cell was flooded with ice-cold water which drenched her while workmen broke down the cell door. Such treatment only made her even more determined,' claims website, www.historylearningsite.co.uk. On another occasion while in prison, Emily threw herself off of a prison upper gallery floor. She was badly injured.

Another prominent suffragette, Emmeline Pankhurst believed that it was Emily's experiences in prison that brought her to the conclusion that only the ultimate sacrifice would bring any success to the Suffragettes. Emmeline wrote in *My Own Story* that Emily decided that only the loss of life: 'would put an end to the intolerable torture of women.'

'Ironically, her self-sacrifice may well have made the position of women worse in Britain' explains www.historylearningsite.co.uk.

Though there had been some movement in the Houses of Parliament with regards to women's rights, some historians argue that Emily's act at the Derby so horrified those in charge that they were even more against the right to vote for women. They argued that Emily was a highly educated person. If a highly educated woman was willing to do what she did, what could society expect of less educated women? An extension of the vote to women would plunge British society into bedlam – so they argued.

What is true is that the monarchy was revered in Britain and any attack on the monarchy was more than just frowned on. However, at the time of her death, even some Suffragettes were concerned at the extreme ideas and plans of Emily Davison. Some felt that she was becoming too extreme in her actions and bringing the movement into disrepute.

Racing writer, Edward Moorhouse was there on Derby Day, 1913, and witnessed the whole, dreadful incident:

They came down the decline to Tattenham Corner. After the first 10 horses had passed at this point a woman suddenly came from under the rails and, eluding the police who were guarding the course, rushed on to the track right in front of Agadir. By a dexterous movement Earl managed to make his horse swerve out of the woman's way.

Unfortunately the strain on Agadir's forelegs instantly caused slight lameness, and thence forward he was a mere 'passenger'. Behind Agadir came the King's horse, Anmer. The woman, who turned out to be a Miss Davison, of Morpeth, Northumberland, a militant Suffragette, made a dash for Anmer's reins. Before the startled onlookers had had time fully to grasp what was happening, they saw the woman, Herbert Jones, the rider of Anmer, and the horse on the ground. Jones and the woman were both unconscious.

Jones, with 'a number of abrasions on his face, and bruises all over his body, was brought to the stands on a stretcher and taken to the ambulance room, where he presently recovered consciousness.' He stayed overnight at a London hotel before returning home.

Davison's skull was badly fractured. She was taken by motor car to Epsom Cottage Hospital. On the Friday night she underwent an operation but, gradually sinking, died on the Sunday without having recovered consciousness.

Miss Davison had become a political martyr, known for sacrificing herself for the greater good of women's rights. There is still controversy as to whether this was a deliberate, politically motivated ploy by the 'Votes for Women' campaigner, or a tragic accident. And, if the former, could it have been possible for her deliberately to target His Majesty's horse?

Jockey Steve Donoghue, who rode Bachelor's Wedding in the race, believed that Miss Davison, who had already distributed her political leaflets and was crossing the track on her way to Tattenham Corner Station to return to London, had assumed that the entire field had passed by, only to duck under the rails and into the path of the stragglers, amongst them Anmer.

Writer John Tyrrel wrote in his *Racecourses on the Flat*, 'The fact that the King's horse was involved was almost certainly pure chance, although it made a good newspaper story.' Said Alistair Burnet in his 1993 book, *The Derby*, 'She left no suicide note. She was certainly intent on publicity, but she got minimal public sympathy, except from her devotees. For her it was probably an unintended martyrdom.'

Whatever her motives, her funeral procession through the streets of London was a spectacular affair. The Suffragettes escorted their misguided comrade's body, seeking to gain the utmost possible advertisement out of an appalling incident.

There was a bizarre postscript to Davison's actions on the racing scene just a few weeks later – at The Ascot Gold Cup, during which a man named Hewitt, flourishing a Suffragist flag in one hand, and a fully loaded revolver in the other, ran on to the course, shouting at Whalley, the jockey riding well fancied Tracery, to stop. Far from stopping, the horse knocked Hewitt over and trampled him, leaving him unconscious and badly injured, while the horse fell over. Whalley was badly shaken but otherwise alright. 'The man was obviously copying the dastardly action of Miss Davison' declared the *Bloodstock Breeders' Review*, although he was not directly associated with the movement.

Women finally received a partial right to the vote in the UK in 1918, when those aged over 30 were allowed to vote – and fully in 1928 when those over 21 were added – 56 years after Wyoming in the USA had become the first place in the world to permit women to vote.

Emily was buried in Morpeth Church in Northumberland. Her headstone has inscribed on it: 'Deeds not words'.

ANTHONY KNOTT
Knott well-known

He'd been a jockey for 28 years, but other than his nearest and dearest, no one had given Anthony Knott a second glance – until November 2008 – when he finally won a race for the first time.

The only time he had looked like coming to public notice had occurred many years previously, back when he was a 16-year-old riding at Badbury Rings point-to-point.

> I had ridden in a race there two weeks earlier, and came down at the open ditch. This time, I was going well in another race when, blow me, I came off at exactly the same open ditch. I couldn't believe it.
>
> Well, I was so piddled off that I grabbed my horse before he could run off and waited until they came round again on the second circuit. When they did, I rejoined the race at the back of the field, which was a bit naughty, I suppose.
>
> The stewards weren't impressed, and I got a seven day ban, which seemed a bit harsh.

The 44-year-old, gap-toothed dairy farmer with 300 cows in his 'real' life, continued to ride for almost another 30 years, because of his overwhelming desire finally to win a race. And that drive almost prevented him from achieving his goal because, with a race at Wincanton – the Racing Post Hands and Heels Novices Handicap Hurdle – at his mercy, Knott began to celebrate extravagantly when there was still half a furlong to run.

Partnering the 7/1 shot, Wise Men Say, his own horse, Knott said, 'I'm a bit unaccustomed to victory, and as I was coming into the final part of the race there was a massive roar from the crowd. It was just instinct to stand up and give them a wave, I wasn't thinking straight for a minute. Then I thought: "Oh God, it's not finished yet" and I could hear another horse coming up behind me, so I sat back down and got on with it.'

His unexpected win really captured the public imagination – and a media frenzy ensued, putting him on TV screens, radio bulletins, internet sites and newspaper front pages – for a few days, there was more interest in his feat than in champion jump jockey Tony McCoy's exploits!

Knott, a father of three from Sturminster Newton in Devon, has ridden since the age of 14 –'I started riding my Dad's pointers when I was about 16 and it just grew from there. I had several horses, but after a while they just went wrong.'

Nonetheless, he plugged away, riding loser after loser on various horses at places like Taunton, Leicester and Lingfield, on the flat and over jumps. But he had virtually given it up as a bad idea never likely to produce the desired result until, firstly, he watched the movie *Seabiscuit* which 'I found so inspiring that I decided to give it one more shot' and, secondly, he acquired the six-year-old Wise Men Say. 'He was really awkward, he was quite a bad boy and used to kick all the time and bite. But ever since I got on him he's never kicked or bitten – I think we're just underdogs sticking together.'

Within a month he had aimed his new horse at the race he felt just might offer the opportunity of finally getting his head in front at the right time.

Knott began getting himself fit by riding a mechanical horse twice a day and swimming 50 lengths a day at the local baths. A less conventional keep-fit discipline involved ballroom dancing. It was working, though – he lost a stone in a few weeks.

Knott was up at 3.30am on the day of the race – but after milking

the cows, went back to bed for three hours – to 'calm myself down.'
Once at the track, he walked the course twice – once with his
daughter, then again with former jockey Steve Smith Eccles – 'this
proved the difference between winning and losing – Steve pointed
out a strip of quicker ground in the middle of the straight, where the
ground was less poached.'

The race finally began – 'Everything goes smoothly until coming
round the home bend where one of the other rides cuts me up and I
lose a bit of momentum' noted Knott in his diary,

> But Joe Tizzard (jockey who had helped him out with
> some tips) had said to try to get a breather into the horse
> on the home turn and then kick and go hell for leather in
> the straight.
>
> I grab that faster strip of ground and he starts to go
> forward powerfully, but when I realise I am in the lead,
> well – that's when everything goes out of the window.
> Suddenly, I say to myself: 'Shit, I'm winning, and this is
> the last we're coming to'.
>
> People have said I mistook the winning post when I
> celebrated, but Wincanton is my local track, and I know
> where the winning line is. As I enter the last 50 yards, a
> great cheer goes up from the stand. My friend Dave
> Coombs later explains that as we are approaching the final
> flight, everyone thought: 'Bloody hell, Knotty's going to
> win this' and they all put down their pints in the bars,
> rushed outside and cheered me up the straight.

Alan Lee of *The Times* described Knott's success as 'surreal' and his
winning flourish as 'celebrating by waving wildly to his agricultural
mates BEFORE riding the final furlong like a bareback cowboy.'

David Ashforth in the *Racing Post* complimented him for
'bringing bouncing, upright, unrestrained, enthusiastic determination to the battle' but pointed out that 'all that was missing was
ability.' He added, though, that the race was 'pure, uplifting
pleasure.' But Knott has ridden one more winner under Rules than
Ashforth!

Knott explained: 'Where I live, if you're walking along and
someone drives past and toots at you, you instinctively wave at them,

and that's what I was doing as I passed the stands.' Not everyone was convinced he would ever break his duck – 'We are astonished. I'm just pleased he finally won but didn't hurt himself' said his wife Sarah.

From unsung journeyman to national hero, the journey took 28 years, and lasted three days as media from all over the world – well, Britain, Ireland, Spain, Italy (*La Gazetta dello Sport*) and America (ABC News) – beat a path to his door and he appeared as ITN News' 'And Finally . . .' story as well as featuring on BBC Radio 4, BBC World News and Setanta.

Reflecting on his triumph for patience and persistence, Knott declared, 'I just wanted to win one race – I've done it now, so I think I'll leave it at that.' And, revealing that his time in the glare of publicity is well and truly over, Knott commented that within three days of the win, be came 'back to earth with a bump when the cows' diet feeder broke down.'

LOSS LEADERS
Always trying and losing

The British love a loser, the pluckier the better. In racing, any regular punter has a personal playlist of unforgettable losers, from the horse who would certainly have won the Grand National but for being carried out at Becher's, to the short-head runner-up whose jockey was blatantly taking a tug. But for the true connoisseur, the most memorable equine losers have nothing to do with betting, and a select few are among the greatest equine characters of racing history.

There are glorious losers, none more glorious than Crisp in the 1973 Grand National, caught on the line by Red Rum after producing the greatest front-running display in the race's history, thereby ensuring himself an immortality far greater than any he would have enjoyed had he held on.

And there are inglorious losers, none more inglorious than point-to-pointers Rossa Prince and Mister Chippendale, whose names are forever linked in racing's Hall of Shame as the pair who in the 1990s each managed to lose a walkover – a one-horse race. Rossa Prince bolted while being saddled and could not be caught in time, while Mister Chippendale's rider forgot to weigh in.

Then there are the career losers, the handful of racehorses whose sheer inability – or sometimes lack of inclination – to win has guaranteed them an honoured slot in the annals.

Most of the major racing nations around the world boast a Losing Legend. The Australian mare Oureone raced 124 times between 1976 and 1983 without ever winning, while Japan has another mare Haru Urara, not quite in Oureone's class with zero wins from 113 races between 1998 and 2004. The Japanese media dubbed her '*makegumi no hoshi*' – 'The shining star of losers everywhere' – and extensive fan merchandise included a branded bra.

In the USA, Zippy Chippy, acquired by trainer Felix Monserrate in exchange for an old Ford truck, did actually manage to win the occasional contest. But since one of these was against a minor league baseball player on foot and another was against a harness racer who had been given a lengthy start, they count as publicity stunts, not proper races. Better to salute Zippy Chippy for the beautifully round number of his more orthodox career: 100 outings up to 2004, and no victories. No wonder he was eventually banned from his local track, Finger Lakes in upstate New York, 'for the protection of the betting public'.

No such gimmicks or commemorative undies are needed to enshrine the name of the best-known British-trained loser: Quixall Crossett, who between February 1990 and November 2001 – when he ran his last race a few weeks before his 17th birthday – posted a winless career total of 103 races in hurdles and steeplechases.

Bred and trained by Ted Caine in a remote corner of North Yorkshire, Quixall Crossett took the first part of his name from Caine's home, High Crossett Farm, and the second from Albert Quixall, the golden-haired England footballer who in 1958 was transferred from Sheffield Wednesday to Manchester United – decimated earlier that year by the Munich air crash – for the then record sum of £45,000. Those racing professionals – and there were plenty – who piously voiced their disapproval of the publicity generated by Quixall Crossett might have taken a different tack had they been aware of the poignant background to the horse's story.

For not long after Quixall Crossett had been born, the Caines' son Malcolm was killed in an accident at High Crossett Farm, and the young horse became the vehicle by which the devastated family came to terms with tragedy and started to face the future. 'It was Quixall that kept us going, really,' said Ted Caine – and winning became an irrelevance compared with the taking part.

For over a decade Quixall Crossett was a familiar spear-carrier in races mostly on the northern circuit, though he did once venture down to Berkshire to sample the glamour of Ascot. On two heady occasions he finished runner-up, at Kelso in October 1996 and, most memorably of all, at Wetherby in May 1998. Ridden by Jim Crowley – now a leading flat jockey – Quixall Crossett was beaten a rapidly diminishing two lengths by 2-9 favourite Toskano in a novice chase: 'Ran a blinder,' said the form book, and the Caines never needed much persuading to slot the video into the machine and relive the closest their hero ever came to winning a race.

In all Quixall Crossett was placed eight times – six thirds in addition to those two seconds – and earned £8,502 in prize money, and like any proper celebrity these days had his own fan club and website.

Next down the list of under-achievers in purely numerical terms is Peggy's Pet, who between 1962 and 1969 ran 94 times under Rules – flat, hurdles and chases – without winning, and for good measure was also defeated in 17 point-to-points.

But while Quixall Crossett and Peggy's Pet were simply too slow to win, perhaps the most iconic loser of modern British racing was a horse who combined genuine ability with a maddening reluctance to deploy it.

Amrullah ran in 74 races between October 1982 and March 1992 and never won, but he was placed often enough to garner over £26,000 in prize money. An 80,000-guinea yearling, he was initially trained by Guy Harwood, and it indicates the expectations harboured about the young horse that his first run came in a hot Newmarket maiden. That race was won by Tolomeo, launching himself on a career which would see him become one of the best middle-distance horses of his generation, his finest hour when landing the Arlington Million in Chicago in 1983.

Amrullah, by contrast, started to slide in the opposite direction as soon as he had finished unplaced in that maiden. He moved on from Harwood to Peter Easterby, and then to John Bridger, but nothing could persuade him to get his head in front where it mattered – though to be fair, he was once beaten by only a neck.

All opposition came alike to him. He lost against the very best – not long before stumps were finally drawn he finished third to the great chaser Remittance Man, though admittedly there were only three runners and Amrullah was a *very* remote third – and he lost against the very mediocre.

There was an individuality, an independence of spirit about Amrullah which appealed to a certain type of racing enthusiast, but – as with Quixall Crossett – not everyone was inclined to share the joke. *Timeform*, the famously upright purveyor of racing information, awarded the horse the dreaded 'double squiggle', the sport's equivalent of the Mark of Cain, and snootily labelled him 'thoroughly irresolute'. We can only guess whether Amrullah himself cared a jot about that – or about the racing journalist who called him 'the sort of slob who given half a chance would stay in bed all day.'

In any case, Amrullah had the last laugh, featuring in the 'And Finally . . .' slot of *News At Ten* when his retirement was announced. In racehorse terms, and in an age when he could yet not be invited onto *Celebrity Big Brother*, that was true fame.

Of course horseracing is about winning, but you can't have winners without losers. And those who have turned losing into a fine art deserve their place in the sun alongside the greatest racing characters of all. So here's to Amrullah and Quixall Crossett and Haru Urara and Zippy Chippy, and to all those horses whose hoofprints will never leave an impression on the grass in the winner's enclosure.

I was at Ascot in April 2009 along with fellow racing writer Sean Magee, who helped with this chapter, and watched, intrigued, as Don't Panic entered the stalls for the 1m race at 3.20. The Peter Chapple-Hyam trained five-year-old had refused to race in his last two outings. He was wearing blinkers for the first time. As the stalls flew open, six of the seven runners jumped out – Don't Panic stayed where he was, just like the horse in the famous Hamlet TV advertisement of some years ago. Aha, we thought, perhaps he is another quirky racing legend in the making . . .

CHARLIE MANN
Oh, man

'I rode in six Nationals and I was pissed for three of them. The horses I rode, you had to be' boasted colourful jockey turned trainer Charlie Mann, once described memorably by Marcus Armytage, as 'Del-boy Trotter meets Valentino.' He still believes he should have won the great race on Doubleuagain which was brought down when 'cantering' in 1986.

Something of a self-publicist, the 1993 Christmas cards emanating from the Mann stables declared, 'There are only two certainties in life – one is dying and the other is owning a winner if it is trained by Charlie Mann.'

Never one to kow-tow to authority, Mann was somewhat aggrieved in February 1994 when his Fifth Amendment was ruled to have dead-heated with Mount Athos, whose nose was obscured in the official photograph of the finish at Uttoxeter. 'Mount Athos would have to have a nose like Pinocchio on his worst behaviour to have any chance of sharing first place' railed the handler, obviously not quite so sure as everyone else that it was purely coincidental that Mount Athos was owned by Hilda Clarke, wife of the racecourse chairman, Stan – after whom the race was named!

Mann handed in his riding licence in 1989 after he broke his neck in a fall at Warwick. He had ridden 149 winners at the time. After his accident he wasn't sure which direction his life would take – 'I never wanted to train, I must say. I spent three years doing things outside of racing. It became apparent that I wasn't qualified for anything else, so I fell into training really.'

He did, though, flirt with an entrepreneurial life, as Richard Edmondson later reported in the *Independent*, in which he also pointed out Mann's preference for 'flat caps with the dimensions of a helicopter landing pad'. 'During his wild entrepreneurial days he dealt in diamonds and tea, chicken legs, vodka and caviar. Most famously, he tried to sell a submarine to a landlocked African nation.' He also reckons he was conned out of £20,000 whilst trying to flog ex-Army tents to Kurdistan. As you do!

He began training in 1993 having spent a year gaining experience with Cath Walwyn. Mann won one of the toughest races in the world in 1995 – the first British success in the event since 1973 – when he sent It's A Snip out to contest the Grand Pardubice, a Czech equivalent of the Grand National, albeit even more challenging, featuring the feared 'Taxis' jump, one of the – perhaps *the* – most feared steeplechase obstacles anywhere in the world.

The year before he had acquired a fine of £1,000 after riding the horse to finish second in the same race – on a riding licence which he had printed up for himself! In a television interview screened in January 2009 Mann confessed with a sly grin that, actually, he hadn't really had a licence to ride the year he won it. When questioned about how he had managed to acquire the necessary paperwork to take part in the race he was ever so slightly vague about it. 'If truth be known, I had to get the licence printed somehow'. He wouldn't reveal further details – probably wisely. He did, though, play down his achievement in winning the race. 'It's a good fun race – it walks a lot bigger than it rides'.

By 1999 he had some decent animals in the yard, and his Celibate, useful if just short of top class, was a fancied runner in the Queen Mother Champion Chase. Mick Fitzgerald, who had won on him in February's Game Spirit Chase – a ride he had deprived an interested Richard Dunwoody of – was supposed to be on board. However, days before the Champion Chase, Fitzgerald was approached by the up and coming Paul Nicholls to ride his classy Call Equiname. With barely a second thought, 'Fitz' accepted. 'Then I had to figure out how I was going to break the news to Charlie'.

He rang the trainer, 'I'm really sorry, but I can't ride Celibate. Paul has asked me to ride Call Equiname'

'You f***ing w****r. You'll never ride for me again.'

Call Equiname won, with Celibate down the field. But here was evidence that maybe the Mann bark is worse than his bite.

'I was walking back into the weigh room, ear to ear grin still on my face, when I met Charlie; "I suppose you were right. Well done" he said.'

'It was very magnanimous of him – and I did ride for him again.'

In 2001, Mann spoke out against what he regarded as the doping problem in his sport, alleging other trainers were using such methods. 'I know that I am not competing on a level playing field' he told racing writer Colin Fleetwood-Jones. 'You see good horses being blown away by animals that are like runaway trains. I know some horses are getting help, almost certainly from EPO (erythropoietin). It is not natural, and I have been suspicious for five years at the way some stables' horses have been winning'.

This was not a stand likely to win him overwhelming support from his peers, and the Jockey Club spokesman John Maxse responded, 'If the scale of the use of EPO was so prevalent, veterinary evidence would have picked it up.' However, he did accept that it was a difficult offence to identify: 'An Australian laboratory said recently that they were close to developing a technique able to detect it – we are ahead of Australia and did not want to make a song and dance about it when we were close to cracking the problem' he added, a little unconvincingly. Maxse continued, 'There are compelling reasons to think that its use in British racing cannot be widespread on account of the effect it would have on the horses' health.'

Mann was back at loggerheads with the racing establishment in late 2007 when he demanded that the British Horseracing Authority withdraw from auction a set of 'cherished' all-brown racing silks expected to make some £50,000. Mann believed that the silks were to all intents and purposes the same as those used for over one hundred years, by the family of his stepfather Edward de Plumpton Hunter, described as 'plain chocolate' – and eventually won the day when, in late November, after his solicitor met with BHA officials, the colours were removed from sale.

Respected *Daily Telegraph* racing correspondent, Marcus Armytage, who pointed out that these two colours would look virtually identical when viewed across a racecourse, weighed in on Mann's side. 'Has racing officialdom gone mad? Frankly, why the Racehorse Owners' Association put up with the ruling body trying to raise more money at their expense through this most dubious of means is beyond me.'

Mann recently discovered an unusual sideline which would not appeal to the majority of trainers – teaming up with the company

Red Letter Days, which offers off-beat holiday and leisure break opportunities to clients. For £73 interested parties were invited to spend three hours at the Mann stable in Upper Lambourn enjoying 'a hearty breakfast with Charlie and his jockey, watching the horses being put through their morning training session.'

'You'll have an early start' warns the blurb for the trip – 'Charlie has trained over 400 winners and can answer all your questions. We can't guarantee that it will turn your donkeys into dead certs, but we can guarantee a morning of enjoyment and insight.'

The Spectator's racing writer, Robin Oakley, was at the Whitcoombe House yard – where Charlie installed innovative Cushion Track gallops – when Red Letter Day clients were present. He recalled one of them asking Mann 'what do you look for in a horse?' and receiving the politically incorrect response: 'Same as you look for in a bird, really – you've got to be attracted. It's important you should like it the first time.' Added Oakley: 'His regular clashes with authority have nearly cost the outspoken Mann dear. He was warned publicly after two cases of mixed-up passports and running the wrong horse that he could lose his licence next time. "OK, one of my staff cocked up, and the buck stops with me." But perhaps he shouldn't have named his daughter's pet orang-utan after a steward.'

Charlie would also doubtless be explaining his training philosophy to visitors: 'Some horses don't want to win, some do, some try and some don't. It's up to me to find out what each horse wants.' He is also happy with the number of horses under his charge – 'I'd rather have 55 horses that are capable of winning than 100 moderate ones. If I don't think a horse is good enough then it's moved on.'

He has been smart enough to source horses from unexpected places – buying from Germany in particular where 'horses you'd pay £80,000 for there, would fetch £200,000 here'. Again his politically incorrect side kicked in when he pointed out a slight oddity in the action of one of his German-breds, stable star, Air Force One: 'See the way he throws his front foot out occasionally? I've never had one do that before – it looks like he's goose-stepping!'

Certainly not one to suffer fools gladly, Mann was approached by a racecourse cameraman, who took a shot of him after one of his horses won a race in January 2009, and then asked him for his name: 'Charlie Mann.'

'Is that your real name?' asked the snapper.

'No, my real name's Aidan O'Brien' responded Charlie.

Mann fears that 'the downside of being so outspoken is that I've possibly lost several owners – but what's the point in keeping your mouth shut if you believe an injustice has been done and needs to be rectified?'

However, this side of his character also ensures that he is never short of a solution to a tricky problem and in early February 2009 when it looked as though his chances of getting to the races with a well fancied couple of runners were being scuppered by the snow lying all around the stables, he thought laterally and had a tractor hitched up to haul the horse-box as far as the snow-free main road 5 miles (8km) away. The horses duly arrived at Taunton, where both Fair Point and Borero won their respective races.

During the same month he revealed the secret of his recent successes – £800 windpipe operations – which he had had carried out on almost 20 of his horses. 'Every horse has improved after it. Horses tire when they don't have enough oxygen.' (I might try it myself!)

Born in 1958, to a mother who was a Yorkshire show-jumper who sold ponies, he left school without academic qualifications, aged 15 after being told that he could do so if he won the Scottish Pony Championship, which honour he duly achieved. He married Susannah Barraclough with whom he had a son and daughter.

Mann's entry in the annual *Directory of the Turf* sums up his approach to life, listing under the heading 'recreations' – 'having fun.'

And he lived up to that in May 2009, announcing stable expansion plans and asking: 'Why is everyone so depressed and talking the sport into a hole?'

DOROTHY PAGET
Larger than life

Imagine being able to bet on horse races which have already been run. And being permitted by your bookie to stake bets of thousands of pounds. Only one big-time gambler has ever been permitted that privilege. She was almost certainly the heaviest backer of her time, definitely the most eccentric and without doubt the most charismatic female ever to grace the Sport of Kings with her presence.

Dorothy Paget, a wealthy heiress, spent much of her time at the races. But when she wasn't there she would turn night into day at her mysterious mansion in Chalfont St Giles where, due to her pronounced dislike of the male half of the human race, she employed an almost entirely female staff, slept during the day and worked overnight. When she did so, her bookmaker, the late, eponymous William Hill, was reportedly quite happy to accept massive bets from her, even though the races had already been run that afternoon, because Ms Paget's honesty and integrity were unimpeachable. That and the fact that she bet enormous sums of money – and lost more often than she won.

She was the biggest owner of racehorses in the land and although she won all the biggest races in the calendar – the Derby, the Cheltenham Gold Cup, the Champion Hurdle – she also owned some extremely moderate beasts. However, such was her commitment to her own horses that she would plunge thousands on them regardless of their chance in the race they were contesting.

Born on 21 February 1905, Dorothy Wyndham Paget was the (very spoiled) daughter of wealthy future MP, Almeric Paget, who would become Lord Queenborough, and the American heiress, Pauline Whitney, whose father was the Secretary to the US Navy, William C Whitney, on whose death she inherited a vast fortune.

She grew up in the early years of the 20th century in a pampered world where money was no object, showing talent in her youth as an accomplished singer. She also became interested and involved in the equestrian pursuits of showjumping, hunting and point-to-pointing, until she began to put on a great deal of weight.

She took up motorsport, racing in public herself as 'Miss Wyndham' and then, perhaps charmed by the personality – albeit almost definitely not the sexual charms – of the dashing driver Sir Henry 'Tim' Birkin, she sponsored him to the tune of tens of thousands of pounds.

The media was enchanted, if not obsessed, by this unconventional debutante, excitedly reporting her every move, although she rarely granted interviews or spoke in public.

In 1930, at the age of 25 and already a hardened gambler at London's card tables, and just two years after women won the right to vote, she deserted Birkin – and his entire sex – and the fast world of motorsport, to burst into the Sport of Kings and become its Queen, albeit a reclusive one, perhaps influenced by the racing successes of her cousin, Jock Whitney, who owned Cheltenham Gold Cup winner, Easter Hero. Money was to be no object – when one trainer asked how much she was prepared to pay for a horse which had caught her eye, she told him, 'Don't ask bloody silly questions. I said, buy him!'

Dorothy Paget didn't just play at racing, she embraced it wholeheartedly and became the champion jump racing owner. Her horse Straight Deal won the 1943 Derby; Insurance won her consecutive Champion Hurdles in 1932 and 1933; and her finest horse, Golden Miller, totally eclipsed every other jumper of the time, running away with the Cheltenham Gold Cup for five straight years from 1932. Chances are, he would have won again in 1937 – but the meeting was cancelled due to bad weather. In 1938 he finished second.

In 1934, uniquely, just 17 days after the Gold Cup, he also won the Grand National. During that race, Paget was said to be 'so overwrought as to be deathly pale' by a contemporary source. Afterwards she greeted Golden Miller, wearing a tweed coat with a beaver collar, low heeled shoes, thick stockings and no lipstick. She made a little more of an effort for the after-race celebration at Liverpool's Adelphi Hotel, organised by her father, turning up at 10pm in a red velvet dress, with her short hair parted in the middle.

She had large chocolate effigies of Golden Miller made for trainer Basil Briscoe and jockey Gerry Wilson to mark the historic occasion. Not all of her celebrations were so lavish – when she won the Derby, during the War in 1943 she shared the contents of her small brandy flask with connections after the race.

Her gambling equalled and almost eclipsed her commitment to the turf as her behaviour became more and more eccentric to the outside world. She would pad around her home during the small hours, clad in her favourite 'woolly teddy-bear dressing gown', phoning her trainers at all hours to demand details of her expensive four-legged assets. One source described her as 'betting like a Chinaman, eating like Henry VIII, and living at night, like Winston Churchill.'

She would risk ten thousand pounds a time on her 'banco' bets – confident tips from her trainers – and twenty thousand on the less frequent 'double banco' selections, depending on the odds. Ms Paget also had an unusual method of occasionally varying her betting stakes – if someone rang her on the morning of a race she would discover their phone number, then stake that number in pounds on her runner.

Otherwise, she would usually stick to backing her selection to make her a profit of £20,000. This caused a sensation once when she took it into her head to back a horse which went off at 1/8 odds – meaning she had to risk £160,000 to make her twenty grand. When she had originally asked for the bet she had anticipated the horse starting at something like 1/2 which would have meant her risking £40,000 to make her required profit. But when the odds shortened dramatically, her bookmaker called one of her secretaries to check whether DP still wanted to place the bet with such an unprecedented sum at stake. Anxious not to be seen to be backing down, she told her secretary that 'I consider his question a piece of gross impertinence.' The bet stayed on, the horse won – and a very relieved DP promptly handed out congratulatory fivers to everyone she could find! It had been her biggest ever wager.

She didn't always back winners, by any means, though. Once, her trainer Fred Darling, told her confidently that her horse Colonel Payne was an absolute certainty for a race at Ascot. She started off with a bet of £10,000 and kept backing the horse, turning up at the course to see the race. Colonel Payne finished nearer last than first and Ms Paget strode to the unsaddling era to quiz jockey Gordon Richards, asking him grimly 'Where's Mr Darling?'

'I wouldn't be quite sure, Miss Paget' replied the 26 times champion jockey, 'But I've a pretty shrewd idea he's on top of the stand cutting his throat.'

Veteran racing journalist Geoffrey Hamlyn, who was on the racing circuit at the same time as Paget, declared in 1994 that she 'lost more money on the British turf than any man or woman before or since'.

Paget shocked the insular racing world by arguing with, and laying down the law to, her male trainers – of whom she had almost 20 – who were used then, as so often now, to acting as the true owners of other people's thoroughbreds and having their word accepted as gospel. Diana Walwyn, wife of trainer Fulke, who oversaw 365 winners for her, eventually put her foot down and banned Paget from ringing him in the small hours. During the eight years he trained for her, Dorothy visited Walwyn's stables just once.

'She would drive you bloody demented' declared Fulke Walwyn, to whom she had once complained that he and his jockey had 'somehow conspired to bring about the defeat' of one of her horses. Furious, Walwyn countered, 'If that's what you think, you know where you can put your horses – all 35 of them – and I've no doubt there'll be plenty of room for them.' They stayed put.

'Training horses is child's play, but it's a hell of a bloody job trying to train Dorothy Paget' said Golden Miller's trainer, the old Etonian, Basil Briscoe.

Paget's eccentricities extended to driving to the races with her staff in two luxury cars – after she had broken down once en route with no replacement to hand. Paget's driving style would not have been out of place on a Grand Prix circuit. She regarded 80mph as a perfectly reasonable cruising speed.

Finding herself in an unfamiliar area on the way to Manchester races, in a broken car she immediately endeavoured to commandeer a local butcher's Baby Austin, offering him £200. When this was rejected, on the understandable grounds that the fellow had arranged to take his mother out for a drive, she upped the ante to £300, plus a trip to the races. When he accepted, he was paid at once from the £5,000 wad of cash routinely carried by her secretary, Miss Clarke, for just such eventualities.

She would sometimes travel to the races by rail, generally booking a whole carriage to herself and making sure she wasn't troubled if dining in the restaurant by booking whole tables at a time – sometimes eating most of the meals served, too.

When she arrived at the races she would disappear into her private box from where she would watch the races. After the last race she would lock herself into the lavatory, the door of which would be guarded by a phalanx of secretaries until almost all the other racegoers had departed, when she would emerge and sit down to eat a huge meal, attended by one or more of her trainers, who would, like her meat, be grilled, and questioned about her horses and their performances.

On one occasion at Manchester racecourse they were left on their own and told to contact the racecourse caretaker when they were ready to depart. When Towcester racecourse refused to put the stand lights on for her when she was there long into the evening, she vowed that she would never run any of her horses there again.

Her superstitions included avoiding at all costs anyone wearing green, and always carrying with her a bundle of precisely nine freshly sharpened pencils – the nine was related to another superstition of usually naming her favourite horses in multiples of three letters – Golden Miller (12); Insurance (9); Straight Deal (12).

Ultimately, horses carrying her famous yellow and peacock blue colours, won her an astonishing 1,532 races and she was leading owner over jumps three times, in 1933/34; 1940/41 and 1951/52 and on the flat in 1943.

Eventually she gave up going racing but maintained her interest in her horses by studying photographs supplied by her trainers and stud managers which she would use to help her plan the matings of her mares.

On 30 January 1960, by which time she was rarely seen on a racecourse, Miss Paget's horse Fortescue won a race at Naas in Ireland. It was to be her last winner.

She drank only Malvern water and tea, except for an occasional snifter of brandy or weak buck's fizz, but smoked up to one hundred Turkish cigarettes through a holder on a daily basis and died tragically early, on 9 February 1960, just short of her 55th birthday. She had complained of feeling unwell the previous day, but had perked up and eaten one of her usual gargantuan meals.

Next morning one of her secretaries visited her room at 4.30am and found her poring over a racing calendar, saying 'We must get these entries (for races to be contested by her horses) off first thing.' An hour later she was found dead of heart failure. Having never made a will her estate of £3,803,380 was mostly seized by the Chancellor, with the remainder of her enormous wealth being passed on to her sister, Lady Baillie, to whom she rarely spoke.

KEN PAYNE
Window cleaner who payned bookies

'Fleecing the bookmakers, that was the name of the game' was the bald statement of intent by Ken 'Duke' Payne, window cleaner turned trainer, who did indeed leave many layers feeling like shorn sheep as another of his heavily backed two-year-olds stormed home.

I have to confess to backing a good few of them at the time, at the behest of a good racing journalist pal who seemed to have a hot-line to the Payne stable. I was only betting in small money but the winners seemed never ending. How was I to know the trainer was not only using gamesmanship and deception to engineer his success, but was also up to something which was pushing the bounds of legality?

Whilst in Malaya serving his country on National Service in the early 1950s, he had met a vet whose manner of treating horses involved giving them a mixture of steroids and vitamin B_{12}. Payne was impressed by this treatment and its success in getting horses 'up' for races.

Unable initially to return to the racing game, in which he had been a stable lad and apprentice jockey, Payne started cleaning windows when he came out of the forces and by the early 1960s had built up a business employing 700 people.

He gradually began to edge into racing as he acquired a horse or two, and began to try out the Malaysian treatments – up to that point, to the best of my knowledge, no vet in Great Britain had ever tried these on a horse. The effect was miraculous. He started by landing a gamble in a pony race meeting at Hawthorn Hill where Fantasia duly landed a £5,000 win for him.

Having acquired premises in the New Forest, in 1967, he was soon handed a horse called Neronton to train by owner Ralph Emery. The horse had seen better days but had decent hurdling form from way back. Getting the horse fit via conventional methods, Payne entered it for a selling hurdle at Catterick – 'I had never before pulled off a betting coup', he said. The racing world was about to make the acquaintance of K Payne. Neronton was backed from 10/1 to 5/1 and, despite almost getting rid of jockey Brian Fletcher at the fifth, the partnership stayed together to win, going away. Payne's first, drug free, coup had won him £20,000.

Payne now began to refine his methods, running horses over the wrong distance, in the wrong class, before placing them where they could win. Bookies soon became suspicious of his runners, taking no chances with the odds they offered.

Then Payne met a wealthy man known as George Pantin from Maidenhead via Australia, who supplied him with some horses and also suggested treating a horse called Raincap with steroids. It transpired that they had both come across the steroid/vitamin B_{12} method before. Payne asked himself 'Was it a drug within the meaning of the term specified in Jockey Club regulations?' He convinced himself that there were no moral objections to using them: 'I never saw steroids do a horse anything but good'. He ceased using them far enough before a race to ensure they didn't show up in any subsequent drug test.

Raincap was entered for a decent Newbury race, which he wasn't meant to win and didn't – a contest at Ripon was his real target, where a four figure sum was invested in the gelding. The steroid treatment produced a startling side-effect, leaving the horse 'strutting around sporting a mighty erection' which caught the attention of a Ripon steward who told the trainer, 'I'd get him cut (gelded) if I were you!' Raincap stormed home.

The winners flowed – upsetting bookies so much that one, from whom he had £500 to collect, literally threw the cash at him 'sending me scrambling round in the mud.'

Payne got his own back via a plot in which he entered two for a race, and put Lester Piggott up on one so that it would be assumed that was the plot horse, only to win with the other one – which he had backed. Another Payne plot misfired when a proud owner 'treated' his horse with gallons of his favourite yoghurt pre-race, 'with the inevitable messy result' and a defeat.

For his next trick, Payne organised coups, then went out to Jamaica to back the horses at inflated odds, flying back with his winnings – until the local laws changed to prevent cash being taken out of the country.

He fell foul of a deal with world champion boxer John Conteh, who pulled out of an agreement to buy £11,000 worth of horse, when, on a night out with Payne, he 'rode' a wooden horse at a

London club, only to fall off – 'he mumbled something about being humiliated by the incident' wrote Payne later.

In his 1978 autobiography, *The Coup*, Payne outlined methods of landing betting scams – 'there are lots of ways to stop a horse legally' he wrote, and outlined some of them:

*Leaving them thirsty then giving them a pre-race bucket of water.

*Tranquilise the horse.

*Have the horse shod with heavy plates.

*Keep the horse untrained at the stalls so that it will be left at the start.

*Tell the jockey to start the horse slowly – 'I would say that at least 10 per cent of slow starts are deliberate.'

*Run your horse out of his best distance, on unsuitable going conditions.

*Tell the jockey to hold him back when he is a front runner.

*Tell the jockey to take a horse wide when he likes to run with the pack.

Payne also explained another of his techniques to make horses run faster: 'By bleeding a horse then transfusing back a couple of pints before a race you give the horse extra oomph.'

Despite his successful coups, Payne, also something of a ladies' man, which caused problems in his personal life, needed a hefty income to pay the not inconsiderable costs of running what had become a large yard, with many employees, all reliant on him.

In 1976 the Payne saga came to a juddering halt. 'Security was my biggest problem. I had the horses to land the coups, but I had to employ the skills of a counter-spy to thwart the bookmakers, the sporting press, the public, my staff and even my jockeys.' Perhaps he was becoming paranoid. He had sent out 39 winners in the year thus far but 'in something like four months I had to take at least £150,000 from the bookies in order to maintain my Middleham establishment and keep me in the lifestyle to which I'd become lovingly accustomed.'

The wheels began to fall off. Planning a Carlisle coup, his horse Mistress X bolted pre-race, using up all the energy needed to win. Payne was staggered to see that when the horse was caught she was taken to the start to race. Thinking quickly, Payne commandeered a Land Rover, bunging the old boy sitting in it £20 to drive him to the start. They went up the course to stop the race getting underway and he told his jockey to feign illness so that he could withdraw the distressed filly.

'I loved the fun and games, but the strain was beginning to tell' said Payne. He received heavy threats before one race in which he was ordered to ensure his horse didn't win. It won. Years earlier he had suffered from malaria, an illness which now struck him again. He owed the banks over £100,000 and the extraordinarily hot summer of 1976 had played havoc with going conditions, foiling his plans for winners. Feed bills were rocketing for the horses, staff wages were due. His youngest son had been tragically killed in a freak accident.

Payne tried to commit suicide, by swallowing a bottle of pills. He was found next morning and saved by the kiss of life from a 'man who had pursued me relentlessly through the courts on an issue involving theft'.

One of the most colourful of racing careers was over. Or was it?

Over a quarter of a century later, the *Racing Post*'s Graham Green would reveal that Payne had popped up in Perth, Western Australia, where he had been working as a car salesman until he applied (only to be rejected) for a trainer's licence in August 2003. And Payne's amazing story continued to surprise when, in June 2007, Corey Maita, a purchaser and reviewer of his autobiography on website amazon.co.uk, added in passing, 'This book gives a great insight to an amazing life. Turns out Ken Payne is my father.'

SIR MARK PRESCOTT
Politically incorrect

You have to love a man who, these days, is entirely unrepentant and unapologetic about his love for, in alphabetical order, amateur boxing, art, bull-fighting, cigars, greyhound coursing, movies, opera and out-smarting the official handicapper!

'All I want out of life is a cigar, to go see a bullfight and have the freedom to turn up the heating when I want to' said teetotal trainer Sir Mark Prescott, a man to whom I will always be grateful for winning with a horse which was expected to lose.

I was on a racing trip to Cagnes-sur-Mer in France several years back, and had been told en route to the track to back Sir Mark's runner, Humoreuse. Ensconcing myself with friends in the restaurant we all proceeded to enjoy an excellent afternoon's wining, dining and betting – cheering to the rafters as Sir Mark's 7/1 shot front-ran to victory. Only afterwards did we wonder why other members of our party, who had also received the news to back the horse, did not seem to be celebrating in the same manner. It transpired that a late message had come through, advising us all NOT to back the horse – wouldn't like the going, badly drawn, some such excuse. Anyway, the message had not been passed on to us – much to our delight and financial enrichment.

An Old Harrovian and son and grandson of Conservative MPs, Sir Mark Prescott's unlikely heroes include Labour stalwarts Tony Benn and 1930s Party leader, George Lansbury.

Sir Mark, who had 200 rides as an amateur jockey, has trained at Heath House, Newmarket since 1970, when, barely out of his teenage years, he took over from the late Jack Waugh, to whom he had been assistant trainer for the previous three years. 'He drilled into me that your duty is to your owner; first, last, always.' Waugh also taught Prescott to recognise his horses by feeling their legs – blindfolded!

Amongst the 1,500 or so winners he has sent out since Belle Royale at Teesside Park on 23 April 1971, were the 2004 triple Group One winner Albanova; dual Champion Stakes winner Albora; and the 13 times winner as a two-year-old, in 1980, Spindrifter. Between 1981 and 1985 his Misty Halo won 21 of 42 starts, a post-war record for a mare. Owned by his great friend, the late *Observer* and *Racing Post* writer, Graham Rock, Pasternak landed huge gambles when winning the Magnet Cup and Cambridgeshire. 2004 was his best season to date, with 76 winners, worth £921,553.78 at a 29.46 per cent strike rate.

'Most in racing would agree that there has never been a better trainer of moderate racehorses' wrote Neil Clark of the *Observer*, in October 2004. His long serving stable jockey George Duffield said, 'He finds it an enormous challenge to place cripples or quirky horses to win races, and when they do he derives as much satisfaction from that as winning a Pattern race.' (The Pattern was introduced in 1971, to highlight the most important annual non-handicap races of the flat season.)

Prescott's ability to take advantage of quirks in the rules to place his horses to best advantage may have made him one of the few trainers to be able to take credit for influencing the rules-makers to change their tactics. In the spring of 2007 the authorities altered the penalty structure for handicap winners, prompting the *Racing Post*'s James Pyman to opine: 'Although nobody at the time directly stated that it was Prescott's expert planning that prompted the amendment, it was widely assumed to be the case.' Pyman wrote that in August 2008 – when Prescott had just sent out Aleatricis to win five times in 24 days.

In a summer 2008 interview, Prescott, 'the bachelor baronet' declared to *Trainer* magazine: 'If I had a family and whatnot, I'd have less time to do all my little scheming wheezes. I'm very happy that everybody else breeds like rabbits and gets into all the expense and often have their lives completely messed up by it. I'm absolutely thrilled for them, but I don't want to do it myself.'

He is one of racing's most loyal employers – to the extent that he once said of stable jockey George Duffield, 'I have looked at many another woman, but I have never looked at another jockey.'

Prescott's career could have been over before it began – he broke his back at the age of 15 and was in hospital for 18 months – 'I couldn't speak, I couldn't swallow, I couldn't blink for nine weeks. It's the most terrible experience, being a prisoner inside your own body with your mind racing.' It happened in 1963 after he slipped up on the flat at now closed Wye racecourse.

When he emerged, his perspective on life had changed: 'I came out believing it was desperately important to do everything as well as I could, but equally to realise it is all completely unimportant in comparison. Training racehorses should never be life and death. That's for other sports.'

Such as bull-fighting, which features prominently in the shape of dramatic photographs in his home, which also houses the skin of the 1884 Ascot Gold Cup winner, St Simon. Well, he WAS once stabled there. Paintings of fighting cocks and statues of coursers are also on display chez Prescott.

Prescott has no problem with justifying bull-fighting, stressing the difference in quality of life between the animals involved in that sport and those served up on a plate as veal. Of coursing, whose main event, the Waterloo Cup, was banned after the 2004 running, Prescott commented: 'The following week, after the government banned hare coursing, 896 hares were shot. Over a total coursing season in Britain, they had never killed more than 159 hares in a whole year. The brown hare would be considerably worse off without coursing'. Asked by the *Spectator*'s Peter Oborne in February 2005 whether he would prefer to win the Waterloo Cup or train the winner of the Derby, he answered: 'I'd rather win the Waterloo Cup.' A couple of years after the ban, Prescott found himself in hot water when he and celebrity TV chef, Clarissa Dickson Wright were accused of allegedly hunting hares with dogs in North Yorkshire.

Prescott is very much his own man – how many other trainers would have politely declined the offer to train for Sheikh Mohammed, on the grounds that at the time, he did not want more than 50 horses in his yard?

Thus it is not surprising that he has said, 'I haven't the slightest interest in being champion trainer. I would like to be the best trainer, though I don't know what that is.' What it certainly is not, according to the great man is, a happy one. 'A happy trainer is a bad trainer, the worse the trainer, the happier he is – because he hasn't noticed what's going wrong.'

He is a stickler for punctuality, as current stable jockey Seb Sanders soon discovered. 'The greatest sin at Heath House is to be late in the morning. It happened just once. It was only by five minutes. But Sir Mark's reaction was . . . well, unprintable.' Almost as unprintable as the time Sir Mark commented scatchingly on a stubbly Sanders chin – 'He has arrived clean shaven since.'

Prescott is under no illusions about racing's place in the wider world, declaring that training is 'unbelievably unimportant. I've wasted what little talent and skill I've got, which should have been spent trying to better mankind in some way.'

He firmly believes most horses do not want to go racing and that, therefore, 'I appreciate how important it is to never, ever run one that is not ready.' Which makes it all the more remarkable that Humoreuse managed to win!

Usually a good loser, Sir Mark once failed to retain a horse which had just won a seller at the subsequent auction. He snatched the bridle off of the horse 'then stomped home, leaving the new, proud owner with his arms around the horse's neck, shrieking for a bridle.' Claimed Sir Mark, 'This fit of pique resulted in a new rule that it was the duty of the trainer of the animal at the time it won to take the horse back to the racecourse stables, whatever the result of the auction – this probably represents my only long term footprint in turf history.'

Sir Mark thinks ahead – farther ahead than most – and once answered 'I'm not prepared to bet against it' when asked whether he believes in life after death. And he has already prepared for that hopefully long delayed event, as he told *Observer* writer Will Buckley in 2001: 'Almost 20 years ago I wanted to find myself a nice plot with some agreeable people around. I had to contact the parks and recreation authority. And there was a very nice fellow, he showed me the graveyard and there was Fred Archer, Mr Dawson, Mr Waugh and lots of nice people. I found a nice corner and said "I want three plots down there." And he said, "Would that be for Sir, and Lady Prescott and your son and heir?"

"Certainly not" I replied, "It's so I don't have to have any f***er next to me".'

ROD SIMPSON
Rod for his own backers?

'Flamboyant' barely begins to describe Rod Simpson, one of racing's greatest survivors, who has disappeared from view time after time only to pop back up a little later in a different location, working for different people – but in the same occupation of trainer.

The nomadic trainer's view of his own lifestyle was perhaps reflected in the title of his 1993 autobiography, *Mainly Fun and Horses* – obviously inviting comparisons with a certain Del Boy Trotter of *Only Fools and Horses* fame. On the front cover Simpson leads a horse in, wearing a bright blue beret and a bright yellow polo shirt, the horse has a colour coordinated light blue sheepskin noseband.

Born on 16 September 1945, and having resisted the urge to join the Horse Guards or the Navy in favour of becoming a wannabe jockey, (he had his first race in public, finishing third of three at Folkestone, and four more losing outings) he sent out his first winner, Lady Tartown, at Warwick on 9 June 1979, when he was private trainer to Mr and Mrs Arthur Zandona, a wealthy family based in Finchampstead.

Rod had his first run-in with the authorities over a Zandona horse called Dollar Pocket – after he decided to adopt wife Eileen's suggestion of easing an unusual and intimate problem the colt had – by smearing their baby son Robin's teething gel on the animal's sensitive balls! Sadly for them the gel contained a banned substance and Dollar Pocket failed a dope test – leading to a £350 fine.

After 12 winners in two seasons for the Zandonas, Simpson moved in to former top trainer Scobie Breasley's yard at Epsom's South Hatch – the stables from which Walter Nightingall had sent out 1943 Derby winner, Straight Deal. Now he began to attract additional owners, vital once the Zandonas dropped out of racing. He later told the *Guardian*'s Greg Wood, 'When I started out as a public trainer in Epsom I had a big owner called Jim McCaughey with lots of horses, and a few months later he hanged himself.'

Simpson, who had been apprenticed to Cyril Mitchell, who told him he'd make a good stable lad, and Frank Muggeridge, as well as being head lad for Alec Kerr, wasted no time in getting up the noses of those conservative folk running the game. Simpson's dress sense was soon making waves. 'I wear leather suits' he told the *Sporting Life* newspaper, 'I get stick from members of the Jockey Club and local stewards, because they look at you as if to say "I don't think he should be allowed in here wearing that" – I don't think they should be allowed anywhere looking like they do!' He once wore 'a multi-coloured ski suit to Devon and Exeter. Some of the old duffers there went crazy.' *Spectator* writer Robin Oakley recalled the time Simpson 'attended a prize giving at Ascot dressed as a punk rocker.'

When his horses Brunico and Tangognat were running at Cheltenham on Triumph Hurdle day in the mid 1980s Simpson was wearing a rather less fashionable item of clothing. He and wealthy owner Terry Ramsden were in the parade ring when the police approached them to explain that they had received a death threat against Ramsden. The pair of them were hurriedly fitted out with bullet-proof vests.

Simpson, good friends with another less than orthodox racing figure, John Francome, married in 1976 to Eileen, and is father to Robin and Rebecca. He is one of the few trainers to boast that his favourite music is heavy metal – and that he had, in earlier days before training, when he was a travelling (to Ireland and France) head lad, dabbled in dubious practices such as smuggling. 'You also learned how many wristwatches you could get around one horse's leg and then cover with a bandage, how many bottles of perfume you could get in the hay net without them rattling.' Mind you, as Rod himself observed, 'Where I was born and bred, just outside Streatham, to be associated with horses was definitely not the done thing. Robbing the sweetshop on the corner was more acceptable.'

He won the Cesarewitch in 1983 with 7/1 chance Bajan Sunshine, tipping it to all and sundry in public, partnered by Brian Rouse. Simpson lost the horse, which had been sold, almost immediately after the triumph.

Simpson landed many considerable gambles for patron and landlord Ramsden and in 1986 he won his first Group One when 33/1 shot Brunico won the Ormonde Stakes – 'I was so pleased that I punched Terry Ramsden's 32 stone minder.'

As the winners flowed, Rod's outgoing personality came into its own – he began bringing a chair into the winner's enclosure *before* races, then sitting on it waiting for his horse to come back in.

Perhaps he went just a little over the top when he told the media before one race, 'He can be lame and win this. He can fall over and win this. The jockey can get off, get on every other horse in the race, get back on and still win'. Ramsden thought he was giving away too much information – 'he gave me a right bollocking about it once'.

In 1987 the Ramsden financial empire collapsed – Simpson had to sell all of his horses. 'The lot. I was left with 10 empty boxes. I had trained 38 winners for him from 25 horses. He was a great character. I remember one time, we took one of his horses to Mussleburgh, which was a long way to go, but we knew that it would win. He rang me 15 minutes before the race and said "how's that horse?". I said, "fine". He said, "it had better be, I've just had a million quid on it."

Not only owners, Simpson had horses with character – his

Fortune's Guest, for example. 'If he saw anything red, he'd attack it. I had to try and train him around missing the postman every morning. Buses, people with red jumpers, he was unbelievable. If he passed a house with a red door he'd go into the garden and kick the door.'

Up to 1990, Simpson was training at Near Down in Upper Lambourn, following a stint at Kelston Stud at Leatherhead. He could no longer afford it, though. He moved on. Walk The Beat won for him on 5 November 1992 at Edinburgh – his final runner out of the Déjà Vu stables at Foxhill, Wiltshire. Deja-Vu? 'I was back at square one, having to start from scratch rather than being able to build on what I had already achieved.'

He moved into Bourne Stables in Lambourn, but by 1994 he had relocated to Cefn Llogell Farm, Coedkernew, near Cardiff.

There later followed a spell of a year out of training whilst he did some corporate hospitality work.

In 1998 Simpson was asked how his horse, Nipper Reed, was, following a race at Ascot. 'He's eaten up well. But then, my girlfriend left me this week, and I'm still eating.' Nipper Reed was gambled on from 20/1 down to 12/1, and *Spectator* racing writer Robin Oakley had got on – 'The shirt was canary yellow. The long, billowing raincoat was emerald green. The beard may now be grizzled but the eyes were shining bright and the tongue, as ever, was in perpetual motion. Rod Simpson, the eternal Comeback Kid was back in the winner's enclosure . . . the first man in the enclosure, ready to relish yet another signpost on his roller-coaster career, greeting his winner characteristically with whooping calls worthy of the hunting field.'

He fell foul of the Jockey Club's Disciplinary Committee in early 2001 when he was fined £2,500 after facing three charges – of using a trainer's badge to gain access to the paddock and weighing room at Royal Ascot in 2000, five months after his own licence had expired; that he had been seen handing money to a ticket tout outside Royal Ascot; and thirdly that he had registered a horse's name against the wishes of an owner.

It was reported that he had been cleared of the touting charge. Wrote the *Independent*'s Greg Wood, 'Given that trainers have been fined rather less when their horses fail dope tests, the size of Simpson's penalty seems to be a little extreme. Simpson's ability to bounce back from apparently terminal blows to his training career has made him a thoroughly popular figure, while his dress sense, from multi-coloured coats to one-piece biker leathers can be a refreshing break from the tweed and trilby norm.'

Simpson was still raging against authority. 'I put my hands up and wrote them a statement explaining how it happened. It was not done as a deliberate scam, it was done in the knowledge that I was a racehorse trainer, but not licensed at that time. What I didn't allow for was the fact the Jockey Club has these ex-policemen aged 90 to 130 with nothing else to do. How can anybody let Lingfield get away with a slap on the wrist (after a recent last minute meeting abandonment) and fine me for anything so trivial?' he asked plaintively and with no hope of receiving a sensible – or, indeed any at all – answer. 'I'm not sure whether anyone wants me any more' mused Simpson – before travelling some considerable distance to discover that they did, actually . . .

He took his unorthodox style of training to pastures new – plying his trade in Dubai and Abu Dhabi where in 2002/03 he had saddled six winners from 94 runners; in 2003/04 six from 149; 2004/05 seven from 143; 2005/06 nine from 91 before taking a brief break. It was reported in January 2006 that he had resigned for some unspecified reason – although Simpson later explained, 'I can't say too much about that, but one thing the press got wrong when they reported it is that they said I walked away from the job, I didn't walk away from it. I ran.'

Shortly after this, he reflected on the fact that perhaps not everyone hated him in the racing game. 'I've been astounded how open doors have been – after all, I've been away a while. I never realised until now I was such a popular bastard.'

The 2008 *Directory of the Turf* listed Simpson, who described himself as a 'sports enthusiast', as training on a dual licence at Upshire Stables, Lambourn and the versatile handler did actually become manager of Wiltshire League side Marlborough Town at one point. But Simpson resumed the wandering in the UAE during 2008/09 when he enjoyed his most successful campaign so far, scoring well into double figures. 'It's pretty tough over there. It's a nice place to go on holiday, but hard to work there' he said.

In December 2008 it became just a little easier when Rod dominated the prestigious National Day Cup meeting in Abu Dhabi – sending out three winners. Then at the end of that month he saddled the first, second and third home in the Listed Abu Dhabi Three-year-old Championship for Purebred Arabians.

The photograph accompanying his entry on the Emirates Racing Authority website suggested that he had toned down at least his appearance, as it showed him sporting conventional shirt, tie and jacket ensemble – no ski suits in Abu Dhabi, and no more a Rod for his own back, perhaps!

Musing on his eventful career, Simpson said, 'Sometimes . . . you think, maybe it's me, maybe I'm the Jonah. If anyone ever had a right to turn around and spit on horse racing, it was me, I can tell you. But the reason I didn't is that I've loved all the people and I've had a lot of fun.'

Simpson's switchback ride around the racing world took an unexpected upward lurch when, in March 2009, his purebred Arabian six-year-old, Fryvolous, became the first horse in the winner's enclosure on Dubai World Cup night after overcoming a poor draw to win the $250,000 Dubai Kahayla Classic over 2000m.

Rod had roared back – again.

ODDS-ON FAVOURITES

JIM BOLGER
Bolshie Bolger

When Jim Bolger sent out his third consecutive winner of the Dewhurst Stakes, 20/1 shot Intense Focus, at the end of the 2008 flat season in which he had won the Derby with New Approach, but seriously upset the media with his procrastinations about whether or not the horse was an intended runner, the hacks were unsure whether to heap him with acclaim or opprobrium.

Most opted for the former – particularly as New Approach had also capped his season that same day with a very impressive victory in the Champion Stakes at Newmarket, the first Derby winner to complete that double for 40 years, since Sir Ivor. The often tight lipped Bolger responded by telling the press pack, 'I'm not sure if he – Intense Focus – is going to run in the Derby, but I'm sure I have him entered. I might tell you next March or April!'

One of his previous critics, Alastair Down of the *Racing Post* called him 'martinet, mentor, man of God and master of making money.' He said of him, that he 'makes his own laws and lives by them.'

An accountant by trade, Bolger's own riding career was brief – producing a good strike rate of 25 per cent as he won three of the twelve races he contested. He put the numbers' game to one side to begin to provide for his wife and two daughters in the less precise world of thoroughbreds.

He got off the mark as a trainer when Peaceful Pleasure won for him at Roscommon on 20 September 1976. Bolger's first English winner was Beparoejojo at Liverpool in March 1978. The Bolger breakthrough hit home in 1982 when filly Condessa won the Musidora Stakes and the Yorkshire Oaks and also finished runner-up in the Irish Oaks.

The stable strongly fancied the chances of Favourite Niece at

Gowran Park on 22 July 1982 – but things went a little awry – 'I fancied her and I backed her. She ran a poor race. When I returned home I found the stables on fire.'

As a result of the blaze he, wife Jackie and family moved to historic Glebe House in Coolcullen, Kilkenny, built back in the 18th century. The testing gallops there soon ensured that few trainers had fitter inmates. Cleverly, he ensured that his gallops could be divided into sections for use at different times of the year.

The attention to detail paid off as Give Thanks became his first Classic winner, landing the Irish Oaks in 1983 and Flame of Tara won Royal Ascot's Coronation Stakes. His 1984 Moyglare Stud Stakes win with Park Appeal entitled Bolger to make a speech at the Moyglare Dinner – which he used to attack the Turf Club and the state-sponsored Racing Board, declaring 'It is not fighting a losing battle, it has thrown in the towel.' That speech failed to endear him to the racing establishment. Bolger showed few signs of caring.

His yard was hit and shut down by a virus during the next season, but by 1987 he could also boast a big international victory, via sprinter Polonia in Longchamp's Prix de l'Abbaye.

He set a new record with 138 wins in one year in Ireland, with Latin Quarter winning at Galway in October 1990, to smash the record of 134, which had stood since 1923 to Senator Jim Parkinson. In the same year he had again laid into the Irish racing authorities when making a speech to the eartern Region of the then Irish Thoroughbred Breeders' Association in which – amongst other matters – he hit out at the fact that just 2 per cent of those governing racing were female. Bolger did though, insist that there was nothing personal against individuals in his criticisms, but that it was the system to which he objected.

Jet Ski Lady won the Oaks for him in 1991 at 50/1. 11 April 1992 was a good day at the office as Bolger saddled five of the seven winners at The Curragh – even with his 8/11 favourite St Jovite, who would go on to be runner-up in that year's Derby and win the Irish Derby, missing out. This was Jim's first flat five-timer, although on 12 August 1991, he had five winners at Gowran Park's mixed card.

Bolger came up with a novel excuse to explain why his much fancied Desert Team finished only third in the Newmarket Stakes in

May 1993 – the handler blamed Channel 4's mobile camera for his failure to win. 'The camera is mounted on a huge truck and this went along in front of the horses for four furlongs. Desert Team had one eye on the truck all the time'

In 1994 Bolger became involved in a bitter dispute with the Turf Club, which resulted in his total vindication after taking his case to the High Court, albeit five years down the line. The case started when Bolger's 12/1 shot Tirolean was beaten by a head at Naas in July 1994, after which jockey Seamus Heffernan was suspended for 28 days, the horse for 30 and Bolger fined £1,000. The implication was obvious and when an appeal merely saw the verdict upheld, Bolger decided to risk taking it all the way – 'I had right on my side. I didn't do anything wrong.' Eventually, on 6 August 1999 the final ruling emerged – the judge finding against the Turf Club. Bolger declared: 'This was a serious setback for the Turf Club. Not only is it a self-perpetuating club but it is also an inept one.'

Having suffered something of a downturn in fortunes, the Bolger stable proved it was no back number when Alexander Goldrun captured two Group Ones in 2004, and in 2006 Finsceal Beo won the Irish and English 1000 Guineas, and was narrowly beaten in the French version.

It isn't only the great and good of racing who get to feel the Bolger wrath, though – in July 2004 after smoking had been banned in the workplace in Ireland he spotted a press hack puffing away in the winner's enclosure at The Curragh and promptly demanded: 'Is this not a place of work?' The fag was soon extinguished, unlike Bolger's unquenchable passion for the sport.

Although racing is his living, Bolger declares that 'the only time I get really excited is when I go to the All-Ireland hurling final if my county, Wexford, is involved, that really gets me going. As regards the excitement in racing, I like to steer a level path. I never get low, and I like to think that I don't get carried away, either, but I enjoy it immensely. I love racing, I love the competition, and I love the people that I compete with, to a person they are very, very generous people, in spirit and personality.'

Amongst those to benefit from Bolger's mentoring at his Coolcullen stables, where smoking and drinking are banned, and attendance at mass encouraged, have been those up and coming youngsters, Aidan O'Brien, Tony McCoy and Paul Carberry. 'Jim Bolger has long been respected among professionals as a grey eminence' wrote Chris McGrath in the *Independent* in October 2008, 'It is only in the past couple of years, however, that the rich texture of that legacy has become more broadly understood.'

Others believe that he would benefit from lightening up a little. 'I was left with a distinct feeling that he would benefit from taking a glass or two of vintage claret' observed racing writer Raymond Smith after an interview, 'and that it would make him relax more.' However, Bolger certainly retains his calm before a big race: 'I will do a bit of pruning, a bit of digging, or a little bit of walking the land – I'll just be concerned that my fellow competitors may be walking their boxes (nervous) – but I will not be.'

Bolger, who was honoured with a civic reception by his local Carlow County Council to mark his 2008 achievements, and his contribution to the local community, will never be everyone's cup of tea. He is not one to dispense goodwill to all men on a regular basis, which makes it all the more noteworthy that he was born in 1941 – on Christmas Day.

WILLIE CARSON
Scot with the lot

D espite having to stand on a box to claim equal stature with his BBC broadcasting partner, Clare Balding, the first ever Scottish champion flat jockey William Fisher Hunter Carson (born in Stirling on 16 November 1942) has had few equals as a major racing character since he first came to national prominence with his first winner, Pinker's Pond, at Catterick on 19 July 1962.

There was no racing connection in his family – his father was a warehouse foreman for Fyffes bananas and Willie's greatest early achievement was that 'I was a good newspaper boy.' The money from that job paid for his first riding lessons on a Shetland pony called Wings, after he had been inspired by a movie to want to become a jockey. Quite when he first revealed his trademark cackling laugh, which endeared him to the public when, starting in 1982, he captained a team on BBC's enduringly popular *A Question of Sport*, is unclear.

The 5ft (1.52m) Carson was set to succeed Doug Smith as first jockey to Lord Derby, whose horses were trained by Bernard van Cutsem in 1967, when he sustained serious injuries (breaking his femur, jaw and wrist) in a car accident, which threatened his future. He had to walk with the aid of callipers at the beginning of the 1968 season but showed great determination and resilience and he was soon riding as strongly as ever again.

Willie was literally dogged by trouble at Redcar in July 1969 when, partnering Javatina, he missed out on a winner when he had to swerve his mount round two invading canines on the course! In 1990 he lost at Lingfield on Aradu when he claimed the horse shied away from an advertising hoarding.

In 1971 he was runner up in the jockey championship with 145 winners, 17 behind Lester Piggott, but the next year made no mistake, winning the title for himself, repeating the performance in 1973 and again in 1978, 1980 and 1983. He once commented in an introspective moment, which perhaps explained some of the huge drive he possesses, 'I seemed doomed to play second fiddle to him (Lester) for life.'

In 1974 Carson exhibited remarkable skill as he partnered Dibidale into third place in the Oaks, riding bareback after the filly's weight cloth fell off two furlongs out. Inevitably, they were disqualified.

Willie became involved in one of the darkest, most controversial incidents of his career in May 1975 at Newmarket where, after talks between the Transport and General Workers' Union and the Trainers' Federation over a pay rise for stable lads had broken down, the lads were trying to picket the course. The average wage for stable staff in Newmarket at the time was reportedly £28 – the equivalent of around £150 today – and Carson was later quoted as saying, 'A lot of us (jockeys) had been stable boys ourselves and knew how badly treated they had been. We wanted them to win the fight.'

Some 200 lads got on to the course and as Carson cantered Pericet down to the start for the second race he found himself surrounded by strikers. 'Pericet pulled right up and I got hit with my own stick' he said in a 2001 interview, '"What are you doing?" I said, "I was with you lot but now you are bloody attacking me."' Some jockeys, including Lester Piggott, retaliated by charging at the strikers and Carson called out to racegoers 'If you want to see horse racing get rid of this lot' whereupon some spectators attacked the lads. Greg Wood of the *Guardian* later wrote of the incident: 'A group of jockeys, including Lester Piggott and Willie Carson, galloped straight through them, waving their whips to clear a path. They looked like 18th-century landowners giving their miserable tenants a taste of leather.' Police had to clear the course and Carson was later given a dressing down by Cambridge's Chief Constable who told him he should have been arrested for inciting a riot.

Carson became first jockey to Major Dick Hern in 1977 and won the Oaks-St Leger double on Dunfermline for the Queen in 1978, whose home he visited in February 1983, to receive his OBE.

In 1982 he was so distracted by his wedding to Elaine Williams in May that when he turned up at Chester for his winning mount on Swiftfoot in the Cheshire Oaks he was almost prevented from taking the ride as he had forgotten his medical record-book, for which he was fined £8.

It took him 11 years to win the 'set' of Classics. He won the 200th Derby in 1979 on Troy. Willie was delighted to win the 1988 St Leger on Minster Son – a horse he bred himself – a unique achievement during the 20th century. Nashwan was Willie's 1989 Derby winner – to whom he paid perhaps the ultimate compliment: 'It's like making love every time I get on the horse.' In 1990 he completed the set when Salsabil won the 1000 Guineas.

On 30 June 1990 he rode six of the seven winners at Newcastle – a 3266/1 accumulator – missing out only in the third race. He later told me that had the third race 'been the last race, I'd have won'! To make this achievement all the more remarkable, he had had the final winner at Goodwood the evening before – and he then also won on his first two at The Curragh the next day, losing on the third but partnering the first three winners at Wolverhampton the day after, giving him 12 winners from 14 mounts. Willie once rivalled even that feat by winning eight of the nine races at a meeting in Madras, India.

In 1990 Willie went to the States to ride phenomenally fast sprinter, the Dick Hern-trained Dayjur, in the Breeders' Cup Sprint at Belmont Park. He looked to have the race in safe keeping only for Dayjur to jump a shadow approaching the finish of the six furlong event, and go down by a frustrating neck to Safely Kept. 'Everybody knows he should have won but, by an act of God, he didn't' reflected Willie.

As an attempted coup took place in Russia in August 1991, Willie rode one of the best topical tips ever, as 100/30 shot Bold Russian obliged at Goodwood.

Willie always believed he was popular with the betting public: 'When other jockeys are beaten on hot favourites you see punters swear at them. When it happens to me they seem to accept it. They understand I am doing my best' he told the *Sunday Express* in April 1993, although former jockey Jimmy Lindley may have been nearer the truth in May 1994, observing 'Some people like him, some don't, but all the horses think he's great.' Not so great, perhaps, if they knew of his opinion that 'people should realise that racehorses only exist because they have been bred to race. They are man-made. They live in five star luxury and if they weren't taught to race they would be no use to anyone and would have to face the bullet.'

Known for his bubbly, outgoing image, there have been hints that beneath the surface he is not entirely at ease with the world, and in 1992 racing writer Michael Tanner described him as 'melancholy-prone' and also suggested that he had 'suffered bouts of gloom during which he frequently contemplated giving up' during earlier stages of his career. And towards the end of his lengthy time at the top he mused in a maudlin moment, 'The phone never rings now. Trainers don't call so much and a few owners don't want me. You can't blame them. Who wants a 53-year-old jockey?' It was the riding which dispersed the blues for Willie: 'People take cocaine to get the buzz I get naturally. When I have won a race, I am as high as a kite.'

He retired in 1996, aged 54 with 17 British and 11 Irish Classic victories to his credit and in fourth place of the most prolific British riders, behind only Sir Gordon Richards, Lester Piggott and Pat Eddery. In 1994 *Business-Age* magazine rated Willie the 14th richest British sportsman, at £6.65 million – half of what they reckoned Lester was worth. In 2001, as well as running his Minster House

Stud, he took on another sporting challenge as chairman of Swindon Town FC, occupying the role until 2007.

In 2008 he was back in the headlines, under a hilarious (!) *Sun* banner: 'Zara Does Like A Little Willie', reporting that he and the Princess Royal's 27-year-old daughter, Zara had strolled arm-in-arm across the Royal Ascot turf, with the popular show-jumper towering above the former champion jockey.

Willie's grandson William Carson has also been booting home the winners of late, going one better than his grandfather Willie, in September 2008, when he partnered Dandy Nicholls-trained 18/1 shot Regal Parade to win the Ayr Gold Cup, a race which always eluded Willie.

MICK CHANNON
Scoring winners

The outpouring of emotion in early September 2008, when Mick Channon was involved in a terrible motorway crash which claimed the life of one of his close friends and racing agent, Tim Corby, brought home to everyone the high regard and affection felt by the public for the former England international footballer, turned international quality trainer.

Channon, who already suffered from 'crippling arthritis from injuries picked up in football' according to fellow player and trainer, Mick Quinn, who also worked in his yard, had to have his jaw wired, broke an arm and suffered a punctured lung, although his incredible fighting nature soon had him returning to the stables from hospital.

Channon, who was born in November 1948, made his name with Southampton, where he played almost 400 games between 1966 and 1977, scoring over 150 goals. He then played for Manchester City; Southampton again, (where they have celebrated the link between player and club by naming one of their luxurious hospitality suites in his honour); Newcastle briefly; Bristol Rovers likewise; Norwich and Portsmouth. He retired in 1986, having won 46 England caps from 1972–77, scoring 21 times. His ebullient character, pacey attacking play and whirring, windmilling right arm goal celebration, made him a very popular player even with those who didn't support the clubs he played for.

He had always been interested in racing, and his horse Cathy Jane won the 1973 Brown Jack Stakes at Ascot for him. The racing sometimes became confused with his football, as he once discovered when he was playing while his horse was contesting a race: 'I went to take a throw-in and noticed the lad was holding up two fingers. I wasn't sure if it meant I was playing like a prat or Jamesmead had finished second.' In 1976 after helping Southampton beat Manchester United to win the FA Cup, Channon and then wife, Jane, did a 'runner' from the after-match celebrations to watch the birth of Royal Final, one of the first foals he had bred, whose mother, Blue Horizon, had been a gift from Saints' chairman, Herbert Blagrave.

Channon enjoyed a flutter as a player and once strongly fancied a horse called Spark Off, which was running at Devon & Exeter on New Year's Day, 1981. Bob 'Larry the Cab' Charles, a great mate of Channon, revealed in the trainer's authorised biography:'Spark Off stormed home at 12/1. Mick won more than £7,000, which was big dough then, but all he could keep saying was how guilty he felt because he hadn't told the other (Southampton) lads that he fancied the horse.' This had ensured that the price was preserved, but, claimed Channon, it was 'also, hand on heart, to save me the cringing embarrassment of having to apologise to all and sundry if I said I fancied them and then they went and got beaten. That rule still applies today. It stops me making enemies.'

At the end of his career with Portsmouth, another future trainer, Mick Quinn, joined the club and said of Channon, 'he would come into the changing rooms with his wellies on covered in horse shit and the *Sporting Life* under his arm.'

He decided to become a trainer, although he wasn't immediately permitted to do so by the racing authorities. When he first applied, 'they asked me if I could ride, as if that was anything to do with it. Unless you are a jockey or from public school they think you know nothing about horses. Well, what jockey apart from Geoff Lewis is a good flat trainer? This attitude is an insult to our intelligence.'

He finally set up in Lambourn with 10 horses and sent out his first runner, the unplaced hurdler Dear Miff, at Wincanton on 22 February 1990. His first winner came five weeks later when Golden Scissors won at Beverley on 30 March – followed just 15 minutes later by Wessex Boy at Wincanton.

He continued the tone for his slightly confrontational approach when, on 21 July he was fined £350 by stewards at Ayr for acting in an 'improper and abusive manner'. He had been reported after one of his owners was prevented from entering the stable block without a pass.

I interviewed Channon early in his training career for an article in a William Hill publication and although he was enormously enthusiastic and chatty it was just as well it was not recorded for radio broadcast as the percentage of swear words in the strongly Wiltshire-accented conversation was somewhat high! As *Daily Mail* writer, Alan Fraser, noted, 'His tongue is the vocal equivalent of that windmill right arm which rotated maniacally when celebrating a goal – quoting Channon requires the removal of swear words, the insertion of grammar and, often, the completion of sentences.'

During my interview with Mick he told me how he nearly ruined Kevin Keegan's training programme after introducing him to racehorse ownership. 'After finally persuading Kevin to come into partnership with me, owning Man on the Run, I got him to come along to the races. Our horse came stone last – so we got drunk on champagne.' A few years later, I was at the Baden Baden racecourse in Germany where Kevin's wife's horse was running. Kevin was there but trainer Channon was missing – from which I deduced that the horse wasn't fancied. It stormed home at very rewarding odds.

Channon scotched rumours that he was considering a return to football as Southampton manager in 1994 when he commented, 'I prefer racehorses to footballers – they don't talk back.'

By this time the racing game was taking notice of the rising star in its ranks and fellow trainer Chris Wall revealed that he had been told the Channon motto by the man himself – 'Proper planning prevents piss-poor performance.'

In 1999 he moved to the West Ilsley stables in Berkshire, formerly owned by Her Majesty and occupied by Classic-winning trainer Major Dick Hern. Channon appreciates and respects what was achieved by Hern and his yard still features brass nameplates of some of the great horses trained there – Brigadier Gerard, Henbit, Troy, Nashwan: 'My late dad, an old cavalry man, polished them every day until he died. Dad now has his own remembrance seat in the middle of the stables where The Queen used to walk. He was a real royalist, like me.'

Channon topped the 100 winner mark for the first time in 2002 when he sent out 123 in all, worth £1.5 million in prize money. The football connections helped him acquire owners, and his stable has sheltered runners owned by Alan Ball and Sir Alex Ferguson.

Channon won the Nunthorpe Stakes, his first Group One success, with Piccolo in 1994 to gatecrash the big time, adding numerous prestigious victories along the way. In 2003 he came his closest thus far to a Classic victory when he sent out Zafeen, the 33/1 runner-up to Refuse to Bend in the 2000 Guineas. His Youmzain, second in the 2007 and 2008 Arcs de Triomphe, won France's Grand Prix de Saint Cloud in 2008, to add to Germany's Preis von Europa, which he collected in 2006.

Yet to win a Classic at time of writing, Channon has been critical of the Derby – 'It's the little things that make English racing special, like the Derby being run on the worst track in world' and also believing 'Racing has shot itself in the foot by moving the race to Saturday. On Wednesday it was racing's big day but now it is just like any other Saturday fixture.'

In 2006 he was overseeing 130-odd horses, which he described as 'like having a classroom full of kids'. He explained with characteristic humour just why training racehorses is such an offbeat profession: 'We put bits of steel in their mouth and chimpanzees on their back, and then expect them not to have problems.'

His is not a gambling stable, however: 'I do my gambling when it comes to picking out the young horses to buy.' However, he is still a favourite with punters, who know that his horses are always trying to win – and he doesn't do excuses: 'I don't think there is any such animal as a racehorse that is not genuine. If they don't give their all, you can bet your life there is something amiss with them, and as the trainer it's your job to find out what it is.'

He told the *Racing Post*'s Paul Haigh about his unorthodox stable tactics – 'I can't be bothered with all the cunning plans and hiding from the handicapper. Throw enough shit at the barn door, and some of it's going to stick.' He has also said that although he has built a reputation for his ability with two-year-olds, 'I would like to move on and get more middle distance horses.'

Channon told website www.britishhorseracing.com that his heroes (sic) are Kylie Minogue and Olivia Newton-John and his favourite movie, *One Flew Over The Cuckoo's Nest*. He also claimed that he enjoys reading autobiographies, most notably that of Sir Alex Ferguson – which does make it a little odd that he was once interviewed by Peter Allen of Radio 5 Live, about his own then newly published 'Authorised Biography' by Peter Batt, only to confess that he hadn't actually read it!

Channon's racing achievements will always be compared with his exploits on a football field, but the man himself once remarked, 'I'd like to be remembered as a trainer who trained racehorses, not just as a footballer who won a few races.' And he is well aware that there are parallels between the disciplines – 'There's no divine right to stay at the top level. It's the same in racing as football – if you haven't produced you take the consequences.'

Let's hope that relegation is not on the cards any time soon for this over-achiever in two sports, who still asserts: 'What gets me up at five every morning is that element of living in a dream factory.'

MICK FITZGERALD
Better than sex

'Johnny Murtagh, the Irish champion jockey, once said to me, "Mick, if you want to do this job you've got to realise you are not a normal person"'. Mick Fitzgerald was certainly no normal jump jockey.

He retired in August 2008, aged 38, with 1,303 career winners (the fifth most prolific jump jockey). The *Racing Post* led its front page with the news, quoting Fitzgerald as saying, 'I didn't feel ready to retire and wanted to retire on my own terms at a time of my own choosing.' He had been off the course since breaking his neck for a second time, in the 2008 Grand National, but the retirement decision was effectively taken away from him when spinal surgeon, Professor Jeremy Fairbanks advised Mick that because of repairs to his injured neck, involving metal and fused bones, further falls could, said the rider 'be pretty catastrophic'. He was not even allowed to sit on a horse or ride out so was forced to break all links with his former life.

Mick's Grand National victory on Rough Quest – a horse which, two weeks previously was set to be scratched and aimed instead at the Irish version – in 1996, was all but overshadowed by his post race comment to the BBC's Des Lynam that 'sex will be an anti-climax after this!' And his 2008 autobiography was duly named *Better Than Sex*. But that wasn't all he said in the excitement of the moment of victory – 'I haven't enjoyed nine minutes so much for a long time. Sex is an anti-climax after this' was one remark, which earned him the instant put-down, 'He's never lasted that long in his life' from then fiancée, Jackie Brackenbury.

Before being assured of victory, Fitzgerald had to become the first winning National jockey to survive a stewards' inquiry after coming very close on the run-in to Encore Un Peu, before being declared the winner.

A year previously Fitzgerald's National fortunes had been a little different. Riding Tinryland, a 50/1 outsider, he fell at the first with the horse adding injury to insult by standing on his private parts. Mick was relieved when a St John Ambulance medic turned up to treat him, but he had mixed feelings when the pain eased up sufficiently for the stricken jockey to notice that his rescuer was wearing drag: 'stockings, a dress, lipstick, the whole Monty. When I finally reached the ambulance I could not help laughing.' The ever-present shadow of injury also loomed after a May 1996 fall when he told those treating him, 'It's the left collar bone – I couldn't have broken the other one as I've already had it removed.'

'As a child I dreamed of riding a winner at Cheltenham' remembered Mick, citing Dawn Run's 1986 Gold Cup win as one of his fondest memories.

He was never known for his modesty, but says, 'I've always had faith in my own ability. Some people confuse it with cockiness, but I don't think I'm cocky. You have to have confidence.'

Michael Anthony Fitzgerald was born in Cork in May 1970 and served his apprenticeship with Richard Lister in County Wexford and John Hayden at The Curragh, before moving to Britain in 1988 where he decided to concentrate on the jumps because of weight problems; he scored for the first time on Lovers Secret at Ludlow on 11 December of that year. His second winner was not far behind – but the third did not arrive for 18 months.

Having decided against a move to New Zealand to ride for trainer John Nicholson, Fitzgerald really began to make an impact as he booted home winners for Exeter trainer Jackie Ritter, then really kicked on after being retained as first jockey to Lambourn trainer Nicky Henderson in 1993, with whom he would ultimately share 762 winners. He knew he was on his way, declaring at the time, 'You could say I'm in the middle lane of the motorway, with my indicator on to go right.' 'He invariably had a plan' said Henderson, 'and while it wasn't always the same plan as mine and wasn't always successful, he'd usually get it right.'

During August 1997 he was one short of the record for a jump jockey in Britain when he partnered nine successive winners – for seven different trainers. He was full of self belief: 'People think there's pressure riding favourites, and I say "I'd rather ride the favourite than a 33/1 shot". It's like taking penalties. If someone said, "Will you take one?", I'd say "Yes, give me the ball". I might miss, but when I ran up to hit the ball I'd be convinced I was going to score.'

His best season was 1998/99 when he rode 121 winners, including Cheltenham Gold Cup winner, See More Business, and as with several of his contemporaries he had to quit without winning the jockeys' title – largely thanks to a certain A.P. McCoy, who said of him, 'He was a brilliant jockey, he's a good lad and a brilliant talker.'

Fitzgerald certainly has the gift of the gab. Henderson suggested when he retired that now 'he can play golf, do his media work, and talk. And talk and talk and talk.' An anonymous weighing room colleague even opined that Fitzgerald can 'talk under water.'

March 2002 saw Fitzgerald bringing home the Queen Mother's last winner, First Love, at Sandown. Then almost a year later he gave the Queen her first jumps winner in 53 years – on the same First Love.

He had a run-in with the shadier side of the racing scene, when in August 2004 he told a BBC Radio 4 programme, *Between Ourselves*, of an anonymous phone call he had received, telling him, 'If you get this horse beat today there will be six grand sat in a brown paper bag waiting for you at Leicester services.' He never went anywhere near the place to check it out.

In that same year Fitzgerald had already contemplated eventual retirement. 'When I retire I'll always look back and feel privileged to have ridden against Scu, Dunwoody, McCoy, and to be mentioned in the same breath as them. If only, as Lorcan Wyer said, "you could bottle that feeling of riding and unscrew it to get a little bit of the fizz whenever you wanted it."'

Only once did his famed vocal ability desert him – after riding Trabolgan to win the 2005 Hennessy Cognac Gold Cup just a day after coming back from a four month absence with a broken neck, acquired as the result of a fall at Market Rasen which put him in a surgical collar for nine weeks: 'I was overcome with emotion. For once in my life I couldn't speak.' To give some indication of the level of achievement, racing journalist Paul Ferguson recalled having seen Mick in fellow jockey Luke Harvey's pub, the Blowing Stone, the night before. He wasn't drinking, but 'he didn't look to be moving with much ease. I really didn't think he looked fit enough to ride, but how wrong I was.' Ferguson saw him in the pub again after the win – 'He had a smile from ear to ear and headed off to the bar where he seemed to have a thousand friends waiting for him to buy them a drink.'

Mick's favourite horse was Fondmort – 'I loved him' – on whom he won the 2006 Ryanair Chase. 'He was a horse who'd never let you down. He'd jump off a cliff for you. Those horses are few and far between. He's one of those horses you'd pull yourself off your deathbed for.'

After his retirement, Fitzgerald was replaced by Barry Geraghty at Henderson's stables. It was a sign that Mick was already en route to a successful new career that, after Geraghty landed his first winner in his new role on Ingratitude at Towcester in October 2008, he was the one to interview and congratulate him on his success for *At The Races*, where he had become a TV pundit.

Might he ever become a trainer? 'As a trainer, you're basically giving up your life. It's like having children, because they are there every day' he told the *Independent*'s Nick Townsend, 'Whether you have had a shit day or a good day, you've still got to go out and feed them, still be on hand to look after them. But if someone came to me and said, "I want you to train 40 or 50 horses for me", well, I'd love that.'

Reflecting on Fitzgerald's career, Alastair Down commented, 'In his formative riding years I used to call him the Bank Robber, because he held everything up.' He added, 'He had about him what all the great ones have – that deep capacity for gloom and fury when they get beat . . . he could look more bleakly furious than any man alive. It's what made him as good as he was.'

Fitzgerald's favourite song is Patsy Kline's 'Crazy'.

DICK FRANCIS
Mystery man

So well established as a writer of racing novels has Richard (Dick) Francis OBE become that some readers have either forgotten, or never knew, that he was, at one time . . . a pilot. And, yes, of course, he was also a jockey.

Born in 1920 at Tenby in Wales, he was called up for the RAF where he served, flying fighters and bombers during the War, but afterwards rode for trainer George Owen, known for bringing on promising young riders. He won for the first time on Wrenbury Tiger in a chase at Bangor in May 1947, then turned professional in 1948.

He soon became second jockey to Martin Molony, getting on board some of the top chasers of the day as a result – winning the King George VI Chase on Finnure and the Welsh Grand National on Fighting Line; and finishing second in the Grand National on Roimond in the same year, 1949. Francis, who had once saved winner, Russian Hero from potentially fatal colic, was not best pleased at the time. 'If I had known what that horse would do to me today, I would have let the bugger die' he moaned.

In 1953/54 Francis became champion jump jockey with 76 winners to his credit. He had his share of spills and tumbles – 'One year at Cheltenham I fell and a horse stood on my face. I was cut open from my eyebrow to the tip of my nose. At the hospital the surgeon asked Mary (his wife) if she'd like to see the inside of a nose. I had 32 stitches. That was on the Wednesday and I rode a winner on the

Friday.' And he also holds a controversial view of the opposite sex taking such risks in racing, having declared, 'Jump racing is as physically wrong for girls as boxing. I would deny them the equal right to cripple their limbs or disfigure their faces.'

In 1953 he was retained by Royal trainer Peter Cazalet and, as a result, began to ride for the Queen Mother, as he was doing when one of jump racing's – indeed, sport's – most baffling and enduring mysteries occurred. Francis was leading the 1956 Grand National (which was not televised) on Her Majesty's Devon Loch and was on the run in with the race at his mercy when the horse collapsed inexplicably. Nobody knows for sure what happened that day – when I interviewed him on the 50th anniversary of the occasion, Dick told me he remains convinced that the horse was 'spooked' by the crowd – 'there were 250,000 at Aintree that day, and 249,999 were cheering Devon Loch. The horse pricked up its ears and thought, "God, what is that?"'

There would be a string of plausible and outrageous explanations put forward over the years. Equine vet Dr Alastair Fraser diagnosed the horse's problem as iliac thrombosis, brought on by an infestation of small, red worms, which make their way to the iliac artery in the hind legs and can cause clotting. If a large clot breaks off the leg can collapse but the symptoms vanish as the horse's blood washes the clots away. Jockey Bryan Marshall, who also rode Devon Loch in a race in which, he claimed, the horse almost collapsed, was reported as saying, 'It was just as though he had broken a blood vessel badly.' An Aintree vet declared at the time that Devon Loch had suffered an attack of cramp.

The incident took place alongside a water jump and another theory was that the horse, sensing a reflection from the nearby water, attempted to jump a non-existent obstacle. An anonymous trainer, quoted by the *Daily Telegraph* after the race, 'felt certain the horse had been electrocuted through an underground cable that shorted on the horse's racing plates.' Former trainer Ivor Herbert blamed 'a sudden, temporary muscular seizure.' Another contemporary suggestion was a minor heart attack. Meanwhile conspiracy theorists outlined an elaborate race-rigging scheme involving whistled signals prompting the horse to collapse.

However, clearly the most likely theory was explained in *The People* newspaper in early 1991 which, after reporting that the horse had an overtight girth, commented via reporter Brian Madley, 'Today, I can reveal that Devon Loch's back legs almost certainly gave way because of the most natural reason in the world – it let rip with a good old-fashioned fart.'

Francis himself movingly described the reaction of the owner to the Devon Loch disaster: 'It was quiet in the Royal box. It was as if the affectionate cheers for Devon Loch, which had died a long time ago in a million throats all over Britain had cast a shadow of silence. There was, after all, very little to be said. Their Majesties tried to comfort me, and said what a beautiful race Devon Loch had run; and in my turn I tried to say how desperately sorry I was that we had not managed to cover those last vital 50 yards.'

It was as though this incident was an omen for the rest of his life as Francis, who had once explained that 'a jump jockey has to throw his heart over the fence, and then go over and catch it', began to write – an autobiography, a *Sunday Express* column and the racing thrillers which eventually made him a household name.

He had given up racing on 31 January 1957 – at the prompting of owner, Lord Abergavenny who had told him while he was out injured with a damaged spleen, 'Look, I'm going to tell you something now. You're at the top of the tree, you're leading the jockey's table, why don't you get out now? The Queen Mother doesn't want you to ride her novice chasers any more.' It worked, and Dick quit, saying he 'wanted to stop before going rapidly down the scale'.

Instead, he worked his way up the scale of literary success with his first novel, *Dead Cert* in 1962, living up to its title. The success of his books was, as much as anything, built on their wholesome appeal. 'The Queen Mother reads my books, you know' he told Corinna Honan of the *Daily Mail* in 1993, who had asked about the lack of sex scenes 'and I'd hate her to read them from my pen. I don't like writing about sex. Everyone knows I write about things that have happened to me or that I've been closely connected with. So I would hate people to think I was writing vivid sex scenes that I'd experienced. It's also probably correct to say that I don't know enough about sex to write about it more than I do.'

Also during 1993, Dick, along with the Queen Mother, Vincent O'Brien, Fulke Walwyn, Fred and Mercy Rimell, Golden Miller, Arkle, Sir Ken, Dawn Run, Jonjo O'Neill and Fred Winter, was inducted into the first Racing Hall of Fame at Cheltenham.

In 1999 an unauthorised biography of Francis by Graham Lord suggested that his wife, Mary, had a big hand in the writing of his books. I must say that my former colleague, the late Peter Blackwell, who was William Hill's on course PR man and a pal of Dick Francis, used to say the same thing. Mary was certainly deeply involved in the research. After her death in 2000 no further Dick Francis novel appeared until *Under Orders* in 2006, by which time his son, Felix was managing him and helping with research.

Aware of changing styles of writing and use of language, Francis mused in 2004 about the title of his first book, 1957's, *The Sport of Queens*, and, deadpan, told the audience at the Sir Peter O'Sullevan Awards lunch, 'One perhaps couldn't have used that title today.'

Daily Mail sports gossip writer Charles Sale committed an embarrassing faux pas in his column of 21 January 2009 when he referred to former trainer Charlie Brooks' entry into the world of racing novels by making mention of 'the late, prolific Dick Francis.' Fortunately, Sale's description was somewhat premature.

PAUL NICHOLLS
Competitive

'You can't do this job unless you are seriously competitive' Paul Nicholls told reporter Sue Montgomery back in 1999 when his target was to establish himself as the country's top jumps trainer – at a time when Martin Pipe had rewritten both the record books and the training manual.

There was respect between them – but nothing more, to judge by Nicholls' 2005 comment to writer Donald McRae that 'I find him quite a hard guy. You have to admire everything he's done in racing, but he is hard to talk to. You can't get to know him – no one can. So you say "well done" but that's it. He's got a business to run and so have I – there's not a lot of time for pleasantries.'

Nicholls, formerly a highly efficient jockey, knew he was in the training game for the long haul, and eventually saw off the Pipe challenge to become champion trainer himself – and therefore the target of similarly ambitious up and coming handlers – but he seems to thrive on the pressure. Like A.P. McCoy he believes, 'The most important race is always the next one you're going to win.'

Unlike Pipe, Nicholls has also made a point of cultivating the public – and his *Racing Post* columns with their frank assessments of his charges' chances in each week's big races, have become required reading for punters. They appreciate the attitude of the man who admits, 'It's a desperately emotional sport. The day I don't want to show what I feel, and that includes disappointment, will be the day I pack it in.'

He has also established good relations with the media, who are always accommodated when contacting him for quotes and information.

These methods compensate for the fact that he doesn't go looking for owners – 'I've never been one for schmoozing, and I've never advertised, either. The way the yard is run is so important. A few years ago, one chap turned up unannounced, saw the set-up and was impressed enough to move his horses. That was Clive Smith, Kauto Star's (2007 and 2009 Gold Cup winner) owner.'

The son of a policeman, (he never wanted to be one, but self-deprecatingly reveals that 'many people said that I rode like one!') Nicholls was born near Bristol in April 1962. Before taking out a training licence in November 1991, he was a first rate jockey during the 1980s, riding 130 winners, twice winning the Hennessy Cognac Gold Cup on Broadheath and Playschool.

On 7 November 1998, Nicholls sent out seven winners and three seconds from ten runners. The 1999 Cheltenham Festival saw him winning the main chase race on each of the three days – as Flagship Uberalles landed the Arkle Chase; Call Equiname the Queen Mother Champion chase, and See More Business – perhaps his favourite horse – the Gold Cup.

In 2000, aged 36 his marriage to wife and business partner, Bridget, (they had a daughter, Megan) broke up. In a statement he issued at the time he said: 'Last season was our best ever but all this success did not come without its casualties.' One of which was their marriage. She then set up as a rival trainer and married a former best pal of Nicholls, and assistant trainer, Jeremy Young. Nicholls himself went on to marry Georgie Harvey, former wife of former jockey Luke Harvey. You can see why some folk liken the world of racing to an edition of *The Archers* or, for those old enough to remember it, TV soap opera *Peyton Place*!

He sent out his 1000th British winner when Noble Action won at Folkestone on 15 November 2004. Shortly afterwards he was a little miffed when fellow trainer Philip Pritchard entered his 500/1 outsider Blazing Batman in the Tingle Creek Trophy in which Nicholls' Azertyuiop and the great Moscow Flyer were lining up. 'If it was a Grand Prix you wouldn't have a Ford Escort lining up against Formula One cars' he observed a little sourly. A similar reaction to a former inmate of his own yard, Cerium, competing in top races as a complete outsider, nearly came back to haunt him when the horse finished fifth in the 2009 Grand National.

Nicholls' pursuit of Martin Pipe saw him lose out on the final day of the 2004/05 season, but he finally landed the title in 2005/06, thenceforth proving most reluctant to part with it. On Saturday, 21 January 2006 Nicholls won six races at Wincanton. 'We came here expecting a good afternoon – but to welcome back six winners is unbelievable' he enthused after Raffaello, 10/11; East Lawyer, 12/1; The Luder, 6/4; Almost Broke, 6/1; Nippy des Mottes, 2/1 and Bold Fire, 4/11 all obliged.

When Kauto Star won the 2007 Gold Cup celebrations were even wilder than they might otherwise be, as the horse was clinching the Betfair Million Pound bonus for winning that race along with the King George VI Chase and the Betfair Chase.

Yet, a year later Kauto himself was beaten into second by a devastating performance from another Nicholls inmate, Denman – and in third place was another stablemate, Neptune Collonges; Nicholls had pulled off the first treble chance since Michael Dickinson sent out the first five in the astonishing Gold Cup of 1983.

Although Denman's owner, Harry Findlay, is perhaps the biggest gambler in British racing, Nicholls himself says he doesn't bet: 'Never have and never will. Ours is not a punting yard. There are people here who like betting on their horses . . . and it's up to them if they have £1 or £500,000 on them. It's of no interest to me.' And it is probably just as well. Paul's wife is the sister of my right hand man at William Hill, Rupert Adams, who relays the odd tip or two from the stable in my general direction, and I'd have been in the poor-house long ago had I heeded them all.

Prior to that Denman–Kauto Star showdown in 2008 Nicholls said that 'Kauto Star is not only the best horse I've ever had, but the best I am ever likely to train, and so I still can't bring myself to believe that the horse in the box next door to him (Denman) is going to turn out even better than the champion.' But he did, by an official margin of seven lengths, which looked rather more to my untrained eye.

But then in December 2008, Kauto Star hit back, winning his third consecutive King George Chase at Kempton – with Nicholls himself asserting that the horse would do just that in his *Racing Post* column. After the race he was scathing about those pundits who had written the horse off – more newspaper selections were against Kauto Star than for him in the race – although the public got right behind him, sending him off as odds-on favourite.

With Denman having had health issues, the stage was set for a re-match between the two in the Gold Cup of 2009 with Kauto Star storming to an impressive victory to become the first horse ever to regain the championship having once conceded it, while Denman was a brave runner-up, who some believe could yet emulate Kauto's achievements.

Like many in the industry, Nicholls, whose yard is at Manor Farm Stables, Ditcheat, Somerset, and who nominates Ayr and Newbury as his favourite tracks, appears to have few outside interests, and when asked what book he would take should he ever be invited on *Desert Island Discs* he eschewed both Shakespeare and the Bible in favour of . . . 'a Dick Francis novel.'

SEA PIGEON
My inspiration

What is it about one horse over another, which encourages you to follow it throughout its career and continue to back it with hard cash even when logic suggests it shouldn't have a hope of winning in a specific race? And even to have a portrait of said beast adorning one's bedroom more than a quarter of a century after he last contested a race?

I am no dewy-eyed anthropomorphic lover of gee-gees, but I've always been attracted to racehorses which appear to have a bit of character about them – and the greatest of these, in my eyes, was Sea Pigeon. It helped that he was one of the classiest and most versatile of horses ever to see a racecourse, but the combination of an animal with these attributes, linked to a charismatic trainer and top class jockeys, an interesting owner and a frequent winning ratio – normally in dramatic circumstances – did it for me. His style of racing – coming with a tremendous late rattle – was also thrilling in the extreme.

Sea Pigeon was born at 4am, on 7 March 1970, in Kentucky, a son of one of the all time greats, Sea Bird II, out of Around the Roses, a daughter of US star, Round Table. He was pretty useful on the flat, finishing seventh in the 1973 Derby won by Morston. After which he was gelded, and bought out of Jeremy Tree's yard for a reported £10,000 by Pat Muldoon, an Edinburgh wine and spirit merchant, spending a brief time at Gordon Richards' yard before moving to Malton-based Peter Easterby, from where he would target top hurdling races.

His flat career certainly wasn't over, though – he went on to win two Chester Cups in 1977 and 1978, and carry an enormous, and unprecedented 10st (63kg) to victory in a last gasp 1979, 17-runner, Ebor Handicap triumph. 'It is a safe bet that there was no more universally popular victory all season' remarked *Timeform*, possibly having heard the relieved cheers from my office at William Hill headquarters as I watched the race on TV. 'Relieved' because Jonjo O'Neill dropped his hands in the last few strides, earning a warning from the stewards. The jockey admitted, 'It was bit closer than I thought'.

Amazingly, Sea Pigeon's opportunity to win the Ebor again in 1980 was forefeited when his entry form was mislaid! The race was won by Shaftesbury, previously hammered by Sea Pigeon when in receipt of 20lbs (9kg) from him in the Vaux Breweries Gold Tankard at Redcar earlier in the season!

However, 1980 did see Sea Pigeon eclipse Boldboy's record for winning the most prize money by an English-trained gelding on the flat – albeit there was one objection on the grounds that Sea Pigeon had won as a two-year-old, before he was gelded.

But over hurdles he was magnificent, contesting five Champion Hurdles at a time when other champions like Night Nurse and Monksfield, together with other quality contenders like Bird's Nest were also on the scene. Sea Pigeon finished fourth at the first attempt, was then twice in succession runner-up to Monksfield in 1978 and 1979, (on the latter occasion trainer Easterby blamed owner Muldoon for briefing jockey O'Neill in the paddock not to come too late – 'It put Jonjo in the wrong frame of mind'). But then he won two in a row in 1980 under O'Neill, at 13/2 by a convincing seven lengths from his old rival, and in 1981 as 7/4 favourite, partnered by John Francome.

To be fair to Monksfield, who had beaten Sea Pigeon five times prior to 1980, shortening the distance of the Champion Hurdle by a furlong may have proved of benefit to the Pigeon.

When he won the later renewal, aged 11, ('It's the old man Sea Pigeon, he's won it at last' exclaimed Peter O'Sullevan in his commentary), the oldest age at which any horse had won the race, 'the ovation Sea Pigeon received on his return to the unsaddling enclosure was among the most enthusiastic we can remember at Cheltenham' reported *Timeform*.

The plan was for Sea Pigeon to go for the hat trick, but when Peter Easterby detected that he wasn't in the type of form necessary to enable him to do so, probably as a result of a virus picked up before the 1981 Aintree festival, he was retired.

Peter Easterby, born in 1929, was a master of his craft – jump racing's champion on three occasions. He was actually born Miles Henry but is forever known as Peter. Why? 'I don't know' he claims, 'Always have been.'

He was the first trainer to saddle over 1,000 winners in Britain in both flat and National Hunt racing. His Saucy Kit was the 1967 Champion Hurdle winner – as was Sea Pigeon's contemporary Night Nurse in 1976 and 1977, while Alverton won the 1979 Cheltenham Gold Cup, Little Owl following up in 1981.

Peter's brother, Mick, is another high profile, characterful trainer – with a pure Yorkshire attitude to life! In 1990 he offered to train a horse for nothing for any dentist who would fix his teeth. He had been suffering with ill fitting false teeth and complained 'I've got five

sets and none of them are any good. My brother Peter's offered me
his, but they don't fit, either.'

Mind you, Peter has his quirks – one of which is apparently
believing himself to be born on a different day from that specified on
his birth certificate. When I tried to confirm his date of birth, as I had
seen different dates in various reference books, I was told by his
daughter 'He says he was born on 4 August, but Mum is positive it is
really the 5th – she says she's seen his birth certificate.' He may not
know his own birthday – but he was certainly aware of the time of
day when it came to training.

On Peter's retirement, his son, Tim, took over the yard.

As an indication of the loyalty Sea Pigeon inspired, when his
retirement was announced his stable lass, Monica Wakefield also
quit. 'There is unlikely to be another quite like Sea Pigeon. He was
the Brown Jack (Champion Hurdler and winner at Royal Ascot in
seven consecutive years) of his day, a figure of heroic proportions'
said *Timeform* in tribute.

The gelding also won two Scottish Champion Hurdles, two
Fighting Fifth Hurdles and a Welsh Champion Hurdle. He raced 39
times over hurdles, winning 21 times, finishing second eight times
and third twice; and 45 times on the flat, winning 16 of them. He
won £277,045 in prize money. He was rated the 10th best Hurdler
of the Century in 1999 – but some of us know better and, as his
stable companion and contemporary Night Nurse finished top of
that list, I believe it to be flawed!

In his retirement Sea Pigeon lived at Polly Perkins' Etchingam
Stud at Slingsby where he was regularly visited by many of those
who had won money as a result of his efforts. One 'super-fan',
Wendy Myers, explained his appeal – 'he is a life enhancer,
enriching the lives of all who enter his orbit – and time spent in his
company leaves one with a tremendous feeling of joy and lightness
of his spirit.'

Which some may feel to be ever so slightly over the top. But
maybe not.

Sea Pigeon died in October 2000.

DEREK 'TOMMO' THOMPSON
Omnipresent presence

Everyone in racing has an opinion about the ubiquitous Derek 'Tommo' Thompson who, for some reason, has done voluntarily to himself what many attempt to do to him, by taking the 'p' out of the diminutive of his name.

Many professionals seem to regard him as an irritant. Jockey Ruby Walsh definitely does – when Walsh opted to ride favourite Kauto Star in the 2008 Cheltenham Gold Cup and was beaten by stablemate Denman, Thompson asked him afterwards:

'Any thoughts now about whether you should have gone for Denman, or whatever?'

'That's probably the most ridiculous question I have ever been asked' snapped the irritated jockey.

'It is, I know, but I had to ask you.'

'No you didn't have to ask.'

Stuff like that makes for good telly, it should be said – so from a viewer's point of view it was an interesting exchange – but you can see why Walsh would get the hump! And *Racing Post* correspondent, Tony Verdie was equally scathing about the Tommo technique in a letter to the paper in July 2005. 'How would he like it if the door to the lavatory suddenly opened while he was ensconced on the can, and someone with a big grin and a foolish chuckle enquired of him how things were going, were conditions underneath a bit on the firm side and could they mar his chances of success?'

A US journalist, observing Tommo in action, once commented, 'Put a cabbage in front of that man and he'd interview it.'

However, the majority of members of the public seem to regard Tommo as a good egg of the highest order – hence the fact that he can be found on a considerable number of days of the year doing the honours at the opening of brand new betting shops the length and breadth of Britain. This is usually after having addressed the nation – well, parts of it – via his regular racing spot on TalkSPORT radio which involves him chatting to whichever combination of Alan Brazil, Mike Parry, Ronnie Irani, Micky Quinn et al might be presenting the Breakfast Show on that particular morning.

Born in July 1950, Tommo has been around, presenting and commentating on TV for over 30 years. A regular on Channel Four's *The Morning Line*, he made his first appearance in 1981 as part of the ITV 7 programme – but is not to be confused with Derek Thompson, the Belfast-born actor famous for his work in long-running TV series, *Casualty*. Tommo now lives in Newmarket – and generously invites those wishing to join his tipping service to do so, 'to save moving lock, stock and barrel to Newmarket' themselves.

Much of what Tommo has to impart each morning – whether he finds himself addressing listeners from the comfort of a chauffeured car as he dashes up the motorway, or from the toilet cubicle of a high speed train, or from the bedroom of the hotel where he laid his head the night before, having probably been addressing those attending a racing or sporting dinner of some kind the night before – is cobbled together from various sources, some more reliable than others.

In January 2009, Tommo was reporting in to TalkSPORT listeners from the cruise ship 'Oriana' in which he was navigating a choppy Bay of Biscay and where he had been earning a crust by regaling his captive audience with regular lectures on his part in the search for Shergar.

Tommo can often appear to be reading out great chunks of the *Racing Post* to listeners who have probably not yet had chance to read it that morning but who will be struck by a curious case of déjà vu when they do. However, he does get the day's going information hot off the presses from the relevant clerks of the course and, when all is said and done, BBC radio stations no longer feel the need to supply such information to licence payers, so bully for Tommo.

His tips are regularly churned out on the programme – and those who missed them are welcome to check out his tipping hotline, on which he shares what his website describes as 'my insider knowledge' on a regular basis. You can pay a mere £1.50 per minute for his pearls of wisdom, which include his 'very popular' Lay of the Day service, his 'Exclusive Maximum' tips, his 'Dark Horses' and 'at least five additional Daily Bets every day' It's a wonder that bookies can still eke out a living! Particularly as Tommo recently revealed that he had 'signed up the top Work-Watcher at Newmarket' to relay information direct from the gallops.

In 2001, the *Observer* newspaper took a look at Tommo's tipping abilities, suggesting, along the way – 'if Derek Thompson was a novel he'd be something by Barbara Cartland'. The paper opined, 'His C4 racing bosses admire him because they know that if a 90-second gap appears, Thompson will ad-lib 90 seconds precisely. Tommo sells himself expertly as the punter's pal. On our evidence he's anything but.'

The piece reported that in the book, *Channel 4 Racing Guide to Form and Betting*, Tommo's advice to readers had been: 'Never bet odds-on – it's as simple as that.' Yet on 11 May 2001 'Thompson plumbed the depths by tipping two 4/6 shots, both of which were beaten.'

Their survey of tipsters produced the worrying stat that 'of the 89 horses tipped by Thompson – many of them obvious and short-priced – 72 were beaten' and that 'over the four weeks Thompson's tips resulted (to a notional £50 stake) in a loss of £1,846.05, which rose to £1,921.37 with the cost of calls.'

Well, anyone can have a bad run – and he's still in business, so someone must rate his tipping abilities!

In 1994 he almost won a life-changing sum of money when he had five winners and a runner-up in a Jackpot bet which could have landed a £100,000 payout – 'Don't worry, Tommo, what you don't have you don't miss' John Francome told him. He also has fond memories of backing 12/1 shot The Drunken Duck, ridden by Brod Munto-Wilson at the 1992 Cheltenham Festival and witnessing the rarity of a Tote lady telling him she didn't have enough money to pay him out. 'Do you mind waiting while I go and get some more?' she asked him. 'I don't mind at all' he said.

Tommo met Grand National-winning jockey-to-be Bob Champion when they were both young lads – Bob is two year's Tommo's senior – living close together in the North East and names Bob's Grand National triumph on Aldaniti as his best racing moment. But, rather oddly, he described it as 'one of the greatest moments in my lifetime' telling *At The Races*, 'I was at Stockton. Bob called me as soon as he had returned to the weighing room and one of the first things he said was "you did well presenting today" – it was typical of him to always be thinking of other people.'

I think Tommo's a good guy. Well, he's never done me any harm, in fact he was very helpful when I wrote a book about the day Frankie Dettori won all seven races at Ascot a few years ago, and I quite enjoy seeing him get involved in some excruciating interview situation or hammed up stunt which the producer of Channel 4 Racing has put him up to, knowing full well that any other member of the team – John Francome, Jim McGrath, even John McCririck or Graham Goode – would probably storm off in a huff if requested to interact with the great British racing public, in such a manner.

Even Tommo can – occasionally – be embarrassed, though, and he once recalled the occasion when he was talking to John McCririck live on air about visiting a female masseuse, adding, 'the beauty about this girl is that she'd drop anything for a jockey.' And presenter Emma Gorman managed to put a blush on his face when he asked her on *The Morning Line*, why John McCririck called her 'Goo-goo.'

'I'll answer that when you tell me why they call you "big fella"' she responded. He didn't answer.

He was also temporarily at a loss for words when he was 'Gotcha-ed' by Noel Edmonds in February 1994 – 'For four or five nights afterwards I had nightmares. I was even waking up in a cold sweat.' He'd deserved it, though – having dropped Edmonds in it when he had asked him to introduce a programme for him when they came back from a break. Edmonds had already told Tommo that he knew little about racing, but Tommo hung him out to dry.

Tommo is never apparently in less than a hearty, chuckling, benign mood, although it can sometimes appear that he is more benign towards female interviewees than male ones. But I'm sure that is just an inaccurate misapprehension as he is a happily married cove, whose son is a very useful rugby union player and whose daughter is called India.

His finest moment was probably at Plumpton in 1980 when, as an amateur, he rode Classified to victory – beating Prince Charles into second in the process.

One of the least edifying incidents of Tommo's professional life came about when, after the *Sporting Life* newspaper accused jockey Kieren Fallon of preventing Top Cees winning the 1995 Swafham Handicap at Newmarket, Fallon, together with the horse's connections, trainer Jack Ramsden and wife Lynda, sued for libel. Thompson appeared in court and claimed that Fallon had told him that Ramsden had given him an order to 'pull' Top Cees. The jury didn't believe him. The *Life* were ordered to pay Fallon £70,000 and the Ramsdens £125,000, plus costs.

There is no end to memorable Tommo quotes. Talking to French jockey Olivier Peslier, in 1997, Tommo told him, 'As we say in England, "bonne chance".' In 2004 he paraphrased a famous David Coleman commentary, when describing a Yarmouth race in which Juantorena, named after the Cuban Olympic gold medallist, was apparently asked by jockey Darryll Holland 'to spread his legs and show his class to the world.'

David Ashforth wrote in the *Racing Post* in October 2004: 'I've got into the probably unwise habit of watching almost all sports, including horseracing, with the volume off. I'm not quite sure how it started. I think it was Derek Thompson.' A few days later, Giles Smith reported in *The Times* that Tommo 'was seen asking a horse, Mr Ed, if it thought it was going to win and then holding the microphone to its lips in anticipation of a reply.'

In January 2005, Tommo was asked to list his 'favourites' by *At The Races*, nominating Red Rum as his favourite horse; *Zulu* his favourite film; The Bee Gees' *Greatest Hits* his favourite album; athletics as his favourite 'other sport' and 'the form book' as his favourite reading matter.

In September of the same year, it was rumoured that Tommo was in the running to succeed the late Richard Whiteley as presenter of *Countdown*. Media commentator Matthew Norman was not impressed by Tommo's claims for the job: 'Tommo is a titan of the airwaves. Best known until now for being criticised by the premium phonelines regulator for a tipping service. Tommo went on to ridicule this baseless attack by losing a tipping contest against a West Highland terrier – there has long been a feeling in the industry that his talents are wasted on horse racing, and *Countdown* could well be the perfect outlet. That or continuity man on one of the smaller Belgian cable channels.' Ouch.

Perhaps his kids – son Jim, born in late November 1984, is a talented rugby union full-back (and grandson of 'the Voice of Rugby', commentator Bill McLaren), with the more than useful Edinburgh club as this is written – are the reason Tommo seems to work so hard and so regularly. How else could one explain the time that I was surfing the TV channels and came across Tommo in full flow of a commentary – on a synchronised swimming competition!

Even as I write these words in mid December 2008, on *Sky Sports News* they are telling the story of a mist shrouded afternoon's racing at Folkestone, and how do they illustrate the piece? Well, by listening in to Tommo's commentary to a race in which the horses were invisible to the racing public . . . 'And here at foggy Folkestone, when we last saw the horses . . . they must be coming now . . . they must have jumped it . . . there they are . . . they're heading for the line . . .'

That's Tommo, though – always prepared to talk first and think later – a strength and a weakness, which was demonstrated well on 13 January 2009 when Tommo became part of a campaign to promote and popularise 'virtual racing' – the cartoon version of the sport, run at 'tracks' with names like Steepledowns, and which is available daily in betting shops. (In passing, I should tell you about the telephone gambler, who once rang his bookie and asked 'What's favourite in the next, please?' The telephonist told him the name of the 6/4 chance, whereupon the caller asked for a £25,000 bet on the runner – which duly won. But to this day I don't know whether that caller was aware that he was backing a 'horse' made out of computer-generated pixels.)

Regarding virtual racing, Tommo told *Daily Star* readers: 'There are no fallers so every horse finishes the race, and no horses or jockeys get injured.' No, Tommo, indeed there aren't, yes they do, and for sure they don't – it isn't real, you see!

But perhaps the classic Tommo-ism occurred when Derek once told TV viewers, 'Further Flight seems to get better and better, although he's not as good as he was.'

PHIL TUCK
Tucked off somewhere

A journeyman jump jockey, Phil Tuck nonetheless had a way of attracting attention during his career in the saddle. At one stage it was because of his almost obsessive superstition. This is a phenomenon not unknown amongst the men whose safety is in the hands of the gods every time they weigh out to ride, but Tuck did take it to excess.

Even his fellow riders thought he took it to extremes – he would salute magpies on his way to the races – he actually named his house The Magpies and painted it black and white, maybe he even saluted the house. He would always wear the same, hole-filled socks, use the same pin on his racing colours, put on the same, tattered t-shirt to ride in. Eventually, towards the end of 1988 Tuck woke up one morning and, before he could touch wood or cross his fingers, decided that he was going to give up all his superstitions – 'It was getting out of hand. Everyone was on about it all the time. I suddenly thought, it's all daftness. I suppose I've grown up, really.'

After all, it would be fair to say that those rituals had not exactly kept him injury-free, in fact a glance at his injury sheet suggested that the superstitions might actually be attracting injuries. In the same year that he scrapped the superstitions, Tuck revealed to the *Sporting Life* his catalogue of calamities over the years:

1977:
2 May . . . Injured bone in foot at Southwell. Off for 4 days.
14 December . . . Concussion, facial injuries sustained at Southwell – off 12 days.
1979:
28 August . . . broken bone in foot at – again – Southwell. Off 23 days.
1 December . . . concussion at Market Rasen – off 9 days.
1980:
20 February . . . Bruised shoulder at Catterick – off 5 days.
27 December . . . multiple bruising at Wetherby – off 16 days.
1982:
21 January . . . badly bruised thumb at Catterick – off 2 days.
17 April . . . chest injuries, coughing up blood at Ayr – off 17 days.
12 May . . . concussion (course not recorded) – off 7 days.

1983:

18 January . . . badly shaken up at Sedgefield – off 3 days.

21 January . . . bruised left thigh, left side of face, damage to gums – off 1 day.

17 March . . . lower back injuries at Cheltenham – off 5 days.

10 October . . . bronchial spasm at Ayr – off 2 days.

23 October . . . dislocated left ring finger whilst lunging horse at home – off 19 days.

1984:

3 January . . . lacerations to face at Ayr – off 7 days.

21 February . . . fractured nose at Sedgefield – off 17 days.

14 April . . . bruised back at Perth – off 9 days.

27 April . . . leg injury at Hexham – off 5 days.

10 September . . . fractured right collarbone at Hexham – off 15 days.

29 September . . . refractured right collarbone at Cartmel – off 7 days.

1985:

1 May . . . went down with flu – off 2 days.

11 May . . . right shoulder muscle injury at Stratford – off 1 day.

1 June . . . right shoulder injury on last day of season at Market Rasen – off 1 day.

5 October . . . broken bone in left hand at Kelso – off 17 days.

1 November . . . bruised hand at Wetherby – off 1 day.

1987:

7 February . . . dazed after fall at Wetherby – off 2 days.

24 February . . . back injury at Sedgefield – off 1 day.

23 May . . . dazed by fall at Cartmel – off 2 days.

1988:

7 January . . . bruised neck at Edinburgh – off 6 days.

15 March . . . suspected fractured collarbone at Cheltenham – off 10 days.

4 April . . . bruised back at Wetherby – off 1 day.

6 April . . . abdominal injury at Kelso – off half a day.

7 April . . . neck injuries at Liverpool – off 7 days.

21 October . . . internal bruising at Cartmel – off 5 days.

30 October . . . broken left arm at Hexham – off 56 days.

But perhaps the most memorable injury Tuck ever suffered is not on that list – albeit the effects were short-lived. Phil had ridden two winners at Cartmel one afternoon and was standing in the winners' enclosure when a waitress, Chrissie Kent, took it into her head to creep up behind him – and sink her teeth into his breeches – leaving behind as evidence a smudge of lipstick and a row of teeth marks on the Tuck posterior. It was, she explained, her way of demonstrating her gratitude for his efforts on the two winners – both of which she had backed. Phil was, well, philosophical – 'I can think of better ways of showing gratitude' he said. Cartmel Clerk of the Course, Major Tom Riley declared, 'As a general rule, we cannot have people going into the winners' enclosure and biting the jockeys' arses.'

Tuck, whose first winner was Persian King at Catterick on 17 December 1975, when he was 19, rode Burrough Hill Lad to win the 1984 Cheltenham Gold Cup, benefiting from John Francome's decision to ride Brown Chamberlin instead – which finished second. 'When we jumped the last I just kicked and screamed at him and he ran all the way to the line – but I waited until the judge said "first number four" before I gave the horse a pat down the neck and thought, "hallelujah!".'

He was runner up in the 1985 Grand National on Mr Snugfit. They seemingly had the race won with 100 yards to run, but Tuck explained 'I heard Last Suspect coming at us – I just felt like a drowning man – there was nothing I could do, and he went and beat us. It broke my heart, it was my ambition to win the Grand National and I came within a length and a half of doing it.'

In 1986 he was on the same horse, which had been enormously backed by its owner, Terry Ramsden, who had staked a reported £100,000+ in each-way wagers. Mr Snugfit went off as 13/2 favourite, but in the final stages of the race, the horse was well down the field until Tuck managed to galvanise him into passing all but three of the remaining runners to take fourth place and make his owner's bets profitable.

Perhaps Tuck's greatest achievement came when, between 23 August and 3 September 1986, he rode an extraordinary sequence of 10 consecutive winners, two short of Sir Gordon Richards' record run.

On 17 February 1990, Tuck partnered Midland Glenn to victory at Newcastle and, at the age of 33, announced his retirement from the saddle, with 423 winners to his credit. 'I went there with five booked rides, the first one finished third but I won on the next one and I decided to call it a day there and then,' he said.

For a brief spell he was working as a salesman before he and his wife Maria set up a livery yard, but racing was in his blood and he was back in the game by 1994 as a Jockey Club starter. A year later he joined the ranks of stewards' secretaries – soon having to deal with a tricky case in September 1995 after jockey Gary Hinds reported Michael Clarke for verbally abusing him about the ride he had given Clarke's wife's horse The Deaconess at Nottingham. Clarke was fined £275, and Tuck commented, 'I can't remember the last time a jockey made a complaint about an owner. He's entitled to his opinion, but the stewards took the view that there was nothing wrong with Hinds' ride.'

Tuck quickly, and importantly, earned the respect of jockeys, some of whom he had ridden against, and he reasoned: 'It has been the best move I have made. I would like to think that having been a jockey is a great help when having to make decisions on the days I am acting as a stipendiary steward – and I would like to emphasise that it is never a "personal thing" when decisions are made and suspensions are imposed.'

In August 2001 Tuck was involved in the decision to fine jockeys Ian Mongan and Adrian Nicholls £100 each at Hamilton racecourse – when they used their mobile phones whilst actually in the saddle on their mounts, albeit still in the parade ring. 'Jockeys may not use mobile phones whilst mounted' said Tuck – the authorities having concerns about the passing of information by jockeys in action at a track.

In November of the same year he was officiating at Wetherby when jockey Adrian Maguire was suspended for six days for hitting fellow rider J.P. McNamara on the back with his whip during the finish of a race.

Tuck said: 'Working in racing is not a job really, it is a way of life. I have been involved in it all my working life and I would like to think I will continue to be involved until I retire.' That was not to be the case, though.

In September 2008 another sudden decision saw him resign as a stewards' secretary at the same time as starter, David Hancock, also quit, both for no obvious reason. Their resignations were both immediately accepted. It was later suggested that a dispute over financial matters may have been to blame for their resignations.

Towards the end of 2008 it was reported that Tuck was heading off to work in Cyprus, helping to sort out problems they were having with starting procedures there. He left with a flourish, as in February 2009, Radio 2 DJ, Steve Wright, played a record request for 'Phil, who's just started his new job in Cyprus and wants to tell his family how much he misses them.' – James Blunt's 'You're Beautiful'.

HAYLEY TURNER
Girl power

'If you had told me a few years ago a female rider would ride a century of winners in a year I would have called for the men in white coats to take you away.' Respected – well, in most circles – racing writer Claude Duval of the *Sun*, wrote that comment on 6 December 2008 when Hayley Turner had a total of 89 victories to her credit for the year, adding, 'her stylish displays make her indistinguishable from the boys.' Many observers of the racing scene were more surprised at her achievement than the confident jockey herself. 'The only difference between me and the boys is that I've got a different changing room' she explained.

The dog-loving rider, (she has two, Jet and Holly who, she says, cost her £7,000 in vet's bills in 2008) booted home 58 winners in 2007. She went on to create history by becoming the first female European-based jockey to score a century of winners in a calendar year when Mullitovermaurice won at 7/1 at Wolverhampton's evening meeting on Tuesday, 30 December 2008. She subsequently received congratulatory messages from Lester Piggott, Tony McCoy and Martin Pipe, amongst others. 'I got more than 100 texts and about 40 letters.'

She had already romped to victory in the Channel 4 Racing Personality of the Year Award 2008, collecting an amazing 67 per cent of the votes and beating the likes of McCoy, Murtagh, O'Brien and Nicholls.

Further proof that she was really making a name for herself was the fact that there was a larger crowd than usual at the Wolverhampton course in anticipation of her achievement – and that bookies immediately issued a slew of odds about what the coming year might hold in store, with Hills making her a shade of odds-on to make the final list of 10 from which the annual BBC TV Sports Personality of the Year Award would be selected by viewers. She was a best priced 9/4 to ride 100 winners again in 2009, and 33/1 to ride a Classic winner during the year.

Ironically enough, Hayley, whose tastes in music embrace Take That and The Killers, was so keen to land the ton that she was found guilty of careless riding on the historic winner – and suspended for two days. 'If you don't get an occasional ban, you can't be trying hard enough' she says, philosophically. It didn't matter, as the girl Alan Lee of *The Times* dubbed 'the self-effacing suffragette of British racing', had already planned to jet off for a skiing holiday to celebrate.

But as a consolation, she was announced as the 'Face of the Derby' 2009, ('I was surprised that I enjoyed taking part in the first photo shoot') following in the elegant footsteps of Catherine Dettori and Claire Dwyer, ('much the finest choice yet' according to Alan Lee) and hoping that she may also get a ride in the Classic. She was also snapped up by the Prince's Trust as an ambassador for its work.

Early in her career, the 5ft 2in (1.57m) and 7st 10lbs (50kg) Hayley was already being noticed – Alan King was quoted in the *Racing Post* in August 2004 as declaring her 'As strong and invigorating as a double brandy.' In April 2005 she told interviewer Geoff Maskell of BBC Nottingham, 'I think being a girl you have to sort of work twice as hard to get rides and prove yourself, but it is getting beter. There's girls around the country now who are riding regularly, so it's looking up.'

Indeed, it was looking up for female riders in general, and Hayley in particular, even though it was inevitable that when she partnered 2009 Derby prospect Taameer from Marcus Tregoning's stable to a 20/1 win at Newbury, he would be asked why he'd given the ride to Hayley. 'I thought that was a very narrow-minded question – a stupid question. It was unnecessary', said Marcus. Tregoning was not phased by it, though, and told the chauvinistic questioner that it had been an easy decision because he rated Hayley amongst the top 10 riders in the country.

Michael Bell, from whom she gets many of her rides, is another supporter – 'She's very athletic, strong, extremely consistent and, tactically, very rarely is she in the wrong place. Very rarely do you want to throw a brick at the television. There were a few doubters initially among my owners. But virtually all now would be more than happy to have Hayley ride their horses.'

And when she rode Sir Michael Stoute's Opera Wings into fourth place in a Wolverhampton maiden in early December 2008, she became only the third female to be given a mount by the redoubtable handler who doesn't do things for show or out of sympathy. It may be an apocryphal story that in her early days at Bell's the trainer would deliberately get her to ride a particular horse so that he could ask her: 'What are you riding today, Hayley?' and receive the reply, 'Turn Me On, Guv'nor', but she soon learned to cope with any chauvinism which came her way.

Hayley's mum, Kate, was a riding instructor who would tell Brough Scott in early 2009: 'I never had a riding school and posh ponies. I was a single mum with three small girls, who made ends meet working as a riding instructor'. It is probably no surprise that Hayley has pursued such a career – 'I've always ridden horses since I was three. But I haven't always wanted to ride racehorses. I started wanting to be a jockey when I was about 16.'

Her career didn't exactly get off to a flying start when her debut mount, 25/1 outsider Markellis broke a leg during the race and had to be put down. 'If anything was going to put me off, it was going to be that moment' she said later. It didn't and it wasn't.

And she was soon off and running with her first winner, on 4 June 2000, at Pontefract, 'my eighth ride, a horse called Generate. A bit of a steering job, really. I watch the video now and I just cringe. I think to myself, "Look at those arms. How did I win that?"' But that would be her only winner in public for more than 18 months.

For someone who rapidly created a name for herself with her rides on the all-weather tracks, it is a useful coincidence that she was brought up near Southwell and rode out for local trainer Mark Polglase, before attending the Northern Racing School. Keen to improve her fledgling talents, young Hayley showed great character – 'I took myself off to America to work at a pre-training centre in South Georgia (she spent three months in New Orleans with trainer Tom Amoss) and when I came back I thought I ought to go to Newmarket.'

Her first double came at Brighton on 19 August 2002 when Blue Streak and Timeless Chick both obliged.

Teaming up with Michael Bell, she rode 27 times for the stable in 2003; 47 in 2004 and more than 60 in 2005, impressing veteran watcher of racing, Brough Scott in the process: 'She's neat, patient and impressively powerful in a finish. One day in July 2005 I saw her win on a horse called Skidrow at Beverley, moving off the rail and pouncing at the furlong pole. No one could have done it better.'

In 2005 Hayley, already dubbed Champion Lady Jockey of the Year by the *Racing Post*, shared the champion apprentice title with Newmarket's Saleem Golam, as both of them rode 44 winners during the turf season.

During the year she did well on a horse named Wunderbra. Prior to one outing, Derek Thompson 'discussed' the combination's chances on TalkSPORT, commenting 'It's win or bust. The jockey could win with a double handful'. Hayley just went about her job, winning on the 5/2 shot.

She has also made her way through the ranks without making enemies along the way. Established jockey Dale Gibson said of her, 'She is very level-headed and universally popular, which is important in our fickle world. She knows where she wants to be in a race and that no one is going to do her any favours.' As Hayley herself said: 'My agent said to me a few times that he knows which trainers to not bother ringing for rides because they won't have a girl on. A lot of them are old school. But luckily the percentage of them is going down, rather than up.'

Hayley has never wanted to use her gender to gain an advantage – when a photographer suggested getting her to don leathers and sit astride a motorbike for a shot to accompany one profile, the shrift she gave him was of the minuscule variety.

But, like any rider, she is aware that falls are an occupational hazard. 'If you go out every time you have a ride thinking about the dangers you're going to have, you've got no chance. You've got to put it to the back of your mind and if it happens, it happens.'

Hayley's growing profile received a major boost when she was named as captain of the home 2008 Shergar Cup team event at Ascot – and she led from the front by winning the stayers' event on Gee Dee Nen. However, an indication of how slowly some attitudes change in the racing world was evident when Willie Carson 'praised' Hayley by suggesting that she rides well 'for a girl'. Professional punter Dave Nevison was outraged, and declared that Carson 'should have been sacked' for his 'outdated and unacceptable attitude.'

In 2008 she was one of four jockeys nominated for the prestigious Horserace Writers and Photographers' Awards – eventually losing out to Johnny Murtagh. In December of that year, after she'd won Ascot's Totesport Cup, worth over £90,000, on Furnace for Hamdan al Maktoum, the *Guardian* commented, 'It is entirely possible that a form student in 2018 will come upon Saturday's result while researching 10 year trends and mutter, "Well, well, well, Hayley Turner. Whatever happened to her?" You can have 100/1 with me!

Top snooker player of his day, John Virgo, a keen racing man, is in no doubt about Hayley's ability – 'I never thought I'd say this about anyone in any sport, but I've seen a woman who's as good as the men.' Gay Kelleway, another female pioneer of the game enthused 'What she has done is remarkable. I'm proud to say that I contributed some winners for her.'

Just as Hayley looked set to dominate the media column-inch championship in 2009, she suffered the first major setback of her career. A February fall whilst riding out resulted in a head injury and a year-long suspension by BHA Chief Medical Officer, Dr Michael Turner. 'I'm absolutely devastated' said Hayley, who put in an appeal and set about becoming a media figure, writing columns and appearing in Channel Four's racing coverage as an analyst.

However, now that she has established a place for herself in the racing hierarchy, boxing fan Hayley, who enjoys the odd glass of dry white wine, is not about to give up the saddle anytime soon – 'I would never do anything else. I'm going to keep riding until I'm old and wrinkly, and a galloping granny.'

As her agent, Guy Jewell, declared, 'When the boys say Hayley's got balls, they are paying her the highest compliment.'

WIN DOUBLES

ARKLE AND GOLDEN MILLER
Two of a kind?

Those of a nervous disposition should prepare themselves for a major shock. Here it comes: I don't believe Arkle was the greatest National Hunt horse of all time. There, I've said it. I've come out at last. I have been moving towards this opinion for some while, but heretofore lacked the strength of character to say it loud and proud – but I do feel much better for announcing it in public.

This is, of course, as close as you can get to heresy in the racing world. I can already imagine that my good friend, and author of the fantastic 2005 book, *Arkle: The Life and Legacy of Himself*, Sean Magee, is preparing a ten thousand word contradiction of my point of view – before he has even read it!

Of course, Arkle's nickname, 'Himself', did indicate the extent of his domination over his rivals of the time. Arkle has basked in the glory of the virtually unchallenged assumption that he is the greatest for as long as I can remember. But I think someone should at least, or at last, challenge that accolade – after all, greatness is not an exact science. Many believe Pele or Maradona to be the greatest footballer. Me, I opt for George Best. Some say Rocky Marciano was the greatest of all boxers. Give me Ali any day of the week. Best golfer, Tiger Woods? Have you forgotten Big Jack Nicklaus already? Federer top tennis racquet wielder? Ask Bjorn Borg how he reckons he'd have got on against him in his prime. But, the immortal Arkle. How can anyone *not* think he deserves the accolade of nonpareil, unmatchable champion?

After all, the evidence is pretty convincing. This is the horse whose superiority over his contemporaries became so overwhelming that the Irish authorities amended their rules and instructed handicappers to draw up different weights for handicaps, depending on whether Arkle ran or not.

Foaled at Dorothy Paget's Ballymacoll Stud in 1957, the bay gelding 'was the nearest thing to a racing machine this country has ever known' enthused *The Encyclopaedia of Steeplechasing* in 1979 – and few have dared to disagree since.

The horse was sold for 1150gns when sent to the sales as a three-year-old to Anne, Duchess of Westminster, and named after a mountain on her estate in Sutherland. He went to be trained by Tom Dreaper in Ireland. In his first season over hurdles he won two of six outings and there was little indication of what was to come from him.

However, during the 1962/63 season he won by 20 lengths on his English debut over fences at Cheltenham. He remained unbeaten and untested during that season and rapidly began to be regarded as a potential Cheltenham Gold Cup winner.

There was another remarkable jumper on the scene, the Fulke Walwyn-trained Mill House, a fellow six-year-old, who had already won the 1963 Gold Cup by 12 lengths, encouraging many to believe that the race was his for the taking for the foreseeable future. When Arkle met Mill House for the first time, in the 1963 Hennessy Gold Cup at Newbury the result was a bloodless victory for the English hope after Arkle made a hash of the third from last fence and could only manage third. But come the 1964 Gold Cup and Arkle, going off 7/4 favourite, put Mill House in his place, beating him into second by five lengths, with no real excuse available to the Walwyn runner.

Over the next three years only four horses would ever finish ahead of Arkle, who was odds-on favourite for the 1965 Gold Cup, and won by 20 lengths again from Mill House. He was even hotter favourite at 1/10 for the 1966 running – this time cruising home by 30 lengths under regular jockey Pat Taaffe. He also won the 1964 Irish Grand National, another Hennessy, the 1965 Whitbread Gold Cup, and the 1965 King George VI Chase at Kempton. His final outing was the 1966 King George VI Chase, in which he finished lame behind Dormant and was discovered to have cracked the pedal bone in his hoof.

His career was over, although an operation enabled him to enjoy his retirement. But the injury eventually led to the rheumatism which caused him such pain that he was put down in 1970. He won 27 races during his glittering career.

At this point I can envisage the National Hunt enthusiasts beginning to foam at the mouth and demanding 'Who the bl**dy hell does this chap think he is? Is he seriously going to argue that Best Mate or Kauto Star was better than Arkle? The man's a fool.' Well, they may have a point there. However, I am not quite that foolish – and terrific though Best Mate was, he was no Arkle. Kauto Star may yet aspire to immortality. But what I am here to suggest is that Arkle was no . . . Golden Miller.

By some cosmic coincidence, Golden Miller and Arkle both won for the first time on the same date of the year – 20 January. The Miller's debut victory was at Leicester in 1931; Himself's at Navan in 1962.

Arkle won three Gold Cups, as did Best Mate. Golden Miller won five, from 1932 to 1936 inclusive (under, it is worth pointing out, four different jockeys) – and might well have won a sixth in 1937, had not the race been lost to the weather. In 1938, well past his prime, he was beaten for the first time ever at Cheltenham, but still managed to finish a gallant runner-up in the race to the top class Morse Code.

Arkle won the Irish Grand National in 1964 under the steadier of 12st (76kg), but never the Aintree version. Golden Miller won the 1934 Grand National under 12st 2lbs (77kg), and in record time, shattering the previous mark by eight seconds whilst carrying 7lbs (3kg) more than Kellsboro Jack, the previous record holder – thus completing a unique double with the Gold Cup.

Arkle often successfully gave away lumps of weight to his opponents to the despair of the handicapper. Golden Miller won the 1938 Prince Chase at Sandown, giving away an incredible 34lbs (15kg) to the runner up.

Arkle won 27 races over six seasons. Golden Miller raced for nine consecutive seasons, and won 28 of his 52 races – during which time he never fell. Golden Miller was owned by the remarkable Dorothy Paget, of whom more is written elsewhere in this book, and lived to the grand old age of 30, when, in 1957, he was put down.

I mean no disrespect to Arkle by making the comparison between two indubitably great exponents of the art of National Hunt racing, but I just want to redress the balance somewhat since it seems to be accepted without comment these days that he was, indeed the greatest and it is only right that someone should stick up for the horse from an earlier generation. Admittedly, there may have been a little less competition around but he could – and did – only beat what was put in front of him in the acknowledged championship race – again and again . . . and again.

CLIVE BRITTAIN AND TIM FORSTER
Two sides of the same coin?

There have been few more optimistic trainers than Clive Brittain – and few more pessimistic trainers that Captain Tim Forster. Yet both – one on the flat and the other over fences – proved masters of their art and attracted great loyalty and affection from staff, patrons and public.

Brittain's willingness to take on horses with big reputations, with his own under-rated but capable inmates had its apogee when he almost stole the Derby with an incredible 500/1 no-hoper.

Tim Forster by contrast, was so convinced that disaster was just around the corner that he once sent out jockey Charlie Fenwick to ride 40/1 shot, Ben Nevis in the 1980 Grand National with vital advice ringing in his ears: 'keep remounting'.

Ben Nevis won the race – and he didn't even have to think about remounting!

Forster was a dyed in the wool jumping man – 'One day I'm going to stand for Parliament, and if I get in, my first Bill will be about abolishing flat racing, and my second about doing away with hurdlers.' And this despite dad, Douglas, owning flat runners, including 1956 Wokingham winner, Light Harvest.

Born in 1934, a year after Brittain, the Old Etonian, Timothy Arthur Forster, later OBE, was at one time a regular Army officer, who served from 1954–60 in the 11th Hussars. When he left the

Forces he learned his training trade with Newmarket handler (Major) Geoffrey Brooke, whose Neasham Belle won the 1951 Oaks and his Our Babu the 1955 2000 Guineas. Forster then worked with another Major, Derrick Candy, formerly of the Intelligence Corps, before taking out a licence in 1962, training a string of jumpers at Letcombe Bassett on the edge of the Berkshire Downs.

He was responsible for ace hunter chaser Baulking Green's string of 22 hunter chase victories – a horse so consistent that he came to my attention when I was just a youngster, convincing me that making money from bookies was simple – just back Baulking Green! I soon learned that it was just a little more difficult than that but still remember the horse – who had a book written about him – with great affection. Given the Captain's background it was probably no great surprise that one of his first noteworthy successes was with Rueil in the 1965 Grand Military Gold Cup.

Forster reportedly had the mottos, 'The situation is hopeless and getting worse' and 'Yesterday was a dead loss, today is even worse, tomorrow is cancelled.' on his office wall, but his Denys Adventure won the 1973 Arkle Chase while Royal Marshall II picked up both the 1974 Hennessy Cognac Gold Cup and the 1976 King George VI Chase.

Royal Marshall II's half brother, Well To Do, won the 1972 National for Forster – a victory which made Forster leading trainer for the 1971/72 season, with 50 winners worth a total of just shy of £50,000, and the first owner-trainer to win the National since the War. Forster's pessimism had revealed itself again when, with minutes to go before entries closed, he was not going to put the horse in. Eventually he did so with 15 minutes to spare. Well To Do's triumph was bittersweet. He was one of five horses which Forster was invited to select from, in the will of owner Mrs Heather Summer who died tragically young from cancer, having correctly predicted the previous year that the horse would win the National.

In 1985 Last Suspect, something of a rogue of a horse, only ran in the National because jockey Hywel Davies talked the unconvinced Forster and owner Anne, Duchess of Westminster, into it. Asked about using the owner's colours again in the race following the National, Forster was back in Eeyore mode when he answered that it would not be possible as 'Last Suspect won't be back in time' before advising connections pre-race – 'Meet me back at the weighing room after we've caught him.'

Not only did the horse return still united with his jockey – he won.

Forster won the Mackeson Gold Cup with Pegwell Bay in 1988 and Dublin Flyer seven years later – and chalked up 13 Cheltenham Festival winners. Pegwell Bay was a decent horse and Forster aimed him at the 1989 Gold Cup, won by the great Desert Orchid, saying, 'In theory he has no chance' but justified his decision to try anyway by gloomily pointing out that 'I might be dead next year, the owner might be dead next year, and the horse might be dead next year.'

Forster was uncharacteristically bullish about the chances of his Uncle Merlin in the 1990 National. It unseated Hywel Davies at Bechers second time round, confirming Forster's pessimism about optimism. Nor was he one to bestow extravagant praise – in public, at least. Trainer Ben Pollock once rode the great chaser and Whitbread Gold Cup winner, Brown Windsor, to victory in a point-to-point in the horse's declining years. Congratulating himself on the achievement, Pollock was brought down to earth by Forster who told him – 'The horse won a Whitbread – and you won a point-to-point on him. Great.' And one of his favourite sayings was – 'There are 60 million people in this country, 20 million of them are idiots. And every single one of them has worked for me.'

Forster moved to Downton Hall near Ludlow in 1994 and won the 1997 Queen Mother Champion Chase with Martha's Son. By now he had developed multiple sclerosis, cancer and heart trouble, which he bore with extraordinary fortitude.

Forster never married – saying once, 'The perfect wife would be a great help – but the imperfect wife might be a grave nuisance.'

His final tilt at the National came in 1997, and he retired in 1999 with 1,346 winners to his credit. He died shortly after, aged 65.

Clive Edward Brittain was born in Calne, Wiltshire in 1933, one of 13 children, and married Maureen – who was his boss's secretary – in February 1957. They are still together over half a century later.

Weighing little more than 5st (32kg) – 'the secretary told me I was too big' – he served his apprenticeship with master trainer Sir Noel Murless, staying with him for some 20 years. He was apprenticed, yet never got a ride in public – but obviously acquired considerable priceless knowledge as a result.

He waited until he was relatively mature to set up on his own at Newmarket's Pegasus House stables with 37 horses in 1972, using, it is said, gambling winnings from a successful plunge on Altesse Royal in the 1971 Oaks. Appropriately enough, some might say, on 1 April he sent out his first winner, Vedvyas, at Doncaster. He was soon making up for lost time.

Three years later he moved to Carlburg stables, also in HQ, and purchased by patron, Captain Marcos Lemos, the London-based Greek shipping magnate whose blue and white colours soon became very well known. Here he acquired rather more ammunition – 84 horses, which he quickly built up to over a hundred.

In 1977 the Brittain name was attached to Royal Ascot winner, Averof in the St James's Palace Stakes and in 1976, amazingly enough, his two runners in the same race – Radetzky and Patris – dead-heated, although the latter was subsequently demoted to third. In 1978 he shocked the racing world when his almost unconsidered 28/1 chance Julio Mariner, won the St Leger – a debut Classic triumph for Brittain, and loyal owner, Captain Lemos. When Starawak won at Redcar on 4 November 1982, it may have been a run of the mill race – but the success took Clive's first place career earnings past the million pound mark.

The *Observer* newspaper said of him, 'If there was an annual prize for the most optimistic trainer in racing it would be won by Clive Brittain. He never, ever thinks that a horse of his might be outclassed'. Confirmation of this came in 1989 when Brittain nearly pulled off perhaps the most astonishing feat of training in the history of the turf; his horse Terimon started at 500/1 (each-way punters got 100/1 to the place part of their bets) to win the Derby – and, partnered by South African rider, Michael Roberts, finished second, beaten only by hot pre-race favourite Nashwan, ridden by Willie Carson. Explained Brittain: 'Nashwan was home and dried as far as we were concerned but we did think Terimon was capable of getting a place. The bookmakers on the hill in the middle of the course were still there at 8pm that night working out how they could pay out so much money. It cost them because punters had each-way bets'.

'I train the horses, not their prices' observes Brittain, adding interestingly, 'Sometimes it's difficult to get a jockey to ride a 100/1 shot, and it can be hard to persuade an owner to run them when they're that price.' His powers of persuasion generally do the job, though. These were the longest odds ever carried to a place in the world's greatest race.

In 1992 the Brittain-trained User Friendly won both the English and Irish Oaks for the stable, only the eighth filly to land that double. She also later added the St Leger to her CV – partly thanks to Brittain's clever kidology to get the going just how she liked it. He kept dropping hints that he might take the filly elsewhere, playing a patient game right up until the eve of the race when Doncaster's clerk John Sanderson finally caved in and turned the watering taps on – thus producing ideal ground for User Friendly, just as Clive had planned.

User Friendly's Classic treble was not an entire fluke. It was the fruition of a plan hatched over a wine-rich dinner involving Clive, owner Bill Gredley and top US jockey Steve Cauthen when Gredley had suggested mating his staying mare Rostova, ridden to victory in the Great Metropolitan over the Derby course and distance by Steve with the Kentucky rider's Derby winner of the same year, 1985, Slip Anchor.

Clive has not always been able to call on the strongest of inmates to go to war with against the big boys. But he is clear about why he has been so successful: 'When people have done well, others tend to forget they started with nothing. We all start with nothing – some people have talent and some have money behind them, but at the end of the day in this game, unless you work and unless you are dedicated, you just don't last'. He has lasted, all right.

Boxing and football fan Brittain is also aware that embracing new ideas can give a stable the edge, even if only temporarily and has always believed in equipping his stables with the best technical innovations available. Mind you, there was one bit of technology which didn't appeal to him – when in 1997 he heard that helmet-mounted TV cameras were to be worn by selected jockeys in an experiment, he suggested, 'They might be better off sticking a camera up a horse's backside to have a look for the non-triers.'

He also embraces the easier to understand belief that the successful ones are the ones who work the hardest – he is renowned for having his string up and about as early as 3.30am, before his rivals are working. 'I wouldn't ask anyone else to get up that early if I wasn't prepared to do it myself.'

Another reason is because he has always been prepared to invest time and thought in his horses – 'The great thing with horses is to have an open mind. Don't prejudge them, for there's always something to like in any horse – even though it's sometimes hard to find.'

Sometimes that 'something' can help to reveal greatness – as Clive said of his and Lemos's great 1984 1000 Guineas winning filly, Pebbles – 'As a foal her cheeky face always caught your eye in the paddock.' Brittain really broadened his horizons when he took Pebbles to the States to win the 1985 Breeders' Cup Turf race, the first British trainer to achieve that feat, and Hardwicke Stakes winner, Jupiter Island to take on the locals in the 1986 Japan Cup – duly winning that too. He has also landed big wins in Germany, France, Italy and Hong Kong.

Some thought he was on the way out in 2001 when he was struggling and in pain with a worn out hip and the Group One winners dried up – but Brittain is made of stern stuff, and an operation put him and his stable literally back on their feet. In 2005 he pulled off another Terimon-style achievement when his written-off 100/1 shot Kandidate finished third in the 2000 Guineas.

Stable jockey Eddie Hide – who was offered that post 'over a glass of champagne with Captain Lemos' – said of him, 'Over the years, Clive was often criticised for running his horses in races that looked beyond them – until his success with Pebbles there were plenty of people who were prepared to have a go at him. But he kept his owners happy with his policy, and it worked for him, too.' Willie Carson is another fan – 'He may have always talked his horses up, but in return his horses have always talked for him.'

An enthusiastic winner and gracious loser, Britttain summed up his approach to the sport in 2005: 'I laugh and dance when I win, but you'll never see me cry if I lose. That's why I've lasted so long.' Brittain's ambition was still burning bright in 2004 when he scotched retirement suggestions as he turned 70; 'I want a Kentucky Derby and 10 English Derbies – then I'll get in my rocking chair', adding on his birthday, 'I get to 70 and suddenly start learning things. Watch out for me in 10 years – I could be dangerous.'

At the start of 2009, Brittain was asked what he wished for in the coming year: 'My wish for 2009 is that I get through it and see 2010.'

GINGER McCAIN AND RED RUM
Almost human

Believe me, I am truly *not* joking. I went to see Red Rum open a new William Hill betting shop in Manchester in the early 1980s. A tremendous crowd turned up to see the triple Grand National winner. One woman had brought along a cake for him and another, seeing the camera I had with me to photograph the occasion for the Hills' staff journal, asked me in all seriousness whether when I got closer to the horse I would get her his autograph.

Rummy was almost certainly the most popular horse of the 20th century, exceeding the affection with which even Desert Orchid was regarded. Red Rum won – well, dead heated – as a two-year-old on his racecourse debut at, inevitably, Aintree in 1967. It was five years before McCain acquired him for 6000 guineas, on behalf of veteran owner, Noel Le Mare. Something clicked between McCain and Red Rum who, shaking off the lack of form he had been showing, promptly won five chases in quick succession.

Yet the horse's first real brush with the public at large almost cast him in the role of villain and party-pooper, when he collared the sensational jumper, Crisp, who had led virtually the whole way in the 1973 National, only to be caught by the fast finishing eight-year-old Red Rum, who was receiving two years and 23lbs (10kg), and beaten by just three quarters of a length in record time. But in 1974 it was Red Rum who was the darling of the crowds as he carried 12st (75kg) to victory as he won the race again. Bookies reflected grimly that the horse's name backwards spelled murder.

In 1975, when 7/2 favourite, and 1976 as 10/1 second favourite, he had to haul top weight around yet still managed to finish second on both occasions, to the top class L'Escargot and to Scottish National winner, Barona. Then, in 1977, Aintree went raucously mental when the horse landed his third victory at the age of 12 in a field of 42, returning 9/1. The horse was subsequently awarded 'Official Freedom to Paddle, Walk or Trot' on the beach at Southport – which is what he'd been doing for years, anyway!

Bookies would have been cleaned out had Rummy won again in 1978, and he was backed down to ante post favourite, only for a hairline fracture of a bone in his foot to rule him out on the eve of the race. The next day he launched a tradition which would endure for 15 years as he led the pre-race parade. He had cleared 150 fences in his five Nationals, never looking like taking a tumble.

Red Rum became so famous that his droppings were sold at inflated prices (80p per bag), he was the first racehorse to be made into a limited company, he switched on the Blackpool illuminations, and frequently appeared on TV – including an appearance on the BBC TV Sport Personality of the Year show during which he appeared to recognise the voice of his jockey. A businessman made a swiftly rejected offer of one million dollars for the horse in order to use him to promote a restaurant chain. With Prime Minister John Major coming under severe political pressure in September 1993, the *Sun* invited readers to vote on who they preferred as PM – Major or Red Rum. Rummy scored nine times as many votes as Major.

And as the Red Rum legend blossomed, so did that of his trainer, Donald 'Ginger' McCain – car dealer and cabbie turned trainer, who exercised his stable star on the sands of Southport. McCain also spoke his mind and had never heard of political correctness. The media loved him.

Never afraid to utter what others only thought, McCain had his say on animal rights protestors in April 1994 – 'I went on a TV programme and met these rabbity, snotty-nosed, insignificant little girls and boys. These so-called do-gooders – cranks is a better word – got on the back of the National, because they get publicity out of it. If it weren't this race it would be something else. Never mind putting horses down, they should put these buggers down.' And his opinion on those who wanted to protest by getting on to the track? 'Let the horses gallop over them.' Another of McCain's satisfyingly old-fashioned prejudices also loomed up when he was asked about female riders in the National – 'I don't think it's a race for women riders, although I expect that eventually a horse will be good enough to carry one round as a passenger to win.'

He listed 'coursing' as one of his favourite recreations in his *Directory of the Turf* entry and his wife, Beryl recalled him going to the since discontinued big event of the sport, the Waterloo Cup, noting that 'he very rarely remembered coming home.'

In 1995 Red Rum died at the great age of 30, shortly after Aintree had staged an evening meeting in his honour, with Rummy getting a 30-candle cake to mark the occasion. The wonderful horse was finally laid to rest alongside the winning post at the course – and his legend continued to grow as he was featured on an Isle of Man stamp and in 2007 voted the most famous horse ever – beating Black Beauty, Shergar and Desert Orchid.

After Red Rum was retired most racegoers thought that McCain would slip back into obscurity as his National luck ran out and he sent out a series of fallers and no-hopers. In 1991 he splashed out to buy a new stables in Cheshire but further National success eluded him. Try as he might, the ageing McCain could not get in another blow at the National – his 14 runners since Red Rum had produced nothing better than a 14th placed finisher. Until in 2003 his 11-year-old, Amberleigh House, complete with lock of Rummy's hair inserted for luck in his headband, ran third at 33/1. Back again in 2004 he gave the 73-year-old trainer his fourth National victory at 16/1. The Princess Royal handed Ginger the trophy: 'Not bad for a bloody taxi-driver' he told her.

Two years later Aintree unveiled a plaque on the stairs leading to the Queen Mother Stand – not in honour of Red Rum – but marking the spot where 'Ginger McCain traditionally watches the Grand National'.

The increasingly curmudgeonly old boy – 'everything's gone soft' – finally bowed out, aged 75, retiring in favour of son Donald junior. But he carried on winding up members of the racing world when, in 2005 Carrie Ford partnered the fancied National runner, Forest Gunner. 'Carrie is a grand lass, but she's a brood mare now and having kids does not get you fit to ride Grand Nationals.' Was he serious? After Carrie finished a very respectable fifth, McCain told her he had 'been out and bought the biggest pair of Y fronts he could find, and had written "Carrie Ford Rules OK" on them. He said if I'd won he would have pulled them over his trousers and posed in them for the cameras.'

But much of the McCain schtick has been about playing up to his image – 'I stick my tongue in my cheek and wind them up. When they ask you bloody silly questions you tell them absolute crap and they take you seriously.'

McCain's final wish is that 'I want to be buried alongside Red Rum by the winning post.'

PAUL AND GAY KELLEWAY
Special K

What better reason could there be to place a horse with trainer Gay Kelleway than to learn that 'I speak to most of my owners by phone when I'm in the bath'? Anyone with such an open, quirky attitude to life and an ability to combine business with pleasure is clearly going about things in very much the right way.

Daughter of a jockey turned trainer with a larger than life attitude to his world, the combative and competitive Paul, she was destined to make an impact in her chosen career. Gay was born on 19 December 1963. She grew up to become champion lady jockey for four consecutive years from 1980, before becoming the first female to ride in the Oaks, in 1986, and the first woman to ride a winner at Royal Ascot when 12/1 shot Sprowston Boy, trained by dad, Paul, won the Queen Alexandra Stakes on 19 June 1987 in a canter, by eight lengths. Twenty years later, and long since a trainer, she renamed her Harraton Stables in Exning, near Newmarket as the Queen Alexandra Stables – after her history-making Ascot triumph. 'My owners bought me the Queen Alexandra plaque at the Ascot memorabilia sale and I have put it above the arch at the stable' she said.

In August 1992 lovers of the double entendre had a field day when at Folkestone, fellow jockey Bruce Raymond was suspended for interfering with Gay Kelleway's Night Gown!

She was the first non American female to ride in the Arlington Million, finishing last on her father's John Rose in September 1992. Then she was the first jockey to ride wearing a jockey-cam, a 4in

(10cm) camera mounted on the rider's helmet to give TV viewers a jockey's-eye view of the action.

She finally gave up riding because 'I used to crave, really crave, a tomato or a grape. It became too much in the end.' After quitting she confessed, 'I am proud of my achievements but it always felt as if I was fighting the odds. In the early days the authorities gave the impression they were against women, to the extent that on many courses facilities were either untenable or non-existent. Although I achieved several firsts I never felt as if I was accepted as a jockey in the eyes of the public. Male jockeys were the first to accept me; after a few dirty tricks they saw that I was serious, and although in 1987 some still did not like being beaten by a woman, it had become accepted.'

She went on to be a most proficient, probably under-estimated trainer – her first winner was Aberfoyle at Lingfield on 5 January 1993 and her first on the flat, Tyrone Flyer at Catterick on 31 March 1993. Unlike many, she has confessed that she is not averse to planning the odd coup – 'I love a bet. I'd be mad not to in my position' she said in the mid nineties. 'I have such a close affinity with my horses. On the occasions we go for a gamble I tell my owners I'll get it right eight times out of ten.' It is said that Gay financed a new BMW thanks to one successful coup.

She once said that in the next life she'd like to be Michael Schumacher and that her favourite food is 'chocolate body sauce.' Also, when asked 'if you were able to change one thing about yourself, what would it be?' she replied 'Let's say Alex Greaves (a buxom fomer jockey) has a wonderful "upstairs" – I wish I had some.'

She demonstrated how inventive she can be to encourage new owners when in April 2005 she said, 'I bought a horse yesterday called Old Bailey and today I flogged him to five barristers I brought racing with me.'

In September 2007, reacting to the decision of trainer Charles Cyzer to quit in protest about levels of prize money Gay, who, according to the *Racing Post*, 'operates as trainer, driver, rider and administrative assistant at her Suffolk base to keep afloat a 25 horse yard', commented, 'I feel like a hamster in a wheel. Everything's becoming more and more expensive. It's a rich man's game – but then a rich man (Cyzer) has just come out of it. I think the small trainers with fewer than 60 horses will be extinct in five or six years' time.'

Gay, who would like Jodie Foster to play her in any film about her life, says that 'I love my life – but I guess I wish I was monogamous. I fall in love too quickly.' Many of the recipients of such feelings are equines – amongst them her Te Quiero; Lygeton Lad; Vortex and Arctic Desert – 'loved them all.' She also once claimed, in 1994, 'It will take a very, very good man to catch me. Plenty have tried.'

Had she not become a trainer her life might have taken a very different direction. 'I love fencing and would like to take it up professionally' she told the *Racing Post* in August 2008 – albeit without making it clear whether she meant of the sword-fighting or wooden constructions variety! One presumes it is the former as Gay is something of a keep-fit buff: 'I like to run two or three times a week, and I don't jog – I run hard.'

In 2008 Gay entered two runners for the Lingfield race commemorating her dad, who died in April 1999 aged just 58, finishing fourth and fifth. One of them, Vortex, a great stalwart for her, was running for the last time. He won 17 races and won over £330,000 in prize money, having originally cost 18,000 guineas. Influential *Times* racing writer Julian Muscat commented that 'Kelleway's father Paul, who excelled in winning important prizes with cheaply acquired horses would have approved of the way his daughter has campaigned Vortex.'

Paul Kelleway, born in 1940, was apprenticed to Harry Wragg and rode his first winner in 1955. He was too heavy to remain a flat jockey though and made his name over the sticks, being retained by both Ryan Price and Fred Winter, winning the Cheltenham Gold Cup on What A Myth in 1969 and striking up a tremendous relationship with the fast finishing, exciting dual Champion Hurdle winner, (1971 and 1972) Bula. Kelleway, a cynical man you might imagine, to judge by his 1996 comment that 'Ability does not get you a glass of water in racing. It is not what you know, but who you know', did not believe in pussy-footing around – 'I'm not a fanny merchant. I don't give owners or trainers the tale. If a horse is a bastard, I say so. I may not get the ride but we know where we stand.'

When Gay became the first female jockey to ride a double at Chester, her hard task-master father, Paul, finally 'told me how proud of me he was for the first time'.

He became a trainer, appropriately enough gaining his first winner, Port Justice in March 1977 at Leicester, on an objection, and then sending out Swiss Maid to win the Champion Stakes in only his second season.

But he continually bemoaned his struggle to attract top owners. Perhaps that was because he said things like, 'I've a reputation as a terrible man to work for. I say what I think' and 'One thing is sure – there is no money to be made from training fees. And I am not going to work my guts out only for an owner to come along one day and take his horse down the road.' He complained to the media in 1994 that 'I am suffering from EB virus', explaining that it stood for 'Empty Boxes'. On another occasion, after saddling a winner he announced, 'That was a brilliant piece of training. I don't know why I've got empty boxes back home at Newmarket.'

He felt he was overlooked in favour of high flying, younger handlers – 'If you needed to rewire your house, would you get a brilliant young electrician to do it, or someone with plenty of experience?' he rhetorically asked fellow trainer Ian Balding. One owner who was very loyal to him, David Sullivan, said of Paul, 'I have had over 100 horses with him, and although he is a bizarre character and always blaming jockeys, I have enjoyed Group One success and made money.'

And there was one particular jockey who never under-estimated Paul Kelleway – John Francome, who says that he had the biggest influence of anyone on his career, 'He gave me some sound advice and was one of those truly great people in racing.'

Gay, a chip off the old block, had been in Dubai before returning to start training in the UK – enjoying her first winner, Tyrone Flyer, at Catterick on 31 March 1983. She acquired Vortex, who would also win at the Dubai Carnival for her, within a year of getting underway, 'I don't have superstars but he has been like a superstar to us. He took us everywhere including Royal Ascot four times and we had some great parties on the way.'

And Gay loves a party – invited to one of the fancy dress persuasion, expect Gaye to roll up in full Madonna kit. The US superstar is one of her musical faves – although she also chills out to Mozart. Asked to describe herself in five words, she opted for 'Passionate, exciting, fun, loving, exhausting.' But maybe she'd like to be a little less of a party girl, revealing at the end of 2008 that her New Year's Resolution was 'personally, to behave myself and to stay on the straight and narrow.'

Gay says she likes to live her life 'working hard and playing hard, because life is so short.' As her website, www.gaykelleway.com, boasted as this profile was written 'Along with my social and organisational skills I ensure that my owners love every part of owning a racehorse with me.' Her favourite recreations were listed in the 2008 *Directory of the Turf* as 'Property, waterskiing, tennis, fencing, theatre'.

A Chelsea (football) and Surrey (cricket) fan, Gay's favourite tipple is pink champagne, and she left *Racing Post* readers who don't live in Lambourn, puzzling over her answer to a 2008 questionnaire asking 'What keeps you awake at night?' by answering, 'The whole of Lambourn knows the answer to that one!'

DANDY AND ALEX NICHOLLS
Fine and Dandy

The combination of former jockey turned trainer David 'Dandy' (after actress Dandy Nichols who played bigot Alf Garnett's wife in the TV favourite of the sixties and seventies, *Til Death Us Do Part*) Nicholls and wife Alex Greaves, one of the pioneer female jockeys of the modern day, has proved to be a family affair success story.

Since turning to training in 1992 Nicholls has justified his 'Sprint King' nickname by cleaning up in many of the top speedster races – including his own favourite target, the Ayr Gold Cup, which he has won five times with Bahamian Pirate (2000), Continent (2001), Funfair Wane (2002 and 2004) and Regal Parade (2008), in whose year he also sent out the runner-up, Tajneed. Furthermore, the Nunthorpe, the July Cup, the Prix de l'Abbaye, the Wokingham, the Epsom Dash and the Stewards' Cup, have all fallen to Nicholls, who set up with just five horses in 1992 but has since boosted his stable strength to three figures plus.

He created a little piece of history in 2007 when he became the first British based trainer to win at the legendary Irish meeting on the beach at Laytown, when he sent out his Quai du Roi to score there.

And in 2008, his Ayr Gold Cup triumph with Regal Parade created racing history as the horse was partnered by 19-year-old William Carson, grandson of legendary jockey Willie – who never won the race himself.

Nicholls often sets punters tricky puzzles with multiple entries for big race targets, and also has to keep all of his owners happy when selecting which jockey will partner which horse – 'If they leave it to me, we don't do too bad; when the passenger tries to fly the plane, it's time for the pilot to bale out.'

When a plan does work out, Nicholls likes to celebrate the fact of a job well done – 'Luca (Cumani) – he's one of the best trainers in the country, but his horse has just won, and he can stand there all articulate and tell you this and that. Me, I'll be screaming me 'ead off!' When Funfair Wane, owned by Kevin Keegan's wife, Jean, gave Nicholls his fourth Ayr Gold Cup winner in five runnings, Alastair Down paid tribute to Nicholls's skills – 'Funfair Wane's win was Dandy all over – blazing off like shit out of a goose, ploughing a furrow nobody else had tried all week and saying "catch me if you can".'

The down to earth – blunt, some may say – Yorkshireman, born in 1956, rode over 400 winners as a jockey, the first at Chester in July 1973, and was perhaps best known for his partnership with flying filly, Soba – inevitably a sprinter. As a three-year-old, Soba won 11 races, including the Stewards' Cup, from 14 starts for Nicholls and trainer David Chapman in 1982.

Nicholls managed to break his leg in early 1985, not in a fall from a horse, but whilst playing football, but he made a rapid return to the saddle and booted home 44 winners during the campaign.

Always a combative rider, in June 1992 he was banned for two successive four-day periods after being hauled before the stewards following two consecutive races at Hamilton's appropriately titled 'Saints and Sinners' meeting.

When he did quit the saddle shortly afterwards, Nicholls recalled 'I went outside, turned the sauna off, put the kettle on and made myself a mug of tea, got the scales and threw them into the field, and I rang Michael Chapman and Neville Bycroft and told them I wouldn't be riding that day or any other day.' There was, though, a postscript. In November 2008 former champion jockey Kevin Darley was asked to recall the funniest thing he'd seen on a racecourse, and replied, 'It would have to be the other year in a charity race up at Newcastle, seeing Dandy Nicholls trying to get into his old riding gear – it was all for a good cause.'

'Short, (5ft 3in/1.60m) solid and striking looking, with a shaven head, he looks like a diminutive but effective bouncer' wrote BBC racing correspondent Cornelius Lysaght, reporting on Nicholls's 2005 Stewards' Cup victory with Gift Horse – which the excited handler not only looked in the mouth, but promptly kissed. '(Kieren) Fallon got a kiss; so did the horse; so did various startled bystanders. Even I got one, a smacker, on the cheek luckily.'

Despite his reputation for producing sprinters, Nicholls has no shortage of confidence in his ability to tackle longer races – 'The Queen, Sheikh Mohammed, Lord Fauntleroy, don't send me their horses, so I have to make do with what folk do send me. It doesn't mean that I cannot do it with other types, though, and I would say to any of 'em, if they want to send me a horse, I'll win the Derby for 'em.' Owner, Edward St George, for whom Nicholls won the July Cup with Continent in 2002, would not disagree: 'They (horses) are his life. He understands them. He talks to them. He will take half witted horses that other trainers throw out and turn them into serious racehorses.'

Born in 1968, Alex Greaves (Mrs Nicholls) became Britain's most successful female jockey despite having to battle weight problems which eventually prompted the end of her career in the saddle in 2005, aged 36, after riding over 300 winners during her 15 years as a professional at a time when very few other females were on the scene.

She started as an amateur with David Barron and rode her first winner at Southwell in 1989, becoming the first female apprentice in Britain to ride out her claim. Alex burst into the racing public's consciousness when she made a big impact on Southwell's all-weather track. By early 1990 she had ridden 19 winners from 33 mounts there, causing her trainer David Barron to enthuse: 'If this had happened on grass it would have been unbelievable, but because it is Fibresand people think it's a fluke. I don't.' Her 50th winner at Southwell, Andrew's First, on 29 December 1990, had also been her first winner just over a year earlier. On 18 January 1991 Alex, by that time known as Queen of the Sands, won on all four of her mounts at Southwell – a female riding record and a 212/1 accumulator.

Later in the year she became the first woman to win the Lincoln, easing 22/1 shot Amenable home and hoping that 'winning the Lincoln will knock on the head the theory that I'm just an all-weather jockey' although she was realistic to accept that 'the chances of me or any other successful lady jockey getting into the big league is nil.'

She was the first woman to ride in the Derby – finishing last on Portuguese Lily in 1996, and in the 1000 Guineas. 'Being a girl in this game, you have to work twice as hard to prove yourself and, after 15 years of pushing hard all the way, I know it's the right decision' she said at the time. Alex was the first woman to ride a Group One winner when she dead-heated on Ya Malak in the 1997 Nunthorpe at York.

But the problems women jockeys have always suffered from in terms of being taken seriously are perhaps best summed up by Lester Piggott's remark that 'their bottoms are the wrong shape', Steve Smith Eccles' that 'women jockeys are a pain', Mercy Rimell's that 'they're not the right make or shape for it' and, in Alex's own case by Frankie Dettori on Channel 4's *Big Breakfast* show, describing her in the following terms; 'an excellent rider, and she has a wonderful pair of big breasts'.

But, great lady jockey and inspiration to many girls in racing though she was, Alex is likely to be best remembered for the comment she made, when receiving the 1996 Lady Jockey of the Year Award (which she won five times in all) at the Jockeys' Association Annual Dinner, aka The Lesters. Alex confessed, 'I've always had my knockers, and I've still got them.'

TERRY BIDDLECOMBE AND HENRIETTA KNIGHT
Hen pecked odd couple

Always a larger than life figure, Terry Biddlecombe battled against the scales throughout his hugely successful career, which saw him win the jump jockeys' championship on three occasions – in 1964/65 when he rode 114 winners; in 1965/66 with 102, (becoming in the process the first jockey to ride over one hundred winners in consecutive campaigns) and in 1968/69 when he shared the title with Bob Davies, when they both scored 77 winners.

Born in February 1941, and coming from a Gloucestershire family, Terence Walter Biddlecombe turned pro in 1960, having tried out show-jumping, pointing and amateur riding. His peak years, from 1962 to 1972, were spent with Fred Rimell's stable and his greatest triumphs included two Mackeson Gold Cups on Gay Trip – but he was injured in 1970 when that horse won the Grand National. Biddlecombe won the 1967 Cheltenham (his favourite course) Gold Cup on 100/8 chance, Woodland Venture and the 1969 Triumph Hurdle on Coral Diver, the horse he would later nominate as his favourite of all – which was why when the horse retired he gave him a home, and went hunting on him.

The rigours of combating his body's desire to weigh more than Biddlecombe required it to were never more starkly spelled out than when he was partnering French Excuse in the 1970 Welsh Grand National. The horse was set to carry 10st 9lbs (67kg), a difficult weight for Terry to make. He spent the morning of the race sweating off pounds in the baths at Gloucester – 'The sweat simply poured out of me. I think I lost almost 9lbs (4kg) in just over two hours. When I came out, I foolishly had nothing to drink. When I got to Chepstow I weighed 10 stone (63kg) stripped.' He had an earlier ride, winning the Tote Investors' Trophy Chase on Chatham, but 'when I came in I felt weak and had a heavy nosebleed in the weighing room. I plugged my nostrils with cotton wool, before weighing out for the Welsh Grand National – over 3m 6f.'

Riding brilliantly, Biddlecombe brought French Excuse, who had been sluggish early on, up the inside of leader Astbury, to win by half a length.

> As I passed the winning post, all my energy drained away. When I pulled up I felt dizzy and almost fell off. My nose began to bleed again and somehow I rode back to the enclosure, dismounted, weighed in and sat down, feeling really rough.
>
> My head was pounding and I could hardly see. I walked to the ambulance room where the air felt freezing cold.

The course doctor told me that I was suffering from exhaustion and dehydration, and prescribed a glass of Guinness – with salt in it. It was horrible. I drank it because I was so thirsty, but the sudden rush of fluids to my insides brought on an attack of colic and I had to have an injection to counteract the spasms. I have never felt so sick in all my life and I did not ride again that day.

That didn't put him off Guinness for long – he now nominates a glass of the black stuff together with a steak tartare as the meal he would choose as his last.

Just 16 days after that incident, Biddlecombe almost died when he fell at Kempton, being pushed along by his mount, King's Dream's knees after it fell and then crushed as the horse knelt on him with his full weight. Biddlecombe was warned that he might lose a kidney, as it had been split. He had suffered multiple injuries, including three broken ribs, and the ruptured kidney, and was in hospital for three weeks and had to miss the mount on Gay Trip – which won the National under substitute, Pat Taaffe. 'My emotions were very mixed – but I have never had a deep ambition to win the Grand National – never in this world has any achievement of mine exceeded the thrill of winning the Cheltenham Gold Cup. When I won the Gold Cup I had a few tears.'

The National also figured in a couple of other memorable moments in his career – he believes that he should have won the ill-fated 1967 race won by 100/1 outsider Foinavon when most of the field fell – as he was going well on Greek Scholar at the time, eventually finishing fourth. And as his funniest racecourse incident he nominated 'Josh Gifford trying to pull me off my horse after he'd come off Out and About in the 1963 National'.

He received one of the great public honours of the day – being the subject of the massively popular *This Is Your Life* TV programme, then presented by Eamonn Andrews, who came into the steam rooms to surprise Biddlecombe. He became a TV pundit, but his application to train under a permit was turned down.

Biddlecombe had his share of run-ins with authority but escaped punishment when winning on The Pouncer, at Stratford in March 1964 when he dropped his whip during the race. He offered his fellow jockeys £10 for a loan of one of their whips, but when the offer was turned down, grabbed one anyway and drove his mount to victory by a head.

He enjoyed one of his best days when he rode five winners from five rides at Ludlow in September 1966.

On one memorable occasion at Wincanton, Biddlecombe was contesting a novice chase when he jumped a fence in close proximity to another horse which, as Biddlecombe and partner negotiated the obstacle safely, somersaulted over, propelling his jockey out of the saddle and catapulting him on to the back of Biddlecombe's mount. 'My horse was slow enough with one jockey on his back, so it was one shove and my uninvited partner was off again' recalled the champ.

He went freelance in 1972 and retired in March 1974, with 905 winners to his credit. It was a difficult decision with which to come to terms – 'I was depressed. I regretted my retirement with a mixture of anguish and resentment. It took me a year to adjust to the vacuum which had replaced my routine.' (His son, Robert, announced his retirement from the saddle, aged just 22, in 2005, to concentrate on earning his living as an artist.)

Despite admitting to admiring cricketer 'Fiery' Fred Trueman and to being a fan of singers Frankie Vaughan and Tom Jones, and enjoying dressing up as John Wayne, Terry is now the partner of the more reserved trainer Henrietta Knight, his third wife – with whom he shared the highs and lows of Best Mate's triple Gold Cup winning career. 'I should have married Hen earlier' the old romantic now says. 'It is well documented that they dragged each other back from the booze brink' wrote the *Independent*'s Sue Montgomery, 'Their other shared passion, horses, has provided headier pleasures; from the pooling of their complementary talents and knowledge has come one of the most formidable partnerships in the game. It would not be too schmaltzy to say that this pair are drunk on life'.

They actually first met in the sixties when Knight 'was in tremendous awe of him because he was a wild one who liked to party. He did a local TV programme called *Terry's Tips* and in one show came to our farm. I wanted to impress him, so I wore a flimsy blue dress and teetered out in high heels, looking like a student nurse. Terry virtually ignored me and, I'm sure, went away thinking he had visited a madhouse. I never met him again until many years later.'

'Hen', born in 1946, the daughter of a major in the Coldstream Guards, is reportedly a former debutante, and unquestionably a former schoolteacher (specialising in biology and history). It isn't clear just how successful her teaching career was, as one report has her being locked in a book cupboard by students and left there for an hour before a fellow teacher released her.

Knight began her equine career in eventing. She finished 12th at Badminton in 1973 and was chairperson of the British Olympic Horse Trials Selection Committee between 1984 and 1988.

She first took out a training licence in 1989, having already been responsible for considerable numbers of point-to-point winners, sending out a winner, The Grey Gunner, at her first attempt. She trains at West Lockinge Farm, in Oxfordshire.

She has also become a very popular figure with the racing public – well, who couldn't love someone who 'watches' races from somewhere she can't actually see them because she is so consumed with nerves? 'I don't want to see a really good horse hurt, or see it make a fool of itself and, I suppose, our judgement, so if something goes wrong I want to be on my own.' She also admits to being happier at home than at the races. 'I very often hate going to the races, but you have to go if you are part of the team. You really have to pull yourself together a bit and face things.' Nor is she the only superstitious member of their household, with Terry admitting to not walking under ladders and counting magpies as well as worrying about seeing a robin in the house – 'it means a death in the offing.'

Terry and Hen spotted Best Mate at a point-to-point meeting in Ireland in February 1999 – 'he did something to us. The weather was dreadful, but Best Mate looked confident and unfazed. We couldn't take our eyes off him' remembered Knight. He didn't win that day, and connections were not prepared to let him go until he did. That detail only delayed the sale by two weeks, though.

Henrietta was riddled with superstitions when Best Mate was strutting his stuff, first winning the Gold Cup in 2002, and remembered how, prior to the horse's seasonal debut at Exeter in November 2004, she had her 'superstitions aroused' when a fox crossed her path and looked at her as she was walking the course pre-race. 'It sent a small shiver down my spine – I prayed it would be lucky for Matey.' However, when he won the Gold Cup in 2004 she did see it happen – 'I thought it might bring a change of luck' she explained, a little illogically, as she had made sure to wear her 'lucky' outfit of blue suit and string of pearls. Another of her superstitions involves hay. 'I don't like seeing hay pass us on the road. It has to be straw. If I see a load of hay, then I might as well go home.'

The pressures of looking after the welfare of a horse which became virtually public property despite being owned, of course, by Aston Villa and sing-song fan, Jim Lewis, (who decided on Knight as a trainer after reading a magazine article about her) and who would receive mail addressed just to 'Best Mate, Oxfordshire', would be enough to persuade anyone to enlist the assistance of whichever gods may be willing to lend a helping hand!

The horse duly won – but you have to question the value of such rituals and illogical beliefs when contemplating that great horse's ultimate fate, when the 10-year-old was killed in a race at Exeter on 1 November 2005, prompting Simon Barnes of *The Times* to write, 'It was a great life, and in a way, a great death. A life worth celebrating, a death worth grieving for.'

'I had a good cry, but not in public. My mother used to instil in us as children that we couldn't cry in public' revealed Hen of the horse which, she confessed, 'changed our lives.' Biddlecombe's reaction: 'I haven't cried because it was a good way for him to go' revealed the true, realistic feelings of genuine racing folk to the inevitable tragedies of their business. 'A few minutes ago I was leaning over the rail watching him in the parade, thinking "you're the most beautiful horse ever created". Horses have to go. We all have to go' reflected Hen. Owner Lewis said, 'He'll be up there in the sky now, taking on Arkle – and he'll probably beat him.' Groom, Jackie Jenner, said, 'I remember looking into his eye just before he died; he was very calm and peaceful.'

Not everyone was sympathetic after the tragedy, with former politician, turned columnist, David Mellor asking, 'I wonder if the thought has stolen across their minds, as it did across mine, that after three Gold Cup wins and a burst blood vessel, should they not have retired him? What more was it reasonable to expect the poor beast to achieve?'

And there was a storm of protest when *The Times*' cartoonist, Peter Brookes combined the horse's death with politician David Blunkett's resignation from the Cabinet in a drawing showing

Tony Blair in jockey silks riding a horse with Blunkett's head, splayed out on all fours, as though he had just fallen, and captioned, 'Best Mate.'

Admiring Philip Blacker's Cheltenham statue of Best Mate, in March 2006, Henrietta maintained a diplomatic silence when Terry declared, 'Look at that power and movement and muscle. It reminds me of me in bed.'

Knight later admitted, 'He – Best Mate – had such a following, we felt a huge responsibility to get everything right, all the time. It was constant pressure. We were nearly exhausted by it all and at times couldn't focus on anything else.'

After Best Mate, not unnaturally, it became harder for the stable to maintain its pre-eminence in the National Hunt world and from May until late November in 2008 they endured a barren run of 179 days and 60 runners without troubling the judge, until Cross Kennon won a Ludlow bumper to stop the rot.

Henrietta is no great supporter of women jockeys over the jumps, telling *High Stakes* magazine in 2003, 'I don't think they are physically strong enough to hold their own against the men over the jumps' This was, of course, before Nina Carberry (the first female rider since 1987 to beat the professionals at the Cheltenham Festival when she won the 2005 Fred Winter Juvenile Handicap Hurdle on Dabiroun) made such an impact. Henrietta is also a great fan of hunting – 'The ban is very sad and is destroying people's lives. Hunters are not bloodthirsty – it's their way of life.'

How long this 'odd couple' – the rough and ready reformed boozer, and the elegant, posh reformed boozer – will maintain their presence at the forefront of the racing scene may be a health-related matter. Terry suffers from arthritis – 'I teased him that he might have to walk the course at Cheltenham on a Zimmer frame' said Henrietta, in March 2006, adding, a little ruefully, perhaps: 'He didn't think that was very funny. At the moment he can cope, but if he got immobile – I don't know.' She also may have been teasing him when she told *Independent* writer Chris McGrath in December 2006 that since Best Mate's exploits, 'People seeing us at the races used to say, "Look, that's Terry Biddlecombe". Nobody knew who I was. But now they say, "Who's that old bald thing with Henrietta Knight?"'

It will be a sad day when the couple take their leave of jump racing and Biddlecombe clearly doesn't want the day to come – 'wonderful horses, a wonderful wife, great owners to work with' – it is difficult to know whose loss will be the greater – racing's, or theirs.

TED AND RUBY WALSH
Irish eyes

In November 2007, Ruby Walsh was 'buried beneath a capsized horse at Cheltenham – many of us thought we would be lucky to see him rise, let alone ride again' reported Alan Lee of *The Times*. After several weeks on crutches, Walsh was back in the saddle on Boxing Day to ride Kauto Star to a second successive King George VI Chase triumph.

Six weeks before the 2008 King George, and almost precisely on the anniversary of the 2007 fall, Ruby Walsh suffered a fall which left him with a ruptured spleen, which was subsequently removed in a serious operation. After a remarkably short spell of just three weeks recovering, Walsh was back in the saddle on Boxing Day to ride Kauto Star to a third successive King George VI Chase triumph. Fellow rider Paul Carberry had taken three months to get over a similar problem, although Walsh was able to explain that – 'Paul was left with part of his spleen – so they had to allow that to recover. I had the whole thing out.'

Contemplating the similarities of approach to the game by Walsh and his contemporary, A.P. McCoy, racing writer Chris McGrath wrote that 'this, too, demands celebration, the way these men routinely tread the margins of mortal peril. For while the two – Walsh and McCoy – share a cadaverous pallor, they approach its hazards with the oblivious, rosy glee of Mr Pickwick himself.'

Johnny Cash's Boy named Sue was driven by his name to become a tough guy. Likewise Ruby – born Rupert in May 1979 – Walsh's name may be a little out of the ordinary, but the Irishman is one tough jockey.

'Stylish in the saddle, companionable out of it, Walsh is a master of his craft' added Lee.

And much of the reason for the young man's pre-eminence in the National Hunt arena is his well regarded father. Ted, also responsible for Irish jump jockey, Katie, first rode, aged 16, in a Leopardstown bumper in 1966. A more than useful amateur jockey (11 times Irish amateur champion, 600 winners) turned trainer, based in County Kildare, Ted Walsh won the 1979 Queen Mother Champion Chase on Hilly Way. He twice landed the Aintree Hurdle –in both 1981 and 1982 – with Daring Run and the 1986 Cheltenham Festival Foxhunter Chase on Attitude Adjuster, appreciating the successes: 'Cheltenham is about excellence. It is the place to win for any fella involved in the National Hunt game. To win there is unbelievable because of the fantastic reception you get in the winners' enclosure.' But after Attitude Adjuster he quit – 'I'd no idea beforehand. I just decided as I came back in that now was the moment to retire.'

Ted's ability in the saddle is often underestimated, but not by former rider turned trainer, Enda Bolger, who described him as having 'the best racing brain of any jockey, amateur or professional, I ever rode against.'

He never rode professionally: 'I regret not having a cut at it.'

But when he became a trainer, Ted dwarfed those achievements. He landed his first winner, Roc de Prince, at Gowran Park in January 1991. He won the 1997 Triumph Hurdle with 9/1 chance Commanche Court. Then he sent out the gambled on Papillon – from 33/1 to 10/1 joint second favourite on the day – to win the 2000 Grand National – together with the Irish equivalent – both partnered by 20-year-old Ruby, who had first walked the famous course eleven years previously, aged nine. Ruby later declared, 'Winning the first on Papillon was my all-time best ride; the feeling was just amazing, all the more because the horse was trained by my father. He has been my biggest inspiration and has taught me pretty much everything I know.'

Ted was hopeful that the Grand National of 2007 would be lucky for him – as it was being run on his 57th birthday. However, his Jack High fell at Becher's first time round.

Says Ted, born in April 1950, of his son, 'My dad's older friends get a great kick out of Ruby's successes now, because it keeps his name alive (Ruby snr died in early 1991 after which Ted took over the licence) – it's an unusual name for a fella.' But Ted doesn't believe that the game his son is involved in is as it was in his day: 'Racing changed from 1980 onwards. There are too many restrictions now. The stewards have destroyed the game with all their new-fangled words and inquiries into everything. It's a high-risk game and there are going to be casualties, but they've managed to take the spark out of it.'

Ted eased Ruby into the game. 'My Uncle Ted guided me in the right direction. He didn't let me ride in point-to-points at first. He'd ridden in so many himself over the years, he just made sure I was mature enough before I tried it. He didn't wrap me up in cotton wool. He just knew that 16 or 17 is old enough for riding in bumpers, but not for getting falls in point-to-points.'

No shrinking violet, Ted Walsh is a popular pundit with a number of racing programmes for channels like RTE, and never short of an opinion. 'He has a mind which rockets across the firmament at a million miles a minute' marvelled Brough Scott, adding, 'There is no horse or jockey or trainer or issue on which Ted cannot give you an instant opinion.' He once threatened, live on Channel 4, to knock John McCririck through the window of the commentary box when they disagreed.

Walsh also understands betting, but even he was at a loss when he once rode a horse for gambling trainer Barney Curley – 'He just said, "I've the price of a good Rolls Royce on him". A good Rolls Royce was worth £50,000 to £60,000 then!' Walsh was beaten and although Curley may not have been over the moon as a result, he didn't take it as badly as some punters at Leopardstown recalled by Walsh – 'If you had been beaten on an odds-on favourite, some of those fellas were ready to dig your mother up out of the grave and throw her at you!'

Ted also has a number of other strings to his bow – displaying fine culinary skills in the Irish series, *The Restaurant*, for example.

He tells a mean yarn, too – one of his best stories involving 'an Irish jockey friend of mine, who shall remain nameless' who had given his false teeth to someone for safe keeping before going out to contest a race that he duly won for no less an owner than the Queen Mother, grabbing the teeth back quickly as HRH came over to speak to him. He popped in the teeth, not realising that the man's pocket was full of horse hair, cigarette ash and God knows what else. When he met the Queen Mother he almost puked on her.'

Ruby was sports mad at school and played at scrum-half in the Leinster Rugby Union Cup Final, and won a Gaelic Football schools medal in the Dublin County Final, aged 17.

He made his racecourse debut shortly after his 16th birthday in May 1995 and a couple of months later, on 25 July, Ted provided him with his first winner, Siren Song, at Gowran Park. Next season he won the champion amateur title, and in December 1997 got off the mark in England when Master Jamie won the William Hill Hurdle at Sandown.

Ruby then turned pro, and was soon making a name for himself, perhaps driven by his father's philosophy – 'I have tried to impress on him that these big days don't last forever, of the importance of enjoying the riding while it is there.'

Ruby became literally a National figure during the 2004/05 season in which he won the Irish Grand National on Numbersixvalverde; the Welsh version on Silver Birch; the Aintree renewal on Hedgehunter – and was beaten by a short head on Cornish Rebel in the Scottish National, which he had, though, won in 2002 on Take Control, giving him a complete set of four.

Ruby's record of injuries is daunting, as already indicated. In 1999 he broke his leg at the Pardubice – an even tougher version of the Grand National – in the Czech Republic. He later broke the same leg again whilst schooling, keeping him out again for five months. He has fractured his wrist twice, dislocated one hip, fractured the other, cracked an elbow, dislocated both shoulders, and suffered cracked and badly bruised vertebrae; Ruby points out, 'Horses either jump the fence or they don't. There is no point worrying about it. They are not trying to fall on purpose.'

He was out of action for a couple of months following a September 2003 fall at Listowel which broke his right hip – so he embarked on something of a busman's holiday, heading off on crutches to watch the Breeders' Cup in the States and the Melbourne Cup.

As for that missing spleen – 'That's jump racing. It was the blink of an eye. You're a bit sore for a few hours, they rip it out, and you're a bit tired after the surgery, but once you're out of the anaesthetic, you're grand. I had a tube down my throat for a couple of days, that was a bit annoying all right.' Walsh doesn't see fit to mention the injections and daily antibiotics necessary for a couple of years after such an operation.

He also confessed that he is not a good watcher of the mounts he misses whilst injured. 'Ten minutes after they've won, you're a bit sick. You go quiet for half an hour, kick the couch, boil the kettle 15 times.' Still, at least he has time to indulge his other passion: football. A committed Manchester United fan he said, 'My greatest moment as a supporter will always be the treble of 1999. I was at the Nou Camp and it was magnificent.'

Despite – perhaps because of – the injuries, Walsh is yet another superstitious racing personality – knocking on wood when making certain statements and admitting, 'I always have to see two magpies.'

Of those injuries he muses, 'I've had some pretty hard times with injuries, but broken bones mend, don't they? The hardest stage of my career was the death of Kieran Kelly.' Kelly, in his early twenties, died after a fall in 2003 and Walsh was deeply affected by the incident – 'Can you believe the stewards tried to make us ride in the race after it had happened. F***ing b*stards.'

The greying Walsh is one of the dominant figures of the Irish jumping scene, riding predominantly for Willie Mullins – winning the title there in 1998/99; 2000/01; 2004/05; 2005/06; 2006/07; 2007/08 – and clocking up his 1,000th Irish winner on Rare Article at Sligo in May 2008.

Based with wife Gillian in Calverstown, County Kildare, Walsh has consistently partnered good horses on the other side of the Irish Sea, too, frequently for the powerful Paul Nicholls yard, and won the 2009 Cheltenham Gold Cup on Kauto Star, causing him to pay tribute to his better half. 'She never puts any pressure on me, but to see her crying her eyes out after the Gold Cup shows just how much it all means to her.'

And, no doubt while he is riding, he has one eye and ear open, picking up the tricks of the trade as he plots his future. 'I'll definitely train one day – racing is my life, and I'm the son of a trainer.'

Although the Kaiser Chiefs' 'Ruby' is often used to accompany footage of the top jockey's latest triumph he is probably more honoured that Irish folk music legend, Christy Moore, chose to immortalise him in his song, 'The Ballad of Ruby Walsh' from his album *Listen*.

The song also name-checks Ted, and it was in the latter's kitchen that the song was first performed in public when Moore visited the pair to ensure that they had no objections to being thus honoured. 'These folk don't normally write ballads about you until you're six foot under' observed Walsh senior – leaving us all hoping that Moore has no reason to write another for many years yet.

YOU BET!

PHIL BULL
Bully for him

'The music loving Marxist' was how John McCririck described Phil Bull, the 'cigar-smoking, bearded guru' who interviewed him for a job at the organisation he founded for the benefit of serious punters, *Timeform*.

'I was amazed that he wasn't impressed with my qualificactions. After all I had been school bookmaker at Harrow' fumed McCririck who soon became aware of 'class warrior' Bull's lack of respect for public shool types, which did not prevent Big Mac from also labelling Bull as 'one of the great geniuses in racing.'

Bull's political feelings may also be detected by his description of racing's early days – 'In the beginning, this game was an exercise for those people, namely the aristocracy, who rode down the course on their hacks. It was almost a kind of circus in the Roman sense, with the riff raff allowed to attend on sufferance' he mused in 1975. Good job it has all changed so much since then, isn't it!

Bull's 'cerise, white circle' colours, carried to third place in the 1956 1000 Guineas by Arietta, returned to the racecourse, after a lengthy absence since 1988, in October 2008 when, in a tribute to their hero, the members of the *Timeform* Betfair Racing Club revived them, and saw them finishing third, courtesy of Golden Bishop at a Great Leighs evening meeting.

Yorkshireman Bull was born in 1910, the son of a miner and a schoolteacher, and educated at Hemsworth Grammar School and Leeds University, from where he graduated with a degree in mathematics, using that skill briefly as a teacher but mainly as a punter. He was an erudite man with a love of music.

Ironically enough, Bull, for whom gambling was such a passion, believed that gambling nearly prevented his very existence. Despite his

Salvation Army background, Bull's dad was a racing man and punter, who lost his life savings of £300 at Doncaster shortly before he was due to be married – delaying the ceremony and Bull's arrival in the world!

The *Biographical Encyclopaedia of British Flat Racing* praises him for 'bringing home to punters the importance of the time factor in the assessment of horses and of their chances in particular races'. Mr Bull 'is not in the least averse to expressing his views and his criticisms' added the volume.

He first invented and sold ratings of horses in 1938, working under the pseudonym of William K. Temple. In his first year of operation his tips produced 19 winning weeks out of 34, 72 winners from 270 bets, and a profit of £166 to a level £1 stake.

Bookie William Hill (the man rather than the eponymous company) had noticed that clients following the Temple tips had been doing uncommonly well and reportedly began to restrict the bets of these punters, resulting in a protest by Bull. A meeting was held between the two parties, after which Bull began to work for and with the bookmaker, to advise him on his bloodstock interests and to manage the horses he had in training. Bull eventually struck out on his own as the *Timeform* project took off.

Although Bull was a great friend of punters, he also became very friendly with the legendary bookmaker, remembering how 'I phoned William Hill one day to complain because I had heard he was closing the account of one of my clients. He asked me to call at his office. I had a great red beard down to my navel, and when he saw me I am sure he said to himself "I'll soon get rid of this bugger". The bugger stayed until two in the morning and for the next 30 years I was never very far away.' And he was close at hand when Hill died in 1971 – 'I gave the address at William Hill's memorial service. An atheist punter giving the tribute to a religious bookmaker – how far can your imagination stretch?' 'The friendship was immediate and real – a two-way exchange of affection and help and advice and ideas and assistance' Bull recalled, shortly after Hill's (he called him Bill or Billy) death.

When Bull teamed his time-based 'racefigures' with colleague Dick Whitford's painstakingly devised form ratings with which he constructed a 'universal handicap' he realised that he had come up with a real winner of a product. '*Timeform* ratings are a co-ordination of these time and form calculations, translated into simple figures, whose level corresponds with the poundage represented by the equivalent marks in an average official Free Handicap'.

In 1948 he formed Portway Press Ltd to advance his plan to establish the mathematical link to horses' performances. The system would triumphantly stand the test of time, making a huge success of his *Timeform* annual publications, launched in 1948 and followed in 1956 by the weekly 'Black Book' and in 1962 by *Timeform* racecards.

Whitford left *Timeform* in 1949 – turning down an offer to work for William Hill, to become racing manager to successful owner Jack Gerber. In 1971 Whitford's ratings began to appear regularly in the *Sporting Life* until he left for health reasons in 1984 to retire to Majorca.

Bull founded the successful Hollins Stud near Halifax in 1947 and was an enthusiastic owner with trainers such as Cyril Ray, Captain Charles Elsey and, after his death, Bill Elsey. He also had horses with Staff Ingham, Barry Hills and North Yorkshire trainer Sally Hall.

Amongst his notable winners were Orgoglio (Champagne Stakes, Victoria Cup); Dionisio (Victoria Cup; Wokingham Stakes); Sostenuto (Ebor Handicap); Vaux Gold Tankard and Whitley Gold Trophy winner, Philoctetes and another Wokingham winner, Charicles, which also won the John Banks Gold Cup.

He had interesting views on breeding – and in 1975 declared, 'There is practically nothing on breeding in print worth reading. The few books on the subject have as much relation to the realities of the matter as astrology has to astronomy – tap roots, inbreeding, outcrossing, sires lines, prepotency etc, overlaid with a dressing of genetics, mostly misunderstood – it is a world of fantasy.'

Bull's racing annual, evolved into the much respected and very collectible 'Racehorses of . . .' series.

In 1969 Bull spelled out his betting philosophy – 'I'm not a gambler. Betting as such doesn't interest me, I couldn't be interested in bingo or roulette, they are pure gambling. Racing is different. It's a continuing play with a fresh set of individual characters every year. Not a who-done-it, but a who'll do it. There's a challenge to solve, and success or failure is reflected in one's bank balance.' Many believe Bull should be declared the patron saint of racing punters.

In 1970 he was interviewed by the *Daily Telegraph* magazine – to whom he provided his own version of the Ten Commandments or the Lord's Prayer for Punters:

* SEEK where thou wilt for winners, but bet only when thou seest value; deliver thyself from the temptation to bet in every race.

* PUT NOT thy faith in luck, nor the law of averages, nor thy trust in staking systems, for these are delusions.

* LET THY stake be related to the depth of thy pocket and to what thou regardest as the true chance of the horse; that which hath the greater chance deserveth the greater stake.

* THOU SHALT not bet each-way in big fields unless thou art well satisfied as to the value of the place bet.

* BET WITH book or Tote according to the judgement: thus shalt thou endeavour to get the best of both worlds.

* THOU SHALT not bet ante-post except upon horses that are known to be definite runners.

* BEWARE the man who would sell thee a system; if thou knowest a profitable one, preserve it to thyself in silence.

* DOUBLE and treble if you must; but bet not upon objections, for thou hast not the evidence and the stewards know not what they do.

* LET THY betting be informed by wisdom and diligence, and tempered by patience and caution, and leavened but a little with boldness.

* LET THY bets be well within thy means: he that maketh his fortune in a week loseth his ducats in a day.

The late racing journalist and owner, Graham Rock began his working life in the racing game at *Timeform*, where he assisted Bull with his time figures. Rock remembered: 'My one disadvantage was that I did not have a driving licence so I could not take Phil to the races, allowing him to sip his Hock as the car sped along the motorway. Occasionally, he would drive and from the passenger seat I would dispense the wine as the car soared along at 90mph (144kmph).

He also recalled:

> Phil was a good snooker player and one evening he invited me to The Hollins, his Gothic mansion in the Pennines for dinner and a game. We went straight to the kitchen. He brought out four thick slices of Wonderloaf, cut hunks off a slightly aged lump of cheddar, assembled them on the bread and tossed them under the grill. These we ate in the dining room, on splendid antique furniture, surrounded by some of the most prestigious trophies in racing. Over the snooker table, he beat me by three frames to two – but for most of the game I was distracted by raging heartburn.
>
> On the racecourse he was no longer the hurricane that had swept through the (betting) ring in the decades following the war. His intellect was still sharp, but we were both opinionated and eventually we fell out.'

Rock moved on in 1975 to the *Sporting Chronicle*, eventually becoming the editor of the *Racing Post* when it launched in April 1986.

Bull was an opponent of taxing betting – 'With betting there is no real article, you are selling to a man. What you are selling him is the prospect of profit, or at least the illusion that he may profit. If you raise the tax to the point where you destroy the illusion then you kill his incentive to bet.' And he confronted the old issue of a Tote monopoly in 1977, saying 'The fact that Tote betting has been available for half a century and approximately 95 per cent of all betting is at bookmakers' odds must be regarded as conclusive evidence of where the punters' preference lies.'

It was down to Bull's constant championing of one mile races for two-year-olds that the *Timeform* Gold Cup at Doncaster was instigated in 1961, still surviving today as the *Racing Post* Trophy.

But for all his love of gambling and racing ('racing's only a piddling little pond really') Bull's obsession was another contest involving horses – only those masquerading as knights. 'I'll never lose my love of chess.

It is the greatest of games. If I ever went blind, I'd get someone to read to me from all those books on the subject I have studied over the years so that I could re-learn the game. I'd be quite content.'

Bull became deeply involved in racing politics as a member of the Racehorse Owners' Association, the Thoroughbred Breeders' Association, the Racegoers' Club and the Horseracing Advisory Council.

In the 1999 book, *A Century of Champions*, written by John Randall and Tony Morris and, admittedly, published by Timeform's own Portway Press stable, Bull was nominated as the 10th most important racing figure of the 20th century, and described as being 'egotistical, dogmatic, stubborn and blunt, but in terms of intellect, logic and vision he dwarfed every other man of his time in a sport he referred to as "a mere triviality".'

Shortly before his own death in 1989 Bull summed up his personal view of life – 'You have a journey through life. It is a short journey, from birth – before which you are unaware of anything – until death – after which you will no longer exist. Seek to enjoy the journey as much as you can, savour the scenery and the people you meet en route. For it is all there is.'

The 1990 *Directory of the Turf* ran a lengthy obituary for Bull and summed him up: 'His often abrasive manner did not endear him to his contemporaries, but few could fail to admire and respect him. In politics his leanings were left of left. He found no contradiction in living a capitalist life, believing in the old maxim that when in Rome one should do as the Romans do, at least as long as they last.'

VICTOR CHANDLER
VC winner?

Victor Chandler, born in April 1951, is the only bookmaker immortalised on canvas by artist Lucian Freud – apparently as payment for one or two losing wagers struck by the legendary painter.

This is just one of the reasons why Chandler is regarded as something of an out of the ordinary character even amongst the realms of flamboyant layers.

The postscript to the artistic yarn, by the way, is that Chandler sold the paintings on 'for a couple of grand' only to see one of them hanging in the Hayward Gallery several years later, valued at the thick end of a quarter of a million pounds. And in 2006, 'Man in a String Chair (aka Victor Chandler) 1988/89' was sold for, ahem, £4,152,000. Chandler may not have sold the lot, though, telling racing writer Jamie Reid in October 2008, 'A lot of my paintings are in storage and I'm looking forward to getting the Lucian Freuds out.'

Chandler was also friendly with artist Francis Bacon, and recalls as 'the funniest supper anyone has ever had', the time when he and his clerk ended up eating at Wheelers' restaurant after a Windsor meeting. 'There was Jeffrey Bernard, Francis Bacon, Francis Bacon's boyfriend, Thora Hird and a friend of hers. We were thrown out.'

Chandler, whose grandfather, Billy – the man who had Walthamstow Greyhound Stadium built, and which stayed in the family until its controversial sale in 2008 – started the business in 1946. Then in 1998, Victor was the first British bookie to take his firm offshore, to Gibraltar, to avoid the tax burden – for himself and his clients – imposed in his native land. 'What I did in coming here (Gibraltar) changed the racecourse market for ever'.

'Chandler has made a career from offering a bespoke bookmaking service. He is, and it is not quite an oxymoron, a gentleman bookmaker' wrote the *Observer*'s Will Buckley in June 2008.

Chandler was public school educated. There was an element of gambling debts being settled involved in his presence at Millfield where he also says he would place bets for the headmaster with the local bookie. At this age he was hoping to grow up to become James Bond, but Victor's career could have been in haute cuisine, having attended catering college in Switzerland. He then went to work in Spain, where, at time of writing, he was living, together with his family, wife Susan and three young boys, along with six dogs, two cats, 16 horses, six pigs, 60 goats, four sheep 'innumerable' chickens – and 'two turkeys that we didn't have the heart to slaughter last Christmas.'

He was 21 when his father died at the age of 50 and he had to take over what was at that time an ailing family business. He began to re-establish the family brand and attracted high rollers to bet with him on course again. 'We had an Indian customer who we used to rent a box for at Royal Ascot. He was losing a million pounds going into Thursday, when he dropped down dead with a heart attack.' Fortunately for the Chandler family fortunes, the man's family paid the debt 'It was not a lot of money to the family. They didn't have to pay, but the wife insisted because she knew how much he had enjoyed the racing.'

The detail there, that Chandler's client could well afford his debts is telling as he insists that his best clients are those that will wager 'a large sum of money for us, but one which doesn't affect their way of life.'

Chandler's most amusing race course memory is 'when bookmaker Lulu Mendoza threw a cigar down and it accidentally landed in his bag. Five minutes later, he and all his staff were throwing money on the ground trying to put out the flames and stamping on it.'

In 1989 at the Cheltenham Festival, a Chandler client gambled £90,000 on 4/9 shot Rusch de Farges, which failed to win. And in January 2004 he revealed he had taken a bet of £250,000 on a losing 2/5 shot – 'He wasn't English and is dead now but I won't even tell you the horse because it would lead to the name of the man and I won't identify any of my clients.' And his most successful day personally on course was when he fancied 100/1 outsider New Halen in the 1990 Mildmay of Flete Challenge Cup at Cheltenham – and trousered a £125,000 windfall when the horse landed the touch.

Chandler rarely operates at the racecourse now, although his company is still represented at several meetings, 'I look back with such fond memories of betting on the racecourse as it was part of my life for so long' he told the *Guardian*'s Greg Wood in January 2009, 'I think I was there at the best of times, and I don't think it's something that is ever going to come back. Now you can go to the racecourse and take five bets all day, and there are people standing right in front of you having bets on the phone.'

Not all of his clients can be described as 'high rollers', including Jeffrey Bernard, who features elsewhere in this book and who once, according to Chandler, was so desperate to hide from him as he owed him a relatively modest amount of money, that he secreted himself under a table upon seeing him approaching the bar he was frequenting. Chandler did not miss a beat and had the cowering Bernard handed a large whisky – under the table.

Chandler operates on the basis that one should 'judge the man, not the deal' and also counsels: 'Gambling and drinking don't go together, and if you don't learn that in the first six months you won't survive long in this business.'

Although he is still very much involved with the firm, you somehow suspect – and rather hope – that Victor may have winced when, in October 2004 his Group marketing director, Alan Randall, described the company's new corporate look – 'The brand is the vehicle by which we will deliver our vision, and it's a brand that's elegant and sophisticated and confident in line with our customers' expectations.' In the same year the company unveiled its new slogan – 'Get more on – get more back' a subtly different message to Victor's own advice to gamblers, 'Never be afraid to win too much' which, I think, I understand but can rarely bring myself to act upon.

Not only has Victor survived such changes in the way betting is now presented to and perceived by the public, he has prospered and is now a wine enthusiast with his own cellar of fine vintages.

During the 2004/05 Premiership season Victor and fellow bookmaker Fred Done struck what they claimed to be the biggest wager ever – a £1,000,000 a head, winner take all on whether Done's Manchester United, or Chandler's Chelsea would win that campaign's title. Chelsea won. Fred paid up.

Recently estimated to be worth £365 million, Chandler looks every inch the wealthy gentleman, always immaculately turned out. He is always on the look out for new markets to break into and as he has already dabbled in Russia, Hong Kong, Singapore and India, he is hopeful that China could pay dividends for him. 'The secret is being introduced to the right person and he knowing that you are not a threat' he told Will Buckley in 2008. 'The more I go, the less I understand China. The Chinese treat gambling as luck – you will have your ups and downs, it is not socially frowned upon.'

Towards the end of 2008 it appeared that Chandler had decided to exploit his personal image for the benefit of the company, and he announced that what had become known as VCBet and VCPoker during 2004 would now revert to the full Victor Chandler nomenclature.

This coincided with a jingle promoting his name appearing over the airwaves to advertise the company on TalkSPORT Radio: 'With so many new competitors entering into the gaming market I thought it was important we portrayed the company history, and the key brand values of trust, honour and integrity. The Victor Chandler name has been synonymous with these values for over 60 years – I want to communicate to customers that they are betting with a real person when they place a bet with Victor Chandler, rather than a faceless organisation.'

Asked by the *Racing Post* in June 2008 to sum himself up in five words, he nominated 'Overweight and over fifty five'. Chandler, who claims to have no superstitions, and is a fan of downbeat singer Leonard Cohen, has a fascinating life story to tell. He has been telling it to a writer friend of mine, who says that Chandler keeps changing his mind about whether and when the book should be published. Perhaps the reversion to putting his name at the forefront of company PR may hasten the arrival of the book onto the shelves. Make sure you get a copy when it does see the light of day.

BARRY DENNIS
Bismarck bookie

Barry Dennis is a rarity – a bookie who doesn't mind upsetting his customers! Probably the most flamboyant layer on a racecourse today, Dennis – who writes a weekly column in the *Sun* which doesn't pull too many punches – came to prominence via his appearances on Channel 4's *The Morning Line*, in which he was responsible in 1998 for the 'Barry's Bismarcks' feature, drawing the attention of punters to short-priced horses which he considered particularly bad value for money, or likely to get beaten at a short price.

He was born in Romford in 1940 and survived the War to become, briefly, a market trader although the writing was on the wall as to his future profession from an early age when he began taking bets from his grandfather to be put on with the local illegal bookie.

He made a book at school and by 1954 was working in an illegal betting shop. He had begun going to the races, and loved the atmosphere.

Barry worked in a betting shop when they were legalised in 1961 then began making a book at Romford dogs – 'I went skint many times. I pawned everything I could find. The bailiffs were regularly round my house taking the furniture.' Eventually he borrowed a significant sum in order to purchase a number of pitches at racecourses, and he began to make a name for himself. 'I work 300 days a year on the southern circuit, clocking up 45,000 miles (72,000km) a year.'

Dennis was on the wrong end of a real hammering on 'Dettori Day' – 'Bookies' Black Saturday' – when Frankie Dettori rode all seven winners at Ascot on 28 September 1996. The betting industry lost the thick end of £50 million on this historic day – and Dennis' description of what it meant to him is startlingly evocative. In 2001 he told me:

> Frankie day. At the start I had been pleased because, for whatever reason, I had got the best move up I had ever had at a full Ascot meeting, about six in from the rails in the back row. A chance to play bigger than usual with the hoped-for bigger rollers.
>
> Nothing unusual for the earlier races, holding about four grand a race, winning a bit, losing a bit, no great alarms. Come the fifth race a few punters commented that Frankie had ridden the first four winners. I just thought – so what, good achievement, but been done before. Didn't even bother to take note of his next mount, didn't notice any undue market moves in the fifth race. After the fifth there was now a buzz going round the ring – the offices must start to take action in the sixth race. I think they did invest, but not in any monster gamble.
>
> Once the sixth race was over, all hell let loose – everyone was speculating what price the offices would take in the final race. I understand that 6/1 was laid to small amounts on the outskirts of the ring. My eldest son, Patrick came rushing up to me and said, 'Coral are out in the ring taking 2/1 Fujiyama Crest' – and he could get 9/4 in the Silver

Ring. I quickly put up 2/1 as well – I wanted to get as much as I could while they were still investing. It's not often – no, never – did I get a chance to mug the offices and lay such a price about a real 10/1 chance.

Shortly after, Hills and Ladbrokes were out doing the same thing. I thought at the time, what absolute cowards, why don't they stand up to the liabilities? It can't win, anyway, it's a bloody great handicap with plenty of horses who can, and will, beat it.

Patrick came up to me and said could I lay a £2,000/£1,000 for him – at the time he was earning about £400 a week. His confidence brought new bravado to me and I called all the offices in and asked them how much they wanted. When they said 'you name it, all in' I laid them £11,000 at 2/1 – ten for me, one for Pat. Remember, at that stage the most I had ever been forced to stand a horse for in my life had been £5,000.

The race is off. I do not feel any anxiety, everyone knows no jockey can ride all seven winners in such big races at an Ascot Festival. During the race I repeatedly switch from my bins to the big screen, but don't panic when he is leading from a long way out. I know, deep down, what he is trying to do is impossible. A furlong to go, still in front. Don't panic, something is coming to challenge him on the outside – this is going to beat him. I knew he couldn't ride all seven winners, it isn't possible. Half a furlong out – I don't know the challenger, but he simply must get up. Twenty yards to go. Reality – it is not going to get up. Frankie's done it.

I stood on my stool, staring into the sky, not hearing a thing. It was like I was in a trance. It was probably about 10 seconds, but time had stood still. I eventually turned back to look at the cheering crowds. 'Patrick, can you handle the cash payout – I've got to go and sit in the car'. I later learned the final damage had been £23,000 on that race alone – £20,000 owed to the offices. Total loss on the day of £26,500. My previous biggest loss on any day during 30 years of on-course bookmaking had been £5,000.

Drove home with the staff in total silence. Everyone frightened to speak. Walked in the door, my wife greeted me in her normal cheery voice. 'Hello, darling – good day?'

'Dettori rode all seven winners' I said.

'Fantastic,' she said, 'What a great achievement.'

I collapsed in my favourite chair, silently crying.

During the next six months, I was lucky enough to have a good run – mainly at Lingfield all-weather – which enabled me to pay off the offices. By February 1997 I had recovered.

My own true story doesn't seem all that unusual now, but looking back at my financial records I now realise as he passed the post first, I fleetingly thought, 'I've gone.'

Although he believed he'd never see such financial carnage again during his working life, cricket loving Dennis suffered to the tune of £50,000 in September 2004 when all six favourites won at Newmarket – 'The only sensible conclusion is that God is a bookmaker – and he sends the odd rotten day to remind us he moves in mysterious ways.'

He has acquired a reputation for not taking bets – particularly small ones – from women. But he protests; 'I do take bets from women. I even take bets from the Welsh. But never from Welsh women – 'cos I'm married to one and I know what they're like.' On another occasion, this time at Royal Ascot, he displayed the message – 'No women or drunks'.

Asked if he had ever fancied going over to the other side and becoming a professional punter, Dennis declared: 'Bollocks to that. I have not got the balls to back horses.'

He is also very sceptical and scathing about politicians, of whom he said once, 'I soon learned it doesn't matter who you vote for, they all tell lies. If I was to follow the politicians' example I'd offer money back on all losers and double odds on all winners. I would just fail to cough up when people came for their money.'

But he is prepared to take big punters on and took a bet of £80,000 from owner J.P. McManus on his horse Baracouda for the 2005 World Hurdle at the Cheltenham Festival – 'I had to put my bicycle clips on to stop the runs going from my rear into my shoes' was his charming description of his situation – until the horse was beaten.

Never afraid to take on officialdom, Dennis was outraged in March 2006 when, at Lingfield, the judge, Jane Stickels – something of a serial offender, it must be said – called 9/4 favourite Welsh Dragon the winner, only to correct herself in favour of 14/1 outsider Miss Dagger, when the jockeys had weighed in. 'This buffoon has cost the industry £7 million', ranted Dennis. 'The real winner was virtually unbacked, but the horse we have to pay out on was a hot favourite. Her eyesight can't be trusted.'

He will also criticise the top racing figures, reacting to John Gosden's decision to run beaten hot favourite Rainbow View in the 2000 1000 Guineas despite adverse ground 'for fear of repercussions from the betting fraternity'. He pointed out: 'There were far many more millions bet on Rainbow View on the day than ante-post – and these punters would have got their cash back had she been withdrawn.'

Dennis has few if any regrets about his time as a bookie, but is not convinced that many will follow in his footsteps – 'The internet has made a complete horse's arse of on-course betting' he complains, predicting, 'People like me will be a thing of the past one day.'

HARRY FINDLAY

'Booming, boorish, bombastic' – the *Independent*

Not since the mid eighties heyday of the flamboyant, long-haired Terry Ramsden, has the world of racing seen an up-front, unrepentant mega-gambler like Harry 'The Dog' Findlay. Ramsden attracted headlines mainly for his losing gambles, which contributed to the £77 million he lost during the decade of big hair and shoulder pads.

Findlay really burst into public consciousness via his Cheltenham Gold Cup-winning horse, Denman, who charged to victory in the 2008 running, leaving the defending champion and stable-mate from Paul Nicholls' yard, Kauto Star, trailing in his wake. Says Findlay of Denman: 'He's got that sort of thing about him, people either want to take him on or they like him, and that's the sort of person I am. There's no middle, grey area with Denman, there's no grey area with me. It's a horse that suits my type of character.'

That Findlay is not exactly your conventional, understated owner happy to go along with the words of wisdom emanating from the direction of his trainer, was already evident when the larger than life character attended the 2008 Derby Awards to collect his Owner of the Year Award. Feeling nervous at the prospect of addressing the assembled multitude of hundreds of the great and good of racing, Findlay popped out for a sneaky puff beforehand, and promptly had his collar felt by a couple of plain-clothes coppers who just happened to be lurking around and who quickly reached the conclusion that the contents of his cigarette did not only consist of tobacco. Findlay told the *Daily Mail*'s Charles Sale, 'The police were bang out of order. I only had one puff and they said I was flaunting the cannabis in their faces. Everyone in racing knows I smoke cannabis because of the allergy (to dogs) and I also needed a quick puff for my nerves. It's a joke this cannabis ban. I'm here with my mum and I recommend it to all her friends to help all their different allergies.'

Undeterred, Findlay made it up to the podium, accompanied by his octogenarian mum, Mary, in whose colours a number of his animals run, where, accepting the award, made by the Horserace Writers and Photographers' Association, he told the assembled masses that 'gamblers live by a moral code not always recognised by the press' and that 'gambling is interwoven with racing' before demanding that the Government must forget all about selling the Tote – and certainly not even dream of selling it to the Pari Mutuel (the French Tote), which would be a 'heinous crime.'

The award went to Findlay and his much older fellow owner, wealthy, tweedy Somerset dairy farmer Paul Barber. The pair of them have become known as the 'Odd Couple' but, as the programme for the event pointed out, 'Which of the pair is Jack Lemmon and which is Walter Matthau I will leave to your imagination – safe to say that Paul has a bet no more than once a year while his racing partner will be investing several times every day and night – whether on horses, greyhounds, tennis, or even rugby – although the latter became a dirty word after the eclipse of the All Blacks in the last (rugby union) World Cup.'

They first met at the Doncaster Sales and Findlay admits, 'But for a chance meeting through a mutual friend I doubt if I ever would have owned a horse.' The crucial difference between them – the importance, or lack of importance – of punting on the horses, is perhaps best illustrated by Findlay's recollection of the time 'Denman was at Bangor when he won at odds of 1/12, and I can remember Paul Barber saying in the paddock – "No bet today, Harry, at that price!". Little did he know that I'd already had £400,000 on him!'

Harry was never going to take a conventional career path; once he told his mum, 'I will just be happy to be alive at 65, but don't expect me to put money away every week for something so many years down the line.'

Findlay's first love was greyhounds (despite that canine allergy) – hence the nickname – and, after getting a job 'walking greyhounds for eighteen quid a week', he worked at the *Racing Post* on the dog desk during the eighties while Ramsden was flaunting his big hair and flashing his even bigger wad of cash around the country's racecourses. Findlay must have looked on in envy at the time, but has now eclipsed the memory of the ultimately jailed-for-fraud Ramsden – although he does admit that he once suffered a similar fate, albeit on a much lesser credit-card fraud charge.

Findlay, who started by playing poker dice when he was at school, is a fearless gambler – when he fancies something or someone, he goes in big – regardless of the price. Recalling the time he staked £400,000 to win £300,000 on tennis star Roger Federer in the 2005 US Open, Harry defends backing odds-on shots – 'It's the biggest myth in racing! It's the biggest myth in life. That is my golden rule. Do not be afraid to back odds-on. It's a myth perpetrated by bookmakers and ignorant punters. Cowards! When people say they never bet odds-on, what they're really saying is that they can't count, or they're a coward. They're afraid of the risk factor. There's no difference between getting 1/2 about a 1/4 chance and getting 4/1 about a 2/1 chance'.

Findlay claimed in a November 2006 interview, 'I lay out literally millions every weekend. There's no point in me betting small. It's all about knowing the right price and how good you are at staking. I have to win to eat. No one makes a good living out of betting in hundreds.'

He is entirely unrepentant about the place gambling holds in his life: 'I have read a lot of the great philosophers, and gambling is a very good parody of life. I see life as a casino, in that I completely and utterly treat money as chips in a casino. Money is chips to play life with.'

His philosophy of life extends to his use of betting exchanges. 'One of the main reasons why I'm pro exchanges is because of the moral argument,' he told the *Guardian*'s Chris Cook, 'You can check how much you're losing, it stops the lies, there's no credit.' However, he is not blind to their faults, 'Betfair's been stagnant for years' he said in December 2006, 'They've lost the heart of what they were trying to do.'

Another plank of his gambling technique involves hedging – or not. 'When you pick a 20/1 shot to win the Grand National, don't have £200 at 20s and then go and lay £600 at 5/2 and, when it wins, get £2500. If you believe in that 20/1 shot, have £200 at 20s and then go and have another £300 at 14s and then £400 at 10s and then, when it goes off at 5/2 or 11/4, don't hedge if you still fancy it.'

Born in 1962, Findlay flirted with life on the 'other side', working in greyhound kennels for under twenty quid a week, standing as a bookmaker for just one week. 'I couldn't do it. A bloke called John, used to work in a factory all day, came in to bet £20. He had sawdust up his nose, in his ears, on his head. He made chairs for nine hours every day. I ended up wanting his dog to win. I lasted a week. I've always been a punter.'

Towards the end of the eighties he finally made inroads towards the big time when an £80 treble on a horse, Holland in the Euro Championships and Stefan Edberg at Wimbledon landed him serious money – £11,000. Then he discovered Asian Handicap betting on football matches – 'By the end of the 1998 World Cup I had won £2 million.'

Harry first made an impression on the turf when his Desert Quest landed him a gamble worth an estimated £1 million by winning the 2006 County Hurdle at Cheltenham. In May 2007 he cleaned up on the newly introduced Race-O pool bet, winning it on consecutive days to land £2,040,791. Mind you, he admitted afterwards that before winning he was £350,000 down.

Denman won him the best part of another million in Cheltenham's 2007 Royal & Sun Alliance Chase, a year before his 2008 Gold Cup triumph, which came as no surprise to this shrinking violet of a man who had predicted to anyone prepared to listen, 'Kauto Star is the speed horse, Denman the crusher. Provided the ground is not too fast I think this horse is a monster.' The monster won him another reported £600,000 in the Gold Cup.

After Denman's triumph, Findlay showed his charitable side when, despite coming from a family of Rangers' supporters, he funded trips to Europe for pupils at a Dublin secondary school to travel to Barcelona and Copenhagen to watch . . . Celtic.

For all his 'Jack the Lad' front, Findlay is not immune to the deeper feelings stirred by horses. Talking of Kauto Star and Denman, he observed, 'Their personalities as horses are very similar to their characters on the course. They were taking pictures of the pair of them the other day, and Kauto was all charismatic, flamboyant, looking like the athlete, the superstar he is. And Denman was there, head down, looking like a black bull, snorting, "Come on! Come and get me!"'

But if all this talk of big money victories has whetted your appetite for a similar lifestyle to Findlay's, consider this tribute to his wife of some 20 years – 'Kay has never moaned, including when we've sold the house, the car and, many years ago, pawned all the jewellery.' She couldn't say she hadn't been warned – on their second date he'd just won £30,000 at the dogs and took her to Scotland to put it all on a horse. 'The horse fell and it was all gone. I was on £52 a week.' And if you still haven't been put off – ponder on the fact that the All Blacks' surprise failure to win the 2007 Rugby World Cup cost him the small matter of £2.6 million. You won't be surprised, though, when he says, 'I still think I should have had more on.'

Maybe his conviction that the All Blacks were some kind of certainty was fostered on one of his regular annual visits down under where, particularly in Australia, he believes that the odds-on shots represent even better value for punting money. During his trip in early 2009, *Racing Post* reporter, Peter Thomas, followed in his footsteps, observing the gambling spree at racecourses, tennis tournaments, cricket pitches and the like, and hearing Findlay explaining, 'I love being amongst gamblers, and these people are all gamblers.' Convinced by the Findlay factor, Thomas even started betting odds-on, 'unloading on a 2/5 shot at Sunshine Coast, which wins', after 'I spy Harry divesting an unsmiling local bookie of a large wad of folding dollars.'

Findlay's return to the snow-covered wastes of England was soured when his Denman, back on course for the first time since recovering from a heart complaint, was beaten convincingly into second place, leaving future Gold Cup plans looking a little uncertain, only for the horse to produce a tremendous effort in the Cheltenham feature event, to run second to Kauto Star.

By the way, Findlay is such an inveterate punter that when he first met his partner, Kay, at The Crucible, where the World Snooker Championship was being played, he asked TV betting pundit, Angus Loughran, 'What price I marry that bird?'

The price Angus quoted is lost in the mists of time but, Findlay reflected in March 2008, 'We didn't get married, because I fell out with the vicar – but we've been together for 19 years, so what a call that was!'

Those who believe that gamblers have to be hard-headed, calculating and unemotional, should know that his good class chaser, Big Fella Thanks, is named after Harry's favourite living thing – the elderly former racing greyhound (and Irish Coursing Derby Champion in 1999) who shares his home. No wonder he is a dogged punter.

CHARLIE HANNAM
Charlie was the bookies' darling

Most characters are recognised as such because of their larger than life presence, or their high profile feats and achievements. Few become known as characters because of lack of awareness of their activities and a downbeat reluctance to play the publicity game.

But one such figure on the turf was a man who died in June 1947 in a quiet residential street in Harrogate at the impressive age of 88 – 'and with him died, unwritten and unspoken, the greatest modern life-story of the betting ring' wrote J. Wentworth Day shortly after Charlie Hannam passed away. Many knew of his betting exploits but most of what they had heard was hearsay or from once or twice removed sources – Hannam himself rarely spoke of his 'working' life.

Born in 1859, he was the son of a Yorkshire farmer of modest means – who met a tragic and extremely unusual end in 1869 when, acting as judge at a racehorse trial over hurdles at Wetherby racecourse, he was killed when one of the horses swerved into him – at North Deighton, near Knightsbridge. Even today little is known of the man who became known on-course as 'Old England'.

He was a former booking clerk for the North Eastern Railway who eventually decided to add spice to his life by making some practical use of his interest in racing, and became a bookmaker, with his older brother Bob acting as his clerk. But he was not just a bookmaker, he was also a fearless punter.

He first realised he could profit from both sides of the betting ring when at a three day Kempton meeting he took on the layers and won himself £8500. 'That decided him. He became the biggest backer of his generation' recalled Wentworth Day, 'He betted two million pounds a year – and he stuck it out for nearly sixty years of regular racing.' He must have gambled in amounts which would have exceeded even those of today's most renowned punters like Harry Findlay.

The neatly moustachioed Hannam cut a dashing figure on the racecourse, always dressed in top quality suits and wearing highly polished black boots with brown uppers. His brother Bob was often alongside him, but did not have the same effortless style nor the same astuteness in his wagering.

'Charles' method was that he made a book against the bookies' – which is what another current day high roller, Dave Nevison, does. 'He always selected three or four horses to win in the same race and he could calculate odds with lightning rapidity.'

But there was no Channel 4 *Morning Line* TV show in those days, no At The Races or Racing UK channels – and Hannam refused interviews and was not interested in offers to write his life story.

He would bet on other sporting events – £100 on a single shot at billiards, for example – and he once lost £10,000 on a game of darts, the same amount on the roll of a dice at Liverpool's Adelphi Hotel one Grand National day.

Trainer Charlie Marlow said of Hannam, 'He is the one man in a hundred million who has made a fortune at gambling, and kept it. I think the secret of his success was his iron resolution. You could not make him budge an inch from his own opinion.' Racing journalist and close friend Meyrick Good concurred: 'It has been faith in his one judgement that has enabled him to wage war on the Ring with such astonishing success for so many years' he declared in 1941. 'Seldom does he visit a paddock to see the horses, and never for the last thirty years have I seen him talking to a single jockey or trainer and seldom is he in conversation with owners except, of course, when asked on occasion to work some extensive commission.'

Hannam did not even listen to tips from his friends. When Good told him that his own horse Fortune's Smile was well fancied in a race at Hurst Park, he assumed that Hannam would also be celebrating when it won at 8/1. 'I backed the two favourites coupled, but, thank you, Good, all the same' he replied.

Hannam had had bad days before, losing £50,000 in an afternoon at Ascot and dropping £10,000 at a 1925 Newmarket meeting. However, he was noted for paying any gambling debts almost instantly, until Cambridgeshire day in 1938 when things went wrong for him and he lost a reported £40,000 on the race after his fancy Domaha, partnered by Gordon Richards, was beaten narrowly into third place by two short heads. The 2lbs (1kg) overweight the horse carried, and the fact that he was drawn 29 of 29 probably did for him – and for Hannam. He asked for time to pay and had to sell some stocks and shares to raise the money.

He had a great deal invested in a Bradford dyeing business and held shares in a number of racecourse companies, most of which he had sold when a Betting Tax was introduced in 1926, after which he had gone to France to race for some while, returning when the tax was repealed.

The Cambridgeshire, though, was the beginning of the end for him and he started to ration his racecourse appearances. His absence caused his more cautious fellow bookies a problem. 'He gave the lead which other, less important professionals or backers would promptly follow' said a fellow layer, 'Charlie would create the prices of the favourites. Then the market against other horses and the varying prices would "settle down" normally.'

Meyrick Good dubbed Hannam 'the Prince of Gamblers' in 1941, several years after scrupulous chronicler of the turf, John Fairfax-Blakeborough had written, 'In an age when men do not wager as they used to, and an epoch when bookmakers will not lay odds to (the) thousands old timers gambled, Charles Hannam is the "prince of plungers"'. Writer and turf personality, C. Morton, dubbed him, 'easily the cleverest backer the turf has ever known'. Fairfax-Blakeborough added, 'Hannam has won in one afternoon what most people would consider a handsome fortune. Equally, he has lost almost as heavily, but in main has gone on winning and proved himself to be the most successful gambler Turf has ever known.'

Good also revealed that there was a 'somewhat eccentric' side to Hannam, rarely appreciated by the public: 'He made three fancy wagers. These were a bet of £1000 that he would never again visit Monte Carlo, £100 to £1 that he would never wear spectacles, £200 that he would never carry an umbrella. Although he never wears spectacles on a racecourse I have seen him with an over-sized magnifying glass when looking at his card! The first named wager he was, I understand, allowed to break.' This latter fact probably related to the fact that Hannam was a keen and successful pigeon-shooter in Monte Carlo, on which he presumably won a great deal of money.

Hannam, who would rarely back horses ridden by jockeys below top class, told Good that he had never wagered more than £10,000 on any individual horse.

Enthused Good:

> That Hannam should have survived his battle with the Leviathans of Tattersalls for so many years has made him in a betting sense one of the marvels of the century. He has been indeed the wonder, the admiration and the envy of every other professional backer of horses. He has stood alone for the fearlessness and independence of his betting, as also for the volume of it. It has been nothing for him to

have thousands at stake, not once during an afternoon, but several times. Yet he has never been an ostentatious personality on a racecourse, which is one reason why he was practically unknown to many racegoers outside that well-known inside circle of speculators.

JOHN McCRIRICK
Misunderstood misogynist

It always seemed to be one of the least likely of friendships – between a small, brilliant, left wing, high political achiever and a large, outrageous, right wing racing pundit. But Labour foreign secretary Robin Cook, the principled Scot who quit the government in protest at the invasion of Iraq, was, in his private life, a keen racing man and, over a 20-year period which began when they first met at Doncaster races in the early eighties, he had struck up a close relationship with John McCririck.

And when Cook died tragically early, McCririck was invited to deliver an address to the 500-plus official mourners at the funeral service for his fellow atheist, which took place at St Giles' Cathedral in Edinburgh on Friday, 12 August 2005. Rather than concentrate as expected on Cook's love of the turf, McCririck, whose normal, highly individual style of dress had already seen him win the 'Best Turned Out' award at the funeral for his purple jacket and hat, teamed with white shirt and bootlace tie, took the opportunity to launch an attack on the Prime Minister, Tony Blair, and his 'petty vindictiveness' for continuing with his Caribbean holiday and missing the occasion. He accused Blair of 'snubbing' Cook by preferring 'to continue snorkelling'.

He stole many of the headlines the next day as a result and also became the target of personal attacks from many of those who only months previously had vented their own political spleen on Cook. Those who were discomfited by McCririck's words, drawing unwanted – by certain factions – attention to the absence of the

Prime Minister from the ceremony, accused him of deliberately seeking self-publicity at the expense of the dignity of a respected politician's final send off.

But the stench of hypocrisy hovered over the criticisms of McCririck, a man who, for all his faults, had been receiving as much publicity as he cared to accept for many a long year and certainly did not resort to tactics of this nature, of whose consequences he would have been well aware, for the sake of it.

To his great credit, McCririck steadfastly refused to apologise for the furore he had caused – 'I was speaking not just for myself but for millions of other people . . . if it was the funeral of Bush or Chirac he would go.' And perhaps he allowed himself a smile of satisfaction when the *Sunday Times* 'leaked' the news that 'Blair has agreed to give an oration at a memorial service for Cook in London in October.'

Up until this point the defining public image of McCririck was of an overweight, sulking show-off of a man who had made his name waving his arms about on the box while talking unintelligible betting-related waffle; and sitting silent for hours on end in protest at being deprived of Diet Coke whilst taking part in the reality TV show, *Celebrity Big Brother*.

Perhaps the outburst at the Cook funeral was his way of re-establishing his credentials as a man to be taken seriously and not just dismissed as a harmless, wilfully eccentric, C-list celebrity, media sideshow. But, just how did such a seemingly unkempt, opinionated, self-declared loudmouth manage to gatecrash the celebrity circuit in the first place?

McCririck is a Harrow public schoolboy turned failed bookmaker and award winning *Sporting Life* journalist. Whilst at that respected paper – to which he initially came as greyhound coursing (the controversial hare-chasing sport now outlawed by the government) correspondent – he exposed a genuine national scandal by the state-owned betting operation, the Tote, which was bending its own rules to the disadvantage of its clients, by allowing bets to be added into the pool from which winning dividends were calculated, *after* races had been run. McCririck's exposure of this outrage caused a sensation and a change in the way the Tote ran its business, winning him a major journalistic award.

His eccentric appearance quickly marked him out as a 'personality' in the usually staid and conservative racing world. But McCririck's unconventional dress sense – capes, deerstalkers, a watch on each wrist, flashy rings – concealed a knowledgeable grasp of the horse racing and betting industries.

It was the latter talent which was to enable him to make a significant breakthrough into the public eye. Channel Four acquired the rights to show the majority of the high quality horse racing broadcast in this country – and unlike the BBC, which had for years tried to pretend that horse racing took place with virtually no associated betting activity, it decided to highlight and focus on the betting element of racing. McCririck was a natural figure to front up this aspect of their coverage. He did so as though to the manner born, standing down amongst the bookmakers and punters on the course, waving his arms about, literally shouting the odds, and attracting gawping crowds of onlookers as he informed viewers about the latest betting moves. This prompted former Harrow School contemporary and face of BBC racing for many years, Julian Wilson, to sniff, 'I always felt his great strength was behind the camera – and whether it's in the interest of coverage to have him in vision is clearly for others to decide.'

The occasion on which one of the spectators handed Mac an ice cream cornet – and then rubbed it into his face – only increased the 'buzz' around the presenter. As did his almost unprecedentedly aggressive interviewing technique when quizzing various horse racing grandees about on-course events. Many of these matters had never been raised in the more subservient days of the Beeb. But McCririck had no problem in asking awkward questions about 'non-triers', the under-representation of ethnic minorities on racecourses, why stewards still addressed jockeys by their surnames as though they were naughty children, and so on.

The lack of publicly voiced criticism in racing journalism had been an on-going disgrace and fact of life for years and remains so, albeit to a lesser extent, to this day. The reason is that racing is such a small, incestuous world, that any journalist upsetting or aggravating trainers, jockeys or owners, would run the risk of being 'blackballed' as a consequence. McCririck did not, and does not, care about that. In May 1998 he said, 'The most reactionary bunch of people in the world are racehorse trainers. As far as they are concerned, the public are a damned nuisance.'

Not everyone in the game condemns him, though – the man Mac

calls 'greatest jockey', former champion jump jockey John Francome, says of his C4 colleague, 'If everyone was as passionate as he is, this would be Britain's number one sport.' Others disagree. Former trainer, turned writer, Charlie Brooks sneered, 'People like McCririck are blind. They've never sat on a horse in their life. They wouldn't know a horse if it kicked them.'

McCririck has often been ahead of public opinion – such as when in 1994 he predicted that despite great internal opposition from the racing establishment, 'I believe that by the end of the century there will be racing on 52 Sundays in the year.'

McCririck appears to be without a normal sense either of restraint or embarrassment. For example, for a man not blessed with conventional good looks or obvious sex appeal he has declared: 'Unlike other sporting types I have got no restraints on physical activity the night before a big race. How lucky the grateful Booby (his wife, Jenny) is.' Then in May 2009 before a trip to Paris for the French Guineas he turned stomachs by revealing: 'After leaving Longchamps, I've arranged to frolic under the bridges of Paris with a busty mademoiselle', before adding, 'She must be in Seine.'

Given the shortage of racing figures instantly recognisable to the outside world, McCririck soon became much sought after as a 'talking head' whenever the broadcast or journalistic media wanted an opinion on a racing-related issue – usually close to Grand National or Derby day. With his willingness to play up to the cameras he became a regular guest on all sorts of shows and as his visibility increased so did the range of topics he was asked to address. And as he did so he seemed to reveal himself as an unreconstructed, unapologetic, right wing Tory – and he was not concerned who knew it.

Nonetheless, well known though he had become after appearing on *Noel's House Party*, *Question Time*, *Children In Need* etc, etc, it was still something of a surprise that he should be selected for *Celebrity Big Brother*, alongside such unlikely 'bed-fellows' as Germaine Greer, Caprice and boy band star Kenzie. Viewers were staggered at the sight of McCririck clad in vast, baggy white underpants, lumbering around the house and making a principled stand when the programme deprived him of what he claimed was a contracted right to drink Diet Coke in the house. He went on strike, refusing to co-operate with the rules of the show, not speaking for almost two days. Finally, he got back his fizzy drink and reluctantly joined back in with the life of the house. He did not win the show, though.

McCririck's public profile boomed at this point – and maybe he even discovered a little 'street cred' with a more youthful audience; a couple of weeks after *Celebrity Big Brother*, at Mac's behest, Kenzie visited a racecourse for the first time, and even sponsored one of the races.

McCririck is intriguing as much for what is not known about him as for what is. He claims never to acknowledge birthdays, but is now well into his sixties. The couple have no children – their dogs are his children, he says. Big Mac is useless domestically: one mutual friend told me that when he visited him once when The Booby was away, they dined on Dundee cake and champagne as McCririck was incapable even of opening a can of beans or making toast for them to eat. 'I'm a failure. I can't do anything of any use to anyone. At least if I made nuts and bolts for a car I'd be useful. But I'm totally irrelevant' he said.

He insists on travelling club class when taking long haul trips – but his wife reportedly has to travel economy class.

He dedicated his one foray into the world of books to his wife – 'To the Booby – so lucky to have hooked her wonderful boy out of the great fishtank of life.' She drives him everywhere, as he does not drive and used to be spotted heading towards and away from the *Sporting Life* offices in High Holborn, pedalling furiously along on a three wheeler bicycle, deerstalker blowing wildly in the wind as he went.

McCririck – unusually, perhaps for a Harrow boy – a school which plays rugby and cricket, but not football – is a fanatical Newcastle United supporter, often flaunting a Geordie-favouring bobble hat whilst appearing on screen and conducting serious interviews.

In 2008 his career looked as though it might be beginning to wind down – or be wound down – as Channel 4 cut back his appearances. However, this had little effect on his public presence, and when the *Racing Post* launched a campaign designed to encourage the BBC to maintain its commitment to racing, the paper was quite happy to enlist the assistance of McCririck. He told them, 'The BBC has a duty to the country's history, and racing is part of the framework and the fabric of the nation. We will all be losers if the public don't know about racing and don't care about racing. The problem is the people running BBC sport don't care about racing in the way they used to.

The last thing channel controllers want is racing – our one hope is that Clare Balding becomes head of BBC sport.'

At the beginning of 2009 yet another extraordinary incident involving McCririck took place. Returning from a day's racing at Cheltenham on New Year's Day, John and Jenny discovered that their mews home had been ransacked. Devastated, they were checking what had been stolen when John's phone rang. He answered it and found himself talking to the man who claimed to have carried out the burglary. 'There was no shouting' said Big Mac, 'I was very calm and found myself saying things like "how many bottles of champagne did you take?".'

The burglar told him he had been looking for John's shotguns – which he promptly denied owning. 'I told him the jewellery he took wasn't worth anything but that it was of great sentimental value to my wife. He said he would give it back and call again to tell me where he would leave it – not that he has. He also told me it could have been worse and that he hadn't taken my racing awards – which was true.' He did though steal two flat screen TVs, several hundred pounds in cash and gold shirt-studs.

McCririck is no short-term, shallow, flash in the pan, here today gone tomorrow, unsubstantial figure who will be forgotten when the tabloids move on to their next passing fancy. He has been around for over 65 years, a public figure for 30, and will remain so until he proves that well known racing adage that everyone is equal on the turf – and under it. And when he does pass on he wants his ashes scattered around the winning post of the now defunct 'Ally Pally' – Alexandra Park – racecourse in north London.

PRINCE MONOLULU
The first McCririck

He wore baggy trousers, a flamboyant waistcoat, a lion's claw mascot round his neck and, on his head, a spectacular plumage. He was always stood in front of a curious crowd of onlookers at the races, waving his arms around and screaming out 'I gotta horse'. But this was some years before John McCririck was even born – and this man was black – the most recognised black man in the country, they said at the time.

He was from somewhere more exotic than most racegoers had ever dreamed of going – a Prince of the Falasha tribe from Abyssinia, he told racegoers. A Zulu chieftain, he told others. And his name was Ras Prince Monolulu.

That much was nonsense – he was plain old Peter Carl McKay, of Scottish descent, who hailed from St Croix (he was born there in 1881) in what would have been then, the Danish West Indies, now part of the United States' Virgin Islands, and who originally hit on the idea of calling himself a Prince, after being press-ganged onto an American cattle-boat in 1902, in which he sailed to England. Once he escaped from that predicament, he joined a travelling circus as a fire-eater and began to travel the world, modelling in Germany, boxing in France, pretending to be an opera singer in Russia and becoming a fortune teller in Italy. Allegedly. He was interned in Germany during the First World War.

By 1920 he had arrived back in England, and headed for the racecourses, where he began to entertain racegoers and earn a living by selling tips for horses – usually one a day.

So flamboyant was he, clad in bright, tropical looking clothes, adorned with horseshoes, flowers, stars, hearts, wearing ostrich feathers on his head, that he was an instant hit with the punters who flocked to see him and listen to him work a crowd. What a showman he was – and when he picked out Spion Kop to win the 1920 Derby at odds of 100/6 – and from which he personally made the relative fortune of £8000 – his reputation was made as word spread about the show he put on and the winners he tipped.

He had tipped the horse 'in trains and buses, in restaurants, in lifts, on street corners – at football matches I would push my way among the crowds, waving my umbrella and implore them to 'have a pound on Spion Kop, and when you've won, don't forget the darkie who told you.' They didn't forget him – 'The crowd mobbed me, they thrust pound notes into my hand, they pushed ten bob notes, half-crowns, shillings and even tanners into my pockets.'

'I gotta horse!' was not only his rallying cry to bring in the punters – it was the title of his autobiography, too.

Even today, those who made his acquaintance back then recall him with affection and nostalgia. 'He was a national icon, renowned for his eccentricity, a racing tipster of such theatricality that even in the days when newspapers carried few photographs and TV was in its infancy, he was still the most recognisable racing personality other than the top jockeys', remembered one fan.

Terry Bond of the *Independent* wrote of him in November 2000, 'In the early fifties, as a little lad, I would accompany my dad to the races. The colour of ebony, Monolulu had an imperious presence. Six feet and several inches tall he dressed in the flash bright robes befitting a member of African royalty. His voice carried across the car parks and racecourses of Britain as he boomed, "I gotta horse . . . gotta horse!" Never a plural.'

A clever touch, that, made it seem all the more plausible that he did have a winner, albeit just the one. It would cost you in those days ten bob (50p) to find out the name of his horse. Sometimes it would win, more often it wouldn't. Didn't really matter, you'd had a free show to go with it.

Brian Lee of the *Western Mail* also saw Monolulu – in the waxworks at Cardiff, where he was depicted alongside champion jockey Gordon Richards. 'He was almost certainly the most famous black man in Britain – undoubtedly the most famous racecourse tipster of all time. I recall his sayings, "God made the bees, the bees made the honey; you have a bet and the bookies take your money!" Another was – "White man for pluck; black man for luck".'

During his life he worked as a lion tamer, street singer, violinist, horseback rider and stable hand, reported Lee, adding, 'He's the only racing tipster to have had his picture in London's National Portrait Gallery.'

Indeed he is – in the shape of a 'modern resin print from original negative, 21 August 1931' taken by George Woodbine, showing him surrounded by a group of kids looking at him as today's equivalent would David Beckham. It was his wedding day – his bride, actress Nellie Adkins, just one of 'several' he acquired.

Another 1931 photo of him at Epsom races in April of that year shows him standing on a box in the rain, wearing what looks like a fisherman's sou'wester and hat, haranguing a flat-capped gathering of racegoers, holding in his hand a clutch of pieces of paper, no doubt bearing the name of a winner-to-be.

What's more, as well as the movie newsreels, he appeared in a number of films – playing himself in 1935's *Dandy Dick*; 1936's *Educated Evans*; 1937's *Wings of the Morning*; 1944's *The Hundred Pound Window*; 1952's *Derby Day*; 1954's *Aunt Clara* in which he was a bookie; 1959's *Make Mine A Million* and 1960's *The Criminal*.

In the early sixties his fading career touched on the new pop music revolution when he appeared in rock star Billy Fury's *I've Gotta Horse* movie – Fury himself was an owner, whose Anselmo finished fourth in the 1964 Derby at 100/1, ridden by 18-year-old Paul Cook, trained by Lester Piggott's father, Keith. In 1933 Monolulu even recorded his 'race-track spiel' on a record, released by the Regal Zonophone label.

He was immortalised as the first black man to appear on TV when the BBC launched its service on 2 November 1936. Popular though he was, Monolulu was not immune from racism. A dinner was given to mark famous jockey Steve Donoghue's 1938 retirement. 'I was at that dinner. At least, I bought a ticket to attend it, but a number of snobs of racing objected to my presence . . . The result was that I had my dinner, not with Steve, but down in the kitchens with the waiters.'

Monolulu was in trouble again when Donoghue died, with the *Daily Mirror* accusing him of using the funeral to sell tips to mourners. 'I went to Warrington, not to sell tips but to pay my last respects to a great little man with a great heart' he insisted.

Monolulu reckoned he gambled his way through £150,000 between 1919 and 1950, and his profile began to decline in the late fifties.

His colourful life finally ended in an equally colourful way – and, bizarrely enough, courtesy of another of the turf's greatest characters, also featured in this book – racing journalist, bon viveur and gambler, Jeffrey Bernard – much later, the subject of the hit West End show, *Jeffrey Bernard Is Unwell*. Bernard's biographer, Graham Lord revealed in 1992 what happened on 14 February 1965 when Bernard was dispatched by his then editor, Dennis Hackett of *Queen* magazine, to interview the poorly Monolulu in his bed at the Middlesex Hospital. 'Bernard took along a box of Black Magic chocolates and when Monolulu proved to be too weak to help himself to one, Bernard pushed a strawberry cream into

Monolulu's feeble mouth. The "prince" tried to swallow it, coughed and started choking. A nurse sent Bernard out of the ward and drew a screen around the bed but it was too late. Monolulu had choked to death.'

There was a poignant postscript to his death when, on 25 October 1992 Monolulu was remembered when relatives and admirers attended a celebration on what would have been his 111th birthday, at a pub bearing his name in Maple Street, London.

ABROAD SPECTRUM

DUQUE DE ALBUQUERQUE
Duke of hazard

There never was before and almost certainly never will there be again, another jockey from the same mould as the Duque de Albuquerque, real name Beltran de Osorio y Diez de Rivera.

In the early 1920s, on his eighth birthday, the Spanish aristocrat saw a film about the Grand National. He fell instantly in love with the race. 'I had loved horses since a child. Now I saw this beautiful race, the greatest test of a horse and rider in the world. I said then that I would win that race one day.' He may never have quite managed his objective – but it wasn't for want of trying, and he darned well near killed himself in the attempt.

In his own 34th year, 1952, the Duque, an amateur rider, managed to achieve the first part of his ambition – taking part in the race. Big punter of the day, Joe Sunlight, even backed him to win him £10,000. He rode his own horse, 40/1 chance, Brown Jack III, putting up 10lbs (4.5kg) overweight. The pair hit the deck at the sixth, leaving the Duque, whose title dates back to the 15th century, hospitalised with a cracked vertebra. 'Poor animal, it was past it' remarked the Duque, overlooking the fact that the same may already have been true of him!

The Duque went back to Spain to lick his wounds, and plot another attempt, duly returning 11 years later – having meanwhile raced all over Europe – to team up with 13-year-old 66/1 shot, Jonjo, who had been favourite for the race in 1961. This time he went well, and got as far as the 21st fence, falling, albeit without inflicting much in the way of damage on either party.

Attempt number three came in 1965 when he purchased and partnered Groomsman, a 10-year-old. Down they came together at Valentine's. Off went the Duque to hospital with a broken leg, an occupational hazard for this adventurous daredevil, whose 22nd break or fracture of a body part, this was.

He found another mount in 1966, by which time he was being described as the 'Iron' Duque, and he and 100/1 outsider, L'Empereur galloped as far as the 26th before the horse decided he'd done enough, and pulled himself up.

Seven years passed, during which time the Duque went elsewhere to get himself injured, succeeding with honours as he collected 10 more fractures.

His fifth attempt to at least complete the course arrived in 1973, this time in collaboration with the seven-year-old Nereo, 66/1, his own horse, trained by Fred Winter – they were a unique combination – the youngest horse and oldest jockey. But for a leather, which broke, causing them to pull up, they might well have made it round the track. 'A leather broke for the only time in my life. I kept on for eight more fences before pulling up before the Canal Turn. I could not give up trying then. It was so often like that. Every year provided the excuse to try just once more.'

Some weeks before the 1974 National, the Duque had an accident in Seville, which necessitated the insertion of 16 screws into his leg. They were removed a mere fortnight prior to the big race. A week before the National he broke his collar bone. Bah – a mere inconvenience. The Duque, aged 55, and wearing a plaster cast, and Nereo, 100/1, (66/1 with some bookies just to get round) now aged eight, not only completed the course, but they finished a highly respectable eighth of seventeen finishers, behind winner, Red Rum. 'I sat like a sack of potatoes and gave the horse no help' he said, modestly, afterwards. During the race, the Duque accidentally barged into top jockey Ron Barry on Straight Vulgan, on the second circuit, who barked at him – 'What the f*** are you doing ?'. The Duque reportedly replied, 'My dear chap, I haven't a clue – I've never got this far before!'

Prior to the 1975 race the Duque managed to break his leg at Newbury, but was still considering taking his chance until Fred Winter stepped in and stopped him, pointing out how unfair it would have been to the horse. 'I have often been afraid on a horse, but fear is like any other habit, you learn to live with it. If a horse crashes, you may break a bone. If a car crashed, you may die. Do you then stop driving?'

The Duque, whose own riding career often resembled a car crash, plotted up ride number seven, again on board Nereo, in 1976. Racing up with the leaders, Nereo capsized at the 13th fence. 'I have been superstitious of that number all my life' observed the understated Duque. Once again he took up residence in hospital, having been trampled on after the fall, and did not regain consciousness for two days. Some days later when he was over the severe concussion he discovered that he had broken seven ribs, broken vertebrae, broken his wrist, and fractured his right thigh bone.

Such a minor setback was not going to deter his Dukeness from his eighth crack at the Aintree marathon. His new ambition was 'to return and complete the course on a Spanish horse, though I admit that my chances of winning seemed remote then, but I do not regard age as something which automatically eliminates a man from doing anything.'

It must have been this intention to bring a horse from his native land which finally stirred the previously unperturbed Jockey Club to endeavour to protect the Duque from himself. They refused him permission to ride over fences, and introduced a rule requiring amateur riders of over 50 summers (the Duque was now 58) to undergo a stringent medical examination. 'I was very sad. I trained hard for the 1977 National' complained the thwarted noble senor, 'I considered myself fitter than I had been for years. Then they banned me. It was my body, my horse and my responsibility.'

However, no complaint was heard from Nereo – even though he would contest the race twice more: in 1977 as a 100/1 faller with Robert Kington on board, with a disconsolate Duque ('it was the saddest National of my life') looking on; and 1978, finishing 14th at 40/1 albeit with a different rider, Mark Floyd.

The Duque never did get back into the National, nor did he ever return to Aintree . . . but at the age of 72 he completed a 700 plus mile pilgrimage on foot. He died, two years later in 1994, in Madrid.

SCOBIE BREASLEY
Wonder of Wagga Wagga

His real name was Arthur Edward Breasley – but the boy from Wagga Wagga in New South Wales became universally known as Scobie – the name of his early hero, Ballarat trainer, James Scobie.

He was born in the year the First World War broke out, 1914 and, having already ridden over 1000 winners in Australia, he would then move to England at the age of 33 and become the most successful Oz jock ever to ride in that country, with well over 2000 triumphs to his name. And, unlike so many great jockeys, he would then become one of the world's highest paid trainers, emulating his boyhood hero.

Scobie's influential manner of riding, sitting high up on his mount's withers, persuaded many young English riders to emulate him. He would rarely win by too far, usually flourishing, rather than using, his whip, thus helping to avoid his mount being burdened with an excessive rise in weight in future races. Another feature of his riding – sometimes costly – was a desire to stick to the rails, come what may.

He learned his trade by riding unbroken horses at an early age and so obvious was it that his future lay in riding that his father took him out of school two years early, aged 12, to begin an apprenticeship with local trainer S.H. Biggins.

A year later he had showed such promise that he moved to Melbourne, where he became apprenticed to trainer Pat Quinlan, riding his first winner, Noo Jee, in August 1928, at Weribee, in Victoria. Although he was suspended for crossing another horse too sharply, following his first big win, Randwick's Metropolitan Handicap, on Cragford, aged 16, he would never once be suspended for foul riding during his half century career. He won big race after big race in Australia – five Caulfield Cups, the Victoria Derby, Sydney Cup, AJC Metropolitan, AJC Derby – but, to his regret, never the Melbourne Cup, despite 16 attempts.

Scobie got married in 1935 to May Weston – on the very day, 5

November, on which thousands of miles away, a certain Lester Piggott was born.

At a time when his thoughts had been turning to retirement, Scobie came to England to ride for wealthy flour mill millionaire owner J.V. Rank's private trainer Noel Cannon in March 1950 and made an instant impression by winning with his first two rides at Liverpool, on Decorum and Promotion. He totalled 72 winners in his debut season and was immediately complimented for his handling of two-year-olds. The next year he won his first Classic, the 2000 Guineas, on Ki Ming and the Cambridgeshire on Fleeting Moment.

The relationship with Rank suffered because of the offhand treatment frequently meted out to Scobie by Rank's heavy gambling wife, Pat, who was not a noted good loser when things went wrong.

Scobie stayed in Australia during 1952 but returned to England when Rank died in early 1953.

The media christened him the 'stop-watch jockey' for his ability to judge pace and time finishes to perfection – this was acquired in Australia where trainers would regularly require their jockeys to clock certain times in pre-race work: 'There were plenty who criticised me and my methods, but I stuck by them. I never wanted a horse to have a harder race than was necessary – and I used to hate losing races I appeared to have won in the last few strides. It probably gave me a lot of pleasure riding them that way, but I honestly could not see any more merit in a 10 length win than a short head.'

As he flourished, Breasley, who could ride without fasting at 8st 2lbs (51kg), opened the way for other Australian riders to follow in his footsteps.

In 1964, aged 50, he captured the Derby on Santa Claus, bringing the Mick Rogers' trained Irish colt to collar leader, Indiana, right at the death, and showed uncharacteristic emotion: 'I've had 13 bashes at this race before I finally made it, and I won't believe it until I read it in the papers in the morning.' There was a bizarre sequel to Santa Claus' victory, recalls racing writer and commentator, Julian Wilson: 'Santa Claus was a short-priced favourite and there were rumours before the race that Breasley had been paid by a bookmaker to prevent the horse from winning. At halfway Santa Claus was in a seemingly hopeless position, and although he eventually won, Breasley was never invited to ride him again.'

Wilson also recalled that 'Rumours and controversy were never far away and the marriage of his daughter to the son of a bookmaker merely fuelled the punters' suspicions . . . much humour was generated by an alleged comment of his wife May in 1975. Breasley, by then a trainer, had won the Middle Park Stakes with Hittite Glory at odds of 9/2. Afterwards, the senior steward Lord Leverhulme, congratulated May, adding "I hope that Scobie had a good bet". "Nah, m'Lord" replied May, "I don't think Scobie's had a bet since he gave up riding"'!

Scobie had suffered a few terrible falls by then – notably a life-threatening one at Alexandra Park in 1954. Just after winning the 1000 Guineas with Festoon, and shortly before his 40th birthday, he cracked his skull in the fall from Sayonara, and both eyes were paralysed as a result, which meant that he had no sense of balance and was unable to ride for the best part of three months. His friend, golfer Norman von Nida, took him out golfing to Sunningdale every day for a month to help with his recuperation. 'Von Nida bullied him mercilessly' recalled Scobie's biographer, Lorin Knight, 'Progress was slow, frustrating and sometimes comic; von Nida was unrelenting but within a month his methods, though drastic, proved to be effective and he knew his friend would ride again.'

Once after falling from a horse, the female owner rang to ask how he was. He replied a little sarcastically, 'Thank you for your letters of condolence and for the fruit and flowers' to which she responded, 'I don't send fruit or flowers to jockeys for falling off my horses.'

Newbury in 1956 saw him take another bad tumble, as did Brighton in 1959 and Lincoln in 1960, but it was someone else's misfortune of that kind, Sir Gordon Richards, which opened the door for another leap forward for Scobie. Richards took a horrendous tumble when his horse Abergeldie fell backwards and crushed him, prompting the great champion's retirement. Scobie became new trainer Richards' stable jockey, with great success.

During the sixties Scobie and Lester Piggott established a fascinating rivalry – with the contrast between Scobie's easy ability to do the weight and Lester's battle with the scales, together with Lester's rushing round the country for winners against Scobie's chauffeur-driven Rolls Royce trips with Richards – capturing the imagination of the racing public. On one occasion, poised to sweep past his older rival during a race, Piggott shouted to Breasley, 'Move over, Grandad!'

That Roller – SB53 – protected Scobie from the one thing he

disliked intently about England – the climate. But it aggravated his employer Gordon Richards once, recalled writer Lorin Knight. 'On arrival (at Richards' stable) chauffeur Bruce would open Scobie's door, remove the comfortable slippers worn throughout the journey and carefully fit warm jodhpur boots on to Scobie's feet.

'One March morning after this Cinderella-like ritual had taken place and Scobie, anointed with a liberal amount of his favourite aftershave, had joined Sir Gordon in the middle of the yard, the big chestnut colt who had stood patiently waiting to be mounted, took one look at his intended rider, sniffed the air, rolled his eyes and started towards him on his hind legs.

'Sir Gordon, blunt Shropshireman that he could be, said "You might as well get back in the car and go back home Scobie – you smell too pretty to ride today".'

Scobie won the 1958 Arc on Ballymoss, trained by Vincent O'Brien, perhaps the best horse he rode, on a muddy, swampy surface and took his second Derby with a masterful ride on Charlottown in 1966, moving off the rails, going wide, then coming back to the inside to get the better of Pretendre by a neck. He was champion jockey in 1957 with 173 winners, becoming the first Aussie to claim the title since Frank Wootton in 1912; in 1961 with 171; 1962, 179; and retained it in 1963. He was also runner-up five times.

When Scobie clocked up 1000 European winners he was weighed against his own weight in Australian sultanas, which were then distributed to children's hospitals! After making it to 2000 British winners he received a double magnum of champagne – which he kept for himself.

The 1963 title was a titanic battle with Piggott – on the final day of the season, Breasley led by 176 to 174 and both had four mounts at Manchester. Scobie drew a blank and Piggott pegged the gap back to one, but the Aussie took the honours by the minimum margin.

During that season, Breasley's victories on seven-year-old Trelawny in the Ascot Stakes and Queen Alexandra Stakes at Royal Ascot and in the Goodwood Stakes were highlights of the entire campaign. Trelawny was one of the most popular horses in training (with George Todd at Manton), who had once faced being put down after breaking a bone only to be saved by trainer and horse doctor, Syd Mercer, who nursed him back to health.

Having retired at the end of 1968 with 2161 winners (and 3251 worldwide) from 9716 rides to his credit, the last of which was Sentier in the Horris Hill at Newbury in October, Scobie set up as a trainer at South Hatch, where he had horses from Lady Beaverbrook, Sir Michael Sobell, Sir Arnold Weinstock and Mr A.J. Kennedy.

He won the Irish Sweeps Derby with Steel Pulse in 1972, then moved in the seventies to Chantilly – partly as a protest against the imposition of VAT on racing – to train for his multi-millionaire patron Ravi Tikkoo, Kashmir-born oil tanker magnate owner of Steel Pulse.

After their Java Rajah was disqualified at Longchamps in 1976, following a positive dope test for caffeine, Tikkoo believed that Breasley and he had been harshly treated by French racing officials, and moved his string to New York's Belmont Park, vowing never to return until he and Scobie were officially cleared of suspicion. Breasley had moved home to the Bahamas and commuted from there to his Belmont Park stables, occasionally visiting England to go racing with sporting pals like Test cricketer Keith Miller and old golfer friend Norman von Nida.

He returned to train at Epsom for the 1979 season, but left again within a year and trained in Barbados where his home was called Lor-Zon-Kel (after daughter Loretta and grand-daughters Zonda and Kelly). He won the local big race, the Cockspur Cup on four occasions.

Scobie died, aged 92, in December 2006.

BROWNIE CARSLAKE
Man of the world

Born in Caulfield, Australia in 1887 (some sources say 1886), the ashes of top jockey Bernard 'Brownie' Carslake were scattered over the Rowley Mile course at Newmarket at the point where he used to launch his famous race-winning charges, when his life ended in 1946.

By this time Carslake, the son of a trainer, had enjoyed a

worldwide career which encompassed numerous dramatic episodes. A skilful judge of pace, Carslake, who was a useful cricketer, and was winning at bush meetings by the age of 12, (including once winning three races in two days on the same horse!) was one of the first Aussie jockeys to come to Britain, arriving in 1906 with the experience of rides in three Melbourne Cups behind him.

He could hardly have had a more appropriately named first winner when he partnered The Swagman to victory at Birmingham.

Brownie (the nickname referred to his sallow complexion, blamed on his diet of, in his own words, 'a cup of tea and hope') had itchy feet and was soon riding in India and on the continent, in Romania, Austria and Hungary, twice becoming Austro-Hungarian champion, in 1912 with 92 winners, and again in 1914. He was in Austria when the hostilities broke out, and was interned by the Germans, but escaped to Romania, disguised as a railway engine fireman. Once there he rode a considerable number of winners over the next year or two, before heading off to Russia where he managed to secure a retainer with a prominent owner and became champion jockey in 1916.

When the revolution broke out in Russia, Carslake had to make himself scarce again and, 'overcoming many difficulties' according to racing writer John Fairfax-Blakeborough in 1931, found himself back in England, assuming that he would be a well off man thanks to the stash of roubles he smuggled out with him – which turned out to be worthless!

However, falling back on his innate ability, he soon made an impression with his talent and his eye-catching late bursts to win races, which would bring cheering spectators to their feet. He won the 1918 1000 Guineas on Lord Derby's Ferry, trained by the influential George Lambton. He won the St Leger in 1919 on Lord Derby's Keysoe and again in 1924 on the Aga Khan's Salmon Trout – being presented with a gold casket in honour of the latter victory, which was not without its controversies.

Prior to the race, in which the colt was entitled on all known form to hold a favourite's chance, his odds began to lengthen, leading to rumours that Carslake was plotting to get the horse beaten. These possibly emanated from an occasion on which, suggested one report, Carslake had enjoyed one or two glasses of mother's ruin (gin) and told the assembled party, which included a couple of well connected bookmakers, that he felt Salmon Trout, at that stage a 4/1 shot, would not stay. The horse's odds began to drift shortly after that, hitting double figures at one point. The Stewards heard the rumours and warned Carlsake in advance that they would be 'watching his riding in the St Leger with particularly close attention.' Salmon Trout, a 6/1 chance, lay well out of his ground, as was Brownie's trademark style, and was still well out of contention with two furlongs to run. Brownie finally launched his effort with one to run and picked up leader Santorb with just a hundred yards remaining to land a stunningly timed victory.

Unusually for those days, Carslake gave a detailed description of the race to the *Sporting Chronicle*, which makes for fascinating reading:

> I had my orders of course, and I made up my mind to be with Polyphontes in the early stages. When we settled down, the last three were Sansovino on the rails, Polyphontes in the middle, while I was on the outside. The others were all streaming away ahead, but I had my policy mapped out, and I meant to stick to it.
>
> When we got to the top corner, Sansovino began to move up a bit, and I saw Polyphontes also go up to take his place. I let him go and made no attempt to follow. There is a long run-in, I said to myself, and Polyphontes will want a lot of reserve if he is to last it out, so I stayed where I was. It was not until seven furlongs from home that I improved my position, and I was able to do this while still keeping a firm grip on my horse.
>
> I was moving up on the outside, but there was some bunching at the turn, and all of them swung wide. I pulled to the inside, and got a clear run in the straight. I must have been ten lengths behind at that time, and I could see Polyphontes and Santorb having a fight.
>
> For a time I let them get on with it, and not until a furlong and a half from home did I make a move. The horse answered at once, as I knew he would, and though I only got up in the last hundred yards I never had an uneasy moment in the last half mile. The fact that I was

a clear winner showed how the horse was travelling at the finish.

Salmon Trout never managed to win again.

The 1920 2000 Guineas fell to Brownie on Tetratema and in 1922 he claimed the 1000 Guineas on Silver Urn.

Carslake was stable jockey to Atty Persse in 1923/24 and first jockey to the Aga Khan in 1925. However, by 1928 his constant battle with his weight began to prove too much for him, and he told a racing paper of the day, the *Pink 'Un*, 'I never had such hard work in my life as in some recent wins over long distances, and felt like flopping out after wasting too hard and eating so little.' He added that he 'never took intoxicants' during the racing season, and that 'I can do all my drinking in the winter and even then, what I buy wouldn't purchase a fashionable yearling.'

A huge dinner took place at the Carlton Hotel on 17 November 1928, to mark his retirement, attended by a veritable 'who's who' of the great and good of the turf, at which he was presented with a silver-gilt cup.

A week later he was a trainer, setting up near Salisbury with 18 horses, from which he managed seven victories.

A year later, though, the lure of the saddle called him back as he believed that he had steadied his weight and could comfortably do 8st 5lbs (52kg). Once again he scored on an appropriately named first winner back – this time Pegasus at Liverpool in March 1930. He eventually had 230 mounts during 1930, for 34 winners, and 56 from 372 in 1931. He won the 1934 Oaks on Lord Durham's Light Brocade and in 1938 hit the Classic heights for the final time when winning the St Leger on Scottish Union.

In April 1940, Brownie rode Ipswich to his usual narrow winning victory at Alexandra Park, getting home by a short head, only to collapse after the race in the weighing room. He was diagnosed with serious heart disease and forced to retire, but died shortly after.

Anyone wishing to check out Brownie's appearance will be interested to know that the National Gallery holds a number of images of him, in and out of silks, which can be found at www.npg.org.uk.

STEVE CAUTHEN
Kentucky Kid

How appropriate is it that your thousandth winner should be called Thousandfold – and how many coincidence punters must have cleaned up as a result! Popular American jockey, Steve 'Kentucky Kid' Cauthen achieved that feat at Doncaster on 15 September 1979 – making the young Yank even more popular in the process. Steve was only 19 years old at the time, having been born on 1 May 1960 in Walton, Kentucky, the son of a trainer and a farrier.

At the age of five he would sit on a bale of hay in the family barn, hunched low, imagining himself riding a winner. He was already familiar with racecourses where he would accompany his parents as they went about their own racing-related careers.

He finished last – some reports say 10th of 11 runners – on 136/1 outsider, King of Swat in his first public ride at Churchill Downs (some say River Downs) on 12 May 1976, but that was not something he was going to make a habit of, and less than a week later he had his first winner when he booted Red Pipe to victory, part of a hat trick which signalled his arrival.

After that he didn't hang about, to put it mildly, and in 1977 ('17, with a 12-year-old's face' wrote one reporter) he scored an amazing 487 victories, to obliterate the previous record of 299. Three times he rode six winners in a single day at Aqueduct and he had to recover from a broken wrist and three broken fingers, suffered when he fell from Bay Streak at Belmont Park in May.

In only his second year of riding he became the first jockey ever to win $6 million in a single season when he rode another appropriately named filly, Little Happiness, at Aqueduct that December. He then acquired more nicknames, '$6m Man' and 'Stevie Wonder' – both well deserved.

Honours were strewn before him – the Eclipse Award for Outstanding Apprentice; Eclipse Award for Outstanding US Jockey;

ABC's Wide World of Sports Athlete of the Year, and *Sports Illustrated*'s Sportsman of the Year, as he even took racing into the sporting mainstream – in the process defeating homer-hitting baseball star, Reggie Jackson, whose World Series-winning displays for the Yankees might have been expected to see off all rivals, let alone a racing guy.

1978 saw him become the 10th, and youngest, jockey to win the US Triple Crown, doing so on Affirmed, in a titanic series of races for the Kentucky Derby, Preakness Stakes and the Belmont, in each of which they had to repel the determined challenge of Jorge Velasquez and Alydar.

After this feat, Affirmed's trainer, Laz Barrera, paid tribute to his 18-year-old rider – 'Steve Cauthen is no 18-year-old. He's an old man. Sometimes he makes me believe in reincarnation. Maybe he had another life where he was a leading rider for 50 years.'

What Barrera may have been unaware of at the time, was Cauthen's pre-Derby preparations. 'I don't think my Dad realised how hard it was to get a room. We ended up in one room. It had two beds and there were five of us, so someone had to sleep on the floor. The night before the Derby, I did it. I didn't want to be bothered by anybody. I slept like a log.'

By 1979, now moving out of his teens and beginning to fill out somewhat, (between 1978 and 1981 he grew by 4 inches (10cm)) he suffered a 110 race losing streak at Santa Anita, then moved to England where he'd be able to ride at slightly higher weights, ('My natural weight is 10 stone (63kg), but I was trying to ride at 8st 7lbs (52kg)') to ride for Robert Sangster. And he made an instant impact when he rode Marquee Universal to victory in the glamorously titled Grand Foods Handicap at Salisbury on 7 April – the Kid had arrived.

He would become British champion jockey on three occasions, winning 10 Classics in the process and riding mainly for the stables of Barry Hills and Henry Cecil. 'When I first saw Goodwood, it freaked me out' confessed Cauthen, 'It took me maybe three years to get on level terms with all these guys who had been riding in Britain all their lives. By the time I left, I hope I added my own legacy to British racing.'

He certainly worked out how to ride at Bath, and on 26 June 1982 he was third and fourth in two of the seven races – winning the other five at accumulative odds of 11,324/1.

Despite continuous success the fresh-faced Cauthen maintained his equilibrium and popularity and in 1984 he won the George Woolf Memorial Jockey Award for the rider whose career and personal conduct 'exemplifies the very best example of participants in the sport of thoroughbred racing.'

The same year he became British champ for the first time, completing a transatlantic double not achieved since Danny Maher managed it in 1908.

Slip Anchor in the 1985 renewal, was his first of two Derby winners – Reference Point was the other, two years later. Both of them were remarkable displays of perfectly judged front-running.

In 1985, despite denying that he was an alcoholic, it was reported that he had entered an alcohol dependency programme in the States. Some years later, Cauthen revealed to *Sports Illustrated*, 'I'd have a drink not to think about going all night without eating. Eventually I got tired and depressed.'

In 1988 he broke his neck and sustained concussion when thrown by filly, Preziosa at Goodwood in August, but he came back as effective as ever, after missing the remainder of the campaign.

Riding Mountain Kingdom in the Ormonde Stakes at Chester in May 1989, Cauthen suddenly felt his nearest rival snapping at his heels – literally. Lazaz had just taken a bite at his riding boot as they raced up the home straight.

He had a run-in with the racing authorities when, in May 1990, despite having already weighed out, he refused to ride three-year-old Nicholas Payne at Leicester – declaring 'I did it because it was in my best interests, and I would do the same again'. He was fined £1000 for 'bringing racing into disrepute.'

When Knifebox won at Chester in October 1991, Steve was completing his 10th consecutive British century.

Cauthen married Kentuckian law student, Amy Rothfuss, in Cincinnati in 1992 and together they raised a family of three daughters, (Katelyn, Karlie and Kelsie) at their spacious breeding farm, Dreamfields, confirming his love of fillies. He won the Oaks three times and completed the Guineas-Oaks-St Leger treble on filly, Oh So Sharp.

The weight issue was a permanent problem, which eventually persuaded him to call it a day – 'When I was riding I could fit my fingers around my legs and wrap 'em over, that's how skinny I was. But

I had to starve muscle off my body to get my weight down. In the end, I was worried that physically I could damage myself long-term. At times I got depressed, because that's what it does to you. Whether you're purging yourself by not eating, sitting in a sauna for six hours a day, or taking laxatives – all that crap is part of being a jockey. Eventually I said, "You've done everything, now it's time to live a life."'

Cauthen returned to Kentucky when his riding career finished, with 2794 winners from 14,630 rides, and a winning percentage of 19.1 to his credit in 1993. It was reported at the time that negotiations for his 1993 retainer with Sheikh Mohammed had collapsed, and he said, 'I could retire'. He did. He had won the Kentucky, Epsom, Irish, French and Italian Derbys along the way.

Part of the reason for his outstanding career may have been his ability to control his mind on the big occasions – 'I don't psyche myself up. I psyche myself down' he said, 'I think clearer when I'm not psyched up.'

He knew precisely what he wanted to do when he quit – 'The whole time I was riding, people may have thought I was sitting around doing nothing out of the saddle' he told the *Independent*'s Nick Townsend, 'In fact, I was studying breeding and trying to learn about conformation, those important factors about what made a good racehorse. I tried to look at horses and maybe a little bit into their soul.' He added, 'My dad told me a long time ago, "if you find something that you love, you'll never have to work another day in your life. And I love what I do".'

Asked once, which of the 'interesting people' he met during his career most stood out for him, he answered, 'The Queen Mother. I became friends with her through Dick Francis. She was an amazing person who led an amazing life. She had such an effect on so many people by the way she led her life. She talked to common people like myself and put them at ease and made them feel important.' Cauthen's own riding heroes were jockeys Jerry Bailey, Edgar Prado, Corey Nakatani, Garrett Gomez and Kent Desormeaux.

On his return to the States, he became an executive at Turfway Park racecourse, the nearest track of any size to his hometown. He also concentrated on becoming as good a golfer as he could – 'He has to have a challenge, and golf has provided it' confirmed Amy.

In 1994 he was inducted into the National Museum of Racing and Hall of Fame.

BART CUMMINGS

No flies on him

Days before his 81st birthday, in 2008, Bart Cummings once again did what he had been doing periodically since 1965 – sent out a horse to win Australia's greatest race, the race which as near as dammit genuinely does stop a nation, the Melbourne Cup.

His horse, Viewed, a 45/1 shot, held off Luca Cumani's Bauer on the line, condemning the Italian handler to a second successive frustration for finishing runner-up, but leaving him and race fans worldwide lost in admiration for the skills of the charismatic octogenarian. Cumani said sportingly, 'Well, Bart Cummings is a genius.' Fellow Aussie handler, John Sadler remarked: 'I say hello to Bart in the mornings – from now on I'll genuflect.' Even Irish racing great, Aidan O'Brien admitted, 'Bart Cummings – he's a special man, isn't he?'

The Cummings' philosophy is perhaps best summed up in his comment that 'Racehorses are bought to win races, not beauty contests – an ounce of good breeding is worth all the conformation in the world' sentiments he first uttered when his pigeon-toed, knock-kneed Galilee won the Melbourne Cup.

What's more, after Viewed's victory, he quickly indicated that he had no plans to remove his considerable presence from the racing world – 'I still love what I do, and I've done okay over the years – you're a long time retired, and anyway, I'd get bored.' Almost lost in the excitement of his 2008 triumph was the fact that Bart's own son, Anthony, saddled the 16th horse home in the race, Red Lord, and said of his old man, 'He just keeps doing it and it certainly gives you something to take aim at.'

Bart was only 23 when he led Comic Court, an inmate of his father of Irish descent, Jim's stables, round the parade ring before the horse went on to win the 1950 Melbourne Cup. It seemed unlikely at that time that he would follow in his father's footsteps as he had discovered that he was allergic to hay! But the die was cast: 'I will never forget the excitement of that win. It fired my imagination to such an extent that I knew there and then I would never be satisfied until I trained a Melbourne Cup winner.'

Bart gives much of the credit for his career to his father: 'Dad got to know all about the endurance of horses from tough days in the bush in South Australia and the Northern Territory. All the experience the old bloke gathered was passed on to me. He was as good as anyone I have ever seen in setting a horse for just one race – and winning it.'

Born in November 1927, James Batholomew Cummings first held a licence in 1953, since when he – up to Melbourne Cup day 2008 – accumulated 250 Group One wins, some 700 stakes race wins, and handled nine Aussie horses of the year.

In 1958 Bart won his first Group One race when Stormy Passage landed the South Australian Jockey Club Derby.

He had to overcome a 1961 setback when he was suspended for a year following an inquiry into the running of his Cilldara who, wearing the still novel for the times blinkers, won a Morphetville Handicap, having finished stone last, unblinkered, a week earlier at Gawler. He lost some owners as a result of the suspension, but by 1968 he was established in his Flemington, Melbourne stables, now known as Saintly Place. He also operates out of stables at Sydney's Randwick, known as Leilani Lodge.

Light Fingers got him off the mark in 1965's Melbourne Cup and, just to prove it was no fluke, he won it again in 1966 with Galileee – and again in 1967 with Red Handed. Oh yes, he'd also been responsible for the runners-up in 1965 and 1966! His 1969 Melbourne Cup favourite, Big Philou, which had already won the Caulfield Cup, was drugged with a large dose of a purgative called Danthron on the night before the race and had to be scratched just 39 minutes before the race was due to start. A $5000 reward was never claimed.

Lest anyone regard him as a specialist with long distance handicappers, he was also winning Group One sprints with the likes of Anna Rose, and Group One two-year-old races like the Golden Slipper Stakes with Storm Queen and others. Cummings has always been a student of bloodlines and their influence on breeding, as well as the importance of horse feeds – 'breeding is half in the feeding' he has said.

Dayana, a four time Derby winner, was his first Champion Racehorse of the Year in 1972/73.

By 1974 he'd become the first trainer in the Commonwealth to train the winners of one million dollars in prize money in a year. In 1988 he was the first to six million. He also won the Melbourne Cup in that year with Think Big – a horse Cummings sold to owner Dato Tan after the two were introduced whilst soaking up the sun around a motel swimming pool. Think Big's triumph deprived what many believed to have been his best hope Leilani of the race and she could only manage second. Some reports suggested that Cummings had advised stable connections to back the mare and that afterwards, according to Cup historian, Maurice Cavanough, he 'had more the look of a mourner than a man who had just achieved a stupendous training feat.' He murmured 'I beat myself.' Think Big would win the race again 12 months later.

After Think Big won for the first time, Cummings could have been forgiven for thinking 'Life's a beach' when he was accused of denuding the local West Beach near his Glenelg stables of 12 metres (39ft) of its sand by working his horses there. The local Trust declared that they would implement a by-law to prohibit him from using the sands, whereupon Cummings promised that if they did he would up and leave – costing the area 30 jobs. He was given a six months stay of execution by the Coast Protection Board, later extended to a year, then another, then another until eventually he did quit the area in 1985.

Cummings explained his recipe for training a Melbourne Cup winner in 1976 – 'It is essential that the groundwork is thorough as a horse generally has to be in training for almost five months leading up to Cup day. It is the muscling up and conditioning that a horse receives in the preparation better than another who has been rushed to get ready for a campaign.'

The Order of Australia was bestowed on him in 1982 for services to the racing industry and his promotion of the sport to the public. 1989/90 saw him win the trainers' premiership in three different states – New South Wales, Victoria and South Australia – another first.

Having again won the Cup in 1991 with Let's Elope, Cummings was asked about the chances of the Brits ever winning the great event and answered, 'Jeez, we gave those Poms a 200 year start. Now we are 100 years ahead of them.'

The nineties saw Cummings facing financial problems which at one stage threatened to bankrupt him, but he managed to come through and remain in business.

He entered the Sport Australia Hall of Fame in 1991 and was an inaugural inductee into the Racing Hall of Fame in 2001, a year after he had carried the 2000 Olympic torch down the Flemington straight prior to the Sydney Olympics.

When the Australian Racing Museum moved to Melbourne in 2004 – and it is well worth a visit, I can tell you from personal experience – Bart's then 11 Melbourne Cup trophies went on display there. His wife, Valmae, had been the source of the original suggestion that trainers should receive miniature replicas of the owners' trophies. Also in 2004 Bart became the first trainer presented with a Lifetime Membership by the Victoria Racing Club, which also renamed a Melbourne Cup qualifying race, previously known as 'The Banjo Paterson' race after another legendary figure of the Oz turf, 'The Bart Cummings'.

Cummings' iconic status in Australia was demonstrated in 2007 when he was honoured by appearing on a postage stamp as part of a series recognising 'Australian Legends'. The Bart Cummings Medal was introduced by Racing NSW in 2008, to be awarded for 'consistent, outstanding performances amongst jockeys and trainers at NSW metropolitan race meetings throughout the racing season.'

Cummings, born and raised in Adelaide, is one of that rare breed, the one-off. Consider what he told the (English) inspector who came to visit his stables and concluded that it contained 'far too many flies'. 'Well' pondered Cummings, 'How many am I allowed?'

SHERGAR
Lost legend

Shergar's name lives on today in racing's only annual team event, the Shergar Cup. It is now over quarter of a century since the Aga Khan-owned and bred, Sir Michael Stoute-trained bay colt with the large white blaze on his head devastated the opposition in the 1981 Derby with a stunning 10 length victory. His handler was hopeful of success – 'I was tense before the race, though I was expecting him to win.' Stoute's tension dissipated as Shergar drew clear of the field. BBC radio commentator Peter Bromley declared 'You'll need a telescope to see the rest.' Great sportswriter, Simon Barnes, wrote of the 'inconceivable brilliance' of the victory. Then up and coming rider, the 19-year-old Walter Swinburn junior, who partnered Shergar, later said, 'He was just something else – a truly great horse'. Few have ever disagreed with that assessment.

Tens of thousands of punters celebrated the victory – not least those who had followed the advice of respected *Guardian* racing writer, Richard Baerlein, who, after Shergar had won his own paper's Classic Trial, wrote of the then 12/1 Derby prospect, 'Now is the time to bet like men!' He took his own advice – and later named his own house Shergar.

The partnership of Shergar and Swinburn had earlier won the Chester Vase in such an impressive manner that bookies rushed for cover, slashing their ante-post Derby quotes to odds-on.

Having landed the Epsom version, Shergar, the 1/3 favourite, was ridden by Lester Piggott (Swinburn was suspended) in the Irish equivalent and cantered to a four length win, looking as untroubled as Usain Bolt when he won the Olympic 100 and 200 metre Golds in 2008. Next up was the King George VI and Queen Elizabeth Diamond Stakes – in which Ascot racegoers thrilled to another four length triumph.

But the run of success stuttered to a halt when he failed to add the St Leger to his list of victories, starting at 4/9, but finishing fourth of eight behind 28/1 shot, Cut Above, who he'd beaten easily in the Irish Derby.

Rock star Steve Harley, of Cockney Rebel fame was a Shergar fan, and he was devastated by this defeat of his equine hero – to the extent that he completely overlooked the fact that he had won £5600 from the £200 he had staked on Cut Above 'just in case.' He had reportedly won enough on Shergar's Derby win to buy a top of the range BMW with his profit. He had been performing that afternoon in Germany, but had cut short his show in order to watch the Epsom race.

Opinions differ as to whether Shergar didn't stay the trip, or that his earlier exertions had caught up with him. His lad, Dickie McCabe believed, 'When he walked round afterwards, I think he felt he had let everyone down.' Trainer Michael Stoute later considered: 'I should have taken Shergar out as the ground was too soft for him'. *Timeform* had little doubt as to what happened – 'we find it astonishing that anyone could be adamant after his St Leger performance that he was capable of staying a mile and three quarters.'

Now the Aga Khan decided to sell shares in the horse as he went off to stand at stud, valued at £10 million. On 8 February 1983, Shergar was kidnapped from his County Kildare stud. A masked gang swooped to steal the horse. Shergar's vet Stan Cosgrove later explained how he felt on visiting the horse's empty box afterwards – 'It was like going into someone's bedroom a week after they've died. You have just been to the funeral and you come back to look at their empty bedroom. It's a terrible feeling, believe me.' Efforts to find the missing stallion were hindered by the fact that there were horse sales on in Ireland at the time, so horse boxes were milling about all over the road system.

The whole episode became even more bizarre as the gang apparently contacted Derek 'Tommo' Thompson, who still dines out on the story of 'one of the strangest weeks of my life' to this day, to try to arrange a ransom payment of £2 million.

Tommo was woken by a reporter from the Press Association news agency at 1.45am to be told that he was one of three journalists nominated by the alleged kidnappers of Shergar to act as intermediaries. The other two were Lord Oaksey and the *Sun*'s Peter Camplin. Tommo set off for the Europa Hotel in Belfast where he was told he would hear from the kidnappers. There, he took a call from a man giving his name as 'Arkle' and claiming 'We have got Shergar.' He was given another number – of a trainer – to call, and he then set off for the trainer's stables, 30 miles (48km) outside Belfast. The three of them drove to meet up with trainer Jeremy Maxwell, who had already taken a call from 'Arkle' asking for a ransom of £40,000 – not the £2m which had been mentioned earlier.

He now changed his code name to that of another, far less well known horse, 'Ekbalco'. When Ekbalco rang again he told Thompson he wanted his ransom demand made public. Tommo tried to ring the Aga Khan and spoke to one of his employees who 'thought everything we were doing was a hoax.' However, Tommo's people later took a call from someone who 'sounded exactly the same as the Aga' who said he would pay the amount being asked. However, Tommo and his team now decided that the Aga's call was a hoax, and then received another call from Ekbalco who now asked for £1000 for a picture of Shergar, as 'a goodwill gesture'. Even Tommo must have begun to fear he was being set up at this point.

Later that evening Ekbalco rang again threatening 'if you don't give us the money by 9am we'll shoot him.' That morning came the call Tommo had been 'dreading' – 'This is Arkle, the horse has had an accident and we've put him down.'

That was the end of Tommo's involvement and it left him wondering 'Was it a hoax call? Was it a real call?' but, perhaps relieved that 'I had never been involved in anything quite like that and I do not expect to be involved in anything like it again.'

Unbeknown to Tommo and his merry men, another journalist was also becoming involved in a convoluted process allegedly leading to Shergar. Irish-born radio broadcaster, Colin Turner, of Independent Radio News took an anonymous call after broadcasting a plea for information, which set him off into 'a bizarre and occasionally alarming series of adventures' so complicated that the full story filled a book, *In Search of Shergar* which he published in 1984, leading to the conclusion that 'Shergar's history cannot be written until he is found and until more people tell what they know'. Which didn't really tell us any more than we knew at the beginning.

The official Shergar kidnap investigation was headed up by Chief Superintendent James 'Spud' Murphy, whose trademark trilby was copied by many of the reporters covering the story. Murphy was happy to include psychics, clairvoyants and mediums in his investigations, who were not always treated with appropriate reverence by the media. He was once reported as telling reporters 'A clue – that is what we haven't got.'

Racing writer, Brough Scott feared a great blow had been dealt to the Irish bloodstock industry: 'What is the point of beautiful stud farms, marvellous limestone soil, understanding men and government tax concessions if horse-napping becomes a popular sport.' Fortunately, it didn't.

No genuine contact to the gang was ever apparently established by the police. A report commissioned by the Aga Khan concluded in 1984 that the horse was probably dead within a week of his abduction, killed by the gang who had originally hoped to raise money through him, but were lacking the expert know-how of stallion-care or bloodstock finances.

Up to time of writing no authenticated trace of Shergar has ever been found – despite many sensationalist claims and stories to the contrary. For example, in January 1989 the *Psychic News* 'revealed', uselessly, that American 'seer' Jeane Dixon was claiming that Shergar 'is alive and well and has been on English soil.' Then, in March 1991, under a banner headline 'Shergar Is Alive', the *Sun* reported that 'kidnapped wonder horse Shergar is alive and happily grazing in a field in the Channel Islands.'

Life-serving prisoner with IRA links, Sean O'Callaghan was reported by the *Guardian* to have said that 'Shergar was destroyed within hours of being abducted. The body was buried in a bog at Aughnasheelin near Ballinamore.' In the same 1994 article, vet, Stan Cosgrove, revealed that he once handed over a substantial amount of money in the hope of discovering the horse's whereabouts – 'I realised then, when that £80,000 disappeared, that the horse was dead.'

Shergar disappeared leaving just one crop of offspring to represent his genes. Authaal went through the ring for 325,000 Irish guineas as a foal and was later bought on behalf of Sheikh Mohammed for a European yearling record price of 3.1 million Irish guineas.

In 1999 Shergar was named as the 18th best Horse of the Century in the prestigious *A Century of Champions* book by John Randall and Tony Morris, and described as having produced 'the best Derby-winning performance of the post-war era.' The 1999 Hollywood movie, *Shergar*, starring Mickey Rourke never threatened to win an Oscar.

In January 2008 the *Sunday Telegraph* claimed to have discovered 'The Truth about Shergar Kidnapping.' An article by Chief Reporter Andrew Alderson linked the IRA to the kidnap and reported, 'The *Sunday Telegraph* has been told that four days after Shergar was seized . . . the Army Council (the Provisional IRA ruling body) realised their equine property was worthless, and told the gang to release the horse.' But, continued the story, the gang did no such thing and instead killed the horse with a machine gun. The story did not pinpoint the location of the horse's remains.

The tragic Shergar tale inspired a rare and moving poetic tribute in 2008 when former apprentice jockey, Jim Anderson, who has generously permitted me to reproduce it here, published an anthology of his poetry, entitled *Shergar & Other Friends*, (SportsBooks Ltd) which opened with 'Shergar':

> So that was it old friend. So much for men.
> The crowns and laurels count for nothing now.
> And those who came like sneak-thieves in the night,
> Have Cain's eternal mark upon their brow.
>
> They did their master's bidding; made their name;
> Not as you did in battle's glorious fire.
> No courage, spirit, heart or talent asked.
> Just worthless souls which cheaply were for hire.

TOD SLOAN
Out on his tod

It is a rare jockey whose name is still used in everyday conversation a hundred years after his prime. But American James Forman Sloan (1874–1933) whose nickname was 'Tod' was immortalised by the cockney rhyming slang 'on your/his/her tod sloan' meaning to be alone, eventually shortened to 'on your tod'.

Sloan was a controversial figure, too. He is credited with being the man who started the 'monkey up a stick', low crouching style of riding when the accepted style of the day was far more upright. In actual fact, the black jockeys on the American scene had already been riding in such a way when then journeyman rider Sloan adapted the style himself after a horse bolted with him one day and he pulled his knees up and crouched over the runaway's neck in order to take a tighter hold on him. The horse responded and Sloan realised that he could develop this way of riding to give him an advantage in races.

A natural horseman, he also spoke to his mounts, and he soon became one of America's leading jockeys, although as biographer

John Dizikes remarked, 'He was involved in a number of questionable races'. He was linked with big time gambler of the day, George 'Pittsburgh Phil' Smith with whom he was believed to have an arrangement which enriched him by $400 every time he rode a winner – the benefit to Smith being that he would always know he had Sloan riding for rather than against him when his cash was down.

Sloan came to England in 1897 to ride US owner James Keene's St Cloud II in the Cesarewitch and Cambridgeshire – finishing a narrow runner-up in the latter. When English jockeys saw Sloan's style he was initially ridiculed, but when he extended his stay and rode 21 winners from 48 outings they soon took him seriously, and many began to copy him, with Classic winning Fred Rickaby declaring that if he were an owner he'd want Sloan riding for him.

However, despite his considerable ability, Sloan was a quirky and not always entirely honest character. He once lay down in the parade ring at Kempton Park and announced that he was too tired to ride in the next race, only changing his mind when he saw how fit the horse, one of top trainer the Hon George Lambton's, looked, whereupon he jumped up and rode the horse to win. Lambton said of Sloan that 'he was a genius on a horse; off one, erratic and foolish. He threw away a career full of the greatest promise.'

Sloan liked to live the high life. He dressed flamboyantly, smoked huge cigars, womanised and mixed with disreputable American betting men, flouting the rules by joining in the massive gambles they launched.

He won his first and only Classic race on Sibola in the 1899 1000 Guineas. Sloan was convinced that he would win the 1900 Cambridgeshire on Codoman and he and his unscrupulous partners pulled every stroke they could manage to ensure victory, only for the gamble to go wrong when J. Thompson on Berrill beat Sloan into second place. Sloan hurled mouthfuls of abuse at Thompson as they rode back, but was overheard by stewards and an official inquiry was launched at which Sloan pleaded ignorance of the rules when accused of standing to win £66,000 on his mount.

Sloan was officially reprimanded and it was made clear that his licence would not be renewed for 1901.

Aged just 26 his English career was over. He appealed for the return of his licence annually for 15 years without success. In total he rode in 801 races, winning 254 of them – an impressive 31.7 winning percentage.

Although a wealthy man when he was banned, he then began to live beyond his means despite having no real source of income.

Ernest Hemingway wrote a short story, 'My Old Man', about Sloan who was also the subject of George M. Cohan's musical, *Little Johnny Jones*.

Sloan was deported in 1915 for running a gaming house and returned to the States, working at the racetrack at Tijuana, Mexico, where he tipped legendary writer Damon Runyan a loser, ending up as a barman in Los Angeles and dying in a charity ward of that city's Sylvan Lodge Hospital on 21 December 1933 of cirrhosis of the liver – on his tod.

His biographer of 2000, John Dizikes, wrote of him, 'Sadly, but commonly, while he couldn't repeat his successes, he continually repeated his mistakes. Still he had also done uncommon things, things remembered a century later; and as the title of his memoirs (*Tod Sloan by Himself*) proudly proclaimed in its double meaning, he had done them, a little man taking on the world, by himself.'

CHARLIE WHITTINGHAM
Bald Eagle

Few trainers ever endear themselves to racing folk sufficiently to be endowed with a widely used, affectionate nickname. US great, Charlie 'Bald Eagle' Whittingham was not only extremely successful, but also extremely popular – not merely for his tremendous sense of humour and approach to life. 'Fast horses and beautiful women are the two things I love best' he said. One American writer said of him, 'He would stare at his horses like he could peer into their souls.'

When the veteran handler died in Pasadena in April 1999, just a week after his 86th birthday, there was an outpouring of feeling seldom equalled amongst racing's hard-bitten population. 'He was tall and lanky and as bald as a bridle, and he strode through the barns and winner's circles of throughbred racing with other giants like Horatio Luro and Woody Stephens for parts of seven decades' said writer Joseph Duro.

Charlie was born in San Diego on 13 April 1913, son of a Yorkshire-born father and Irish mother – learning his trade walking horses and cleaning stables at the Caliente track in Tijuana, Mexico as a teenager during the Depression.

He had first taken out a trainer's licence in 1934 – he was there when the Santa Anita racetrack opened on Christmas Day of that year – and his career hit its stride when in 1940 he met Horatio Luro, (amazingly, they were introduced to each other by Bing Crosby) an elegant, urbane horseman from Argentina who would saddle a good number of champions. The pair hit it off and teamed up, (Luro was the boss, Charlie the apprentice) bringing over horses from Argentina and touring the States with a number of horses. The War intervened at a time when he was working at the Longacres track.

He would become a Marine, marrying Peggy Boone whilst still serving in 1944, but continued his racing career with her blessing after the War. During the conflict he had seen action in the Pacific, contracting malaria in the process – the cause of his hair loss, which resulted in the famous nickname, bestowed by childhood pal Joe Hernandez, who became Santa Anita track announcer.

Luro and Whittingham evidently discovered the secret of how to enjoy a long and successful life, as Luro died in 1991 aged 90. Once asked what he had learned from Luro, Whittingham said, 'Patience. You've got to let the horse tell you when he's ready. Listen to anybody else and you're in trouble.'

Whittingham secured his big break when Liz Whitney Tippett hired him to work for her at her Llangollen Farm stable – from where in 1953 Porterhouse earned US top two-year-old colt honours. But it would be a long journey from Tijuana to becoming, aged 76, the oldest trainer ever to win the Kentucky Derby, doing so in 1989 with Sunday Silence – having also done it aged 73. Sunday Silence went on to beat Easy Goer in the Preakness but went down to the same rival by eight lengths in the final Triple Crown race, the Belmont Stakes. Whittingham was philosophical – 'I'm trying to feel bad. But they handed me this cheque for $1 million, the horse is fine and I plan on waking up tomorrow.' Sunday Silence went on to win the Breeders' Cup Classic.

Despite his success in the race he wasn't in thrall to it, believing, unlike many, that too many good horses were ruined by being aimed purely at the Triple Crown races. He'd taken two horses, Gone Fishin' and Divine Comedy, to the 1958 and 1960 Kentucky Derbys, talked into it against his better judgement by owner Liz Tippett. They ran eight and ninth – after which he vowed, 'I'd never take a horse to Churchill Downs again unless I thought I could win.'

When he acquired Ferdinand, he decided this was, at last, a horse ideal for the Kentucky Derby. In the hands of the great Bill Shoemaker, 18/1 shot Ferdinand picked off the 1986 field one by one as he came through from 16th to win by two lengths from British challenger Bold Arrangement. Whittingham, not represented in the race for many years, said, 'It took me 26 years to get here because I said I wouldn't come till we got a good horse. We've got one now.'

He dedicated his working life to horses, arriving at the stables before dawn every day and staying there until after dark – 'I get five hours' sleep a night – but I haven't had a headache in 73 years.'

In 1974 he was inducted into the sport's Hall of Fame, having already won the Eclipse Award as top trainer in 1971. He did it again in 1982 and 1989. Amongst the champions to emerge from his barns were Ferdinand, Sunday Silence, 1953 National champion, Porterhouse; Ack Ack, Horse of the Year in 1971; Cougar II in 1972; Estrapade,1986; Miss Alleged and Flawlessly. He won the 'national earnings' title seven times – from 1970–73; 1975; 1981/82. Over 20 of his stable's inmates had career earnings of over $1 million.

Amongst the best remembered and loved Charlie chat-lines were his comment on jockeys when asked whether he gave his riders a lot of pre-race instructions. He looked incredulously at his questioner, and asked, 'Have you ever seen the size of their hats?', following up the remark by insisting that 'they are incredible, because their hat size, shoe size and IQ are all the same number.' He had reasons to support his stance on jockey intelligence – recalling the time in the fifties when top rider Ralph Neves had lost on one of Charlie's fancied horses, telling the trainer after the race, 'This horse needs blinkers'. Charlie replied – 'Uh – he HAS blinkers.' 'Then take 'em off' responded Neves.

Charlie was never afraid to express his confidence in his horses. When a trainer once told him he thought he could beat one of

Charlie's runners, Whittingham advised him: 'Bring extra blankets'. The other trainer asked 'Does it get chilly, then?' whereupon Charlie answered 'No, because that horse is gonna go by you so fast, you're gonna catch cold!'

An incorrigible, lifelong joker, Charlie once applied to train in New York, listing his hair colour as 'brown'. When challenged, he explained, 'That's the way I remember it.'

Charlie, who spent most of his career on the West Coast, was a perfectionist in preparing his horses which he always said would be 99 per cent right the day before and 99 per cent after a race – but always 100 per cent on raceday itself.

Whittingam's son, Michael also became a trainer and inherited his father's barn at the course where he was most successful, Santa Anita. His last day at the races was, appropriately enough at Santa Anita shortly after enjoying a family party to mark his 86th birthday.

His death was announced to the crowd at Santa Anita – and it was marked by a perfectly observed silence. He was later honoured by the track, which erected a bust of Whittingham and his dog, Toby, in the paddock.

Charlie posted an estimated 2534 lifetime wins and his horses earned a total of $110,602,295.

Perhaps the incident which really summed up Whittingham's attitude to his horses was when the great Sunday Silence kicked out at him, catching and badly gashing his head. As people rushed to help stem the bleeding, Whittingham commented, 'I hope he hasn't hurt his foot.'

PAST THE POST

FRED ARCHER
19th century Lester?

'Fred Archer captured the public imagination as no other jockey had ever done' declared the authoritative *Biographical Encyclopaedia of British Flat Racing.*

As single minded as Lester Piggott and Tony McCoy and as charismatic as Frankie Dettori, it was front page news throughout the land when, not even 30 years of age, he shot himself on 8 November 1886 with a weapon he kept in his bedroom as a precaution against burglars.

Archer had ridden for just 17 years – and had been champion jockey for 13 of those, riding 2748 winners from fewer than 8100 mounts. 'Archer's up' became a greeting amongst London cabbies, to indicate their well-being.

Thousands lined the streets for his funeral on a cold, wet Friday, 12 November in Newmarket. 'The public dismay that greeted his suicide by all accounts must have been similar to the news of the sudden death of Princess Diana in 1997' said his great grandson Alex Tosetti in 2003.

The shrewd, driven Archer was, as would be Lester Piggott, believed to be extremely careful with his money, to the extent that he would frequently 'borrow' coins in order to weigh in at the correct weight, only for repayment to slip his mind. As a result, Archer acquired the nickname 'The Tinman' from the Victorian slang word for money – 'tin'.

He would bet on and against his own mounts, but was so honest that on several occasions he cost himself dear by beating his own chosen investments.

There was never any doubt that Archer would be a jockey as the son of jump jockey William was apprenticed at the age of 11 and rode in public for the first time in 1869, landing his first victory on Athol Daisy at Chesterfield on 28 September 1870, aged 13, weighing 4st 11lbs (67kg).

After Archer rode Sterling to win the Liverpool Autumn Cup in November 1873, grateful owner, Thomas Roughton, presented the jockey with a short-barrelled gun – the one he would kill himself with.

Archer achieved national prominence when he rode the unfancied Atlantic, owned by Lord Falmouth, to win the 1874 2000 Guineas. He went on to win 21 Classics, amongst them five Derbies. Archer, still just a 6st (84kg) teenager, won the 1874 jockey title, and never surrendered it until his death, his best year coming in 1885 when he rode 246 winners. However, unusually tall (5ft 10ins (1.78m) for a jockey, he began to put on weight and would suffer all sorts of agonies to take it off.

Natural ability was harnessed to a shrewd racing brain. He made it his business never to lose ground at the start – 'I've always got my horse ready to go but not pulling at him, and then when we do start I'm off at full speed at once' – and in a close finish, 'most sit back when they finish and I sit forward and you know, that may just catch the judge's eye.'

He became a superstar, attracting the attention of celebrities and even Royalty. He was applauded in theatres, trains were delayed if he was late and women buzzed around him. But the Hon George Lambton said of him: 'He was courted and flattered by every kind of man and woman, and early in life he became the idol of the public, and yet he never suffered from that disagreeable complaint, "swollen head".'

His relationship with owner Lord Falmouth and trainer Mathew Dawson proved all conquering with 12 of his Classic triumphs emerging from that source, although in the Derby, of the 13 Falmouth owned runners he partnered, only Silvio won.

Archer's Derby win on Bend Or in 1880 showed his character in all its determined glory. Despite having had his arm savaged by a horse which also knelt on the jockey, just over three weeks before the Derby, Archer had his arm strapped to a steel brace under his silks and rode a brilliant race to win the Derby, despite also having to fast continuously while he was out of action through the injury.

His favoured way of losing weight was to imbibe a dreadful purgative, known as Archer's Mixture, complemented by his lunch, consisting of a biscuit or slice of toast, warm castor oil and a tiny glass of champagne. Asked once if he would make the weight for a ride he said, 'I shall sit in my Turkish bath and no doubt elsewhere until it's time to go to the races.'

A public favourite, Archer courted controversy over his partnership with Dutch Oven, winner of nine races as a two-year-old in 1881, but slow to regain that form next season. She won the Yorkshire Oaks but two days later could only finish third, convincing Archer that she would not win the St Leger.

Archer, in an early example of a tactic Lester Piggott would later adopt, tried to desert 40/1 chance Dutch Oven to get up on the favourite, Geheimniss, trained by John Porter. Dawson refused to permit him to do so and Archer duly put in an inspired ride to force Dutch Oven over the line in front of Geheimniss.

Now rumours began to spread in the sporting papers of the day that Archer had pulled Dutch Oven last time out in order to push her odds out for the Leger. He wasn't over-worried about such stories, particularly when he collected a five figure sum from gamblers John Hammond and Arthur Cooper (believed to be Archer's go between with the bookies when he fancied a gamble) – who won £60,000 between them on the filly. Hammond received in return Archer's whip while Cooper was given his saddle.

In 1883 Archer was beaten on Lord Falmouth's Galliard in the Derby when the favourite finished only third behind winner St Blaise and runner-up Highland Chief. This time the rumours suggested that Archer pulled his horse to give a better chance to Highland Chief, trained by Archer's brother, Charles, a heavy gambler who stood to win a significant sum. This seems unlikely, given that when the two had ridden against each other in a race some years previously Fred had done his best to force his brother over the rails, almost breaking his neck, as Charles tried to come up his inside. However, the whispers continued, particularly when Lord Falmouth decided to withdraw from racing, ostensibly because of his age.

Archer's continuous wasting took a terrible toll on both his mental and physical condition. He rarely socialised with fellow riders and until marrying Helen Rose Dawson – the daughter of his trainer's brother – on 31 January 1883, he still lived in one room at the Heath House stable. The happy couple took up residence at Falmouth House which Fred had had built in Newmarket's Snailwell Road, naming it in honour of his loyal owner. Helen Rose gave birth to a child in January 1884, but the boy lived for only a few hours. She was pregnant again later that year and she gave birth to a baby girl. But Helen Rose died shortly after the baby was born. Archer visited the United States in an effort to overcome his sorrow but although his riding did not suffer, his mind was clearly grief-stricken.

When he landed the Derby in 1885 he even attracted the attention of the great wit of the times, Oscar Wilde. After Archer on Melton had outsmarted his great friend, Fred Webb, who was on Paradox, by putting the favourite, Melton's head in front right on the line, Wilde sent a congratulatory telegram: 'I understand that Milton's *Paradise Lost* is being revised, and will be published under the title of "Paradox Lost by Melton"'. The foiled Webb said of Archer, with whom he had been an apprentice, 'It is not wasting that makes Archer so thin and worn. He wears that worried look because he cannot ride two winners in one race.'

Archer won the 1886 Derby on Ormonde but later in the year had to waste hard to win on two mounts in Ireland in October and he was clearly sickening on his return; and when he was narrowly beaten by a head in the Cambridgeshire after weighing out a pound overweight on St Mirrin, he had developed a fever. He rode on for a few more days but illness eventually got the better of him and the balance of his mind was clearly affected when he committed suicide, shockingly enough in the presence of his sister, Emily, who tried desperately to prevent him, and leaving behind an estate worth £60,000.

Archer's ghost is said to haunt Newmarket Heath, and as recently as 1993 his spirit was reportedly present when stable lads held a séance at his former stables.

GEORGE ALEXANDER BAIRD
The Squire

A man whose local paper could say of his fortune that it 'had been squandered on horse-racing, prize-fighting and harlotry' and who once abducted a marchioness, and numbered amongst his mistresses, Lillie Langtry, must have had plenty going for him.

George Alexander Baird certainly had a hefty fortune to squander in the first place, having inherited an estimated £3 million jointly from his father, whose wealth had been made from the emerging railways, and an uncle who had also donated £200,000 to the Church of Scotland in what one cynic of his day described as 'the largest insurance premium against fire ever paid!'

Born in 1861 he became one of the most fascinating of turf personalities and even today there is confusion over the man's innate honesty – or otherwise.

Baird's biographer, Richard Onslow said of his subject: 'He spent many thousands of pounds as a patron of prize-fighting, and otherwise found his amusement in heavy betting, cock-fighting, dog-fighting, brawling and any other pursuit that made a noise, all of which may seem hardly edifying for a product of Eton and Cambridge.'

With his future inheritances to support his interests, Baird rapidly became one of the best amateur riders on the scene. However, the arrogance of youth and the flamboyance of his lifestyle may have offended the straitlaced old boys of the Jockey Club, who in April 1882 were able to bring him down a peg – or three.

Baird partnered his own Billy Banks in a selling race at Birmingham. The horse drifted in the betting market from 6/4 to 4/1 but won by eight lengths – only to be subsequently disqualified, for carrying the wrong weight. Not only that, but another rider in the race accused him of making 'highly offensive' remarks about his competence in the saddle and threatening to push him over the rails if he came too close to him.

The stewards included two men whose wives were believed to be on 'friendly' terms with Baird and the *Racing Calendar* duly reported that Baird, 'having been reported for foul riding . . . be warned off every course where the Grand National Hunt Rules are in force, for two years from this date.' To add to this, 'no horse his property, nominated by him, trained by him, or in any way under his care, joint care, management, or superintendence, be allowed to run for any race at any meeting.'

Down the years one can almost hear the 'chaps' declaring 'that'll sort the damned fellow out'. Not a bit of it, Baird just switched his horses into the nominal ownership of his best friend, 'Stiffy' Smith, who apparently returned the friendship by leeching cash from his wealthy pal.

Whilst under the warning off, Baird came of age and plentiful amounts of money was delivered into his bank accounts. He also became part of the rough-edged following of the boxing world, where he came into contact with many shady, unscrupulous figures, who referred to him as 'The Squire'.

Baird's contrary character showed itself off – he would have no compunction at playing often offensive, cruel 'pranks' on strangers, whose objections would merely occasion the intervention of Baird's gang of prize-fighters – however, 'a number of men about town in London, who put up with his nonsense and let him smash their hats or drench them with a brandy and soda, had no difficulty afterwards in touching him up for a substantial sum.'

Yet he was often generous and thoughtful to those in his circle – whether they were deserving of such treatment or not. Once, learning that a former friend, Captain Jimmy Shaw, was ill in Paris, Baird hired and paid for top medical assistance to rush to treat him.

The public prints had a field day with the activities of the man who adopted 'Mr Abington' as his nom de course.

Allowed back on the racecourse, his horse Busybody won both the 1000 Guineas and Oaks in 1884, then in 1887 Merry Hampton, who had cost him 3100 guineas, won the Derby, ridden by John Watts – who he paid a £5000 per year retainer. But once again Baird's behaviour caused a stir, when he refused to accompany the horse.

'Dash it all, George' said his friend Tom Spence, after congratulating him, 'go and lead your horse in.' But Baird refused point blank, 'remaining in a corner of the enclosure, apparently the least moved personage in the crowd' said one report. Another opined, 'I really believe he would have been far happier had he himself just ridden the winner of a selling race.'

He did very well when in the saddle himself and he kept his weight down by breakfasting on weak tea and castor oil. He would travel far and wide for his rides – 'he has been known to charter a special train in order that he might reach a northern racecourse in time to ride a horse for a £100 plate' noted Charles Adolph Voight, a close observer of the amateur riding scene of those times.

Generally riding on the flat, he did win a valuable hurdle race at Kempton on his own Theophrastus – betting £2000 on his mount.

He was very popular with the betting public, who were confident that his runners were allowed to run on their merits and would back them heftily. But his riotous lifestyle soon took its toll. Baird was in New Orleans with 'the boys' when he fell victim to a serious attack of pneumonia and malarial fever. He retired to his bed in the St Charles Hotel – and would never rise from it.

With his friend, pugilist and 'ruffian', Charlie Mitchell, maintaining a less than useful vigil over the sick-bed – all the time puffing away on a huge cigar and blowing smoke in Baird's direction whilst singing music hall songs and telling unsavoury jokes – The Squire grew weaker, before becoming delirious, and despite the tender ministrations of a concerned nurse, breathed his last on 18 March 1893.

Baird's body was repatriated on the *Majestic*, which sailed from New York, and his body was laid to rest beside his father in the family vault at Stichill in Roxburghshire.

When his Will was revealed it showed he had left £831,719, from which it was seen, reported one contemporary source 'that in his short life of 32 years he had run through something like £2 million'.

Baird's death came as a huge shock to his paramour, the Jersey-born actress, married beauty and society figure, Lillie Langtry. Lillie was an inveterate racegoer, and she had met Baird at Newmarket in April 1891 when The Squire insisted that she change her intended bet to place her money on his own horse, Quartus, which duly obliged at 5/2, after which he handed her a roll of cash to put on his Macunas in a later race – which also won at 4/7. Langtry, known to be partial to the odd shilling or two, was impressed and immediately accepted an invitation to dine with Baird. They became an item.

Reported chronicler of characters of those times, J. Wentworth Day, said: 'Baird had a notorious affair with Mrs Langtry, which he crowned by staging a rat-pit in the foyer of the Haymarket Theatre one Sunday afternoon, where all his friends were invited to try their dogs against cagefuls of London sewage rats.' How grateful Langtry must have been to be so honoured!

Born Emilie le Breton in 1853, the daughter of a clergyman, the famous actress and lover of the Prince of Wales (later King Edward VII), Lillie was known as the 'Jersey Lily' after the island where she was born. She raced as 'Mr Jersey' to conceal her identity as it was not the done thing for women to own horses. In that guise she saw her Milford, given to her by her lover, Baird, win the Coventry Stakes at the 1892 Royal Ascot meeting, after which there were hopes that Milford might win the Derby, thus making her the first female owner to do so. He didn't – but he did win her 10 more races.

She owned two Cesarewitch winners, Merman in 1897 and Yentoi in 1908. Following her second marriage she allowed her horses to race under her real name of Lady de Bathe.

She became the mistress of the Prince of Wales, later King Edward VII, in the 1870s, and they shared a love-nest in Bournemouth, now the Langtry Manor Hotel. She also gave some of her favours to Prince Louis of Battenberg, father of Lord Mountbatten.

Amongst her other prominent horses were Brayhead, winner of the 1897 Liverpool Cup; Maluma, the 1898 Lewes Handicap and the 1899 Prince Edward Handicap. Uniform took the 1899 Lewes Handicap for her. Her colours as 'Mr Jersey' were turquoise and fawn hoops, turquoise cap.

The *Sporting Life* reported on 22 March 1893 in a despatch from Nice, that 'Mrs Langtry heard of the death of Mr 'Abington' Baird while cruising in the Mediterranean on the *Whyte Ladye*. She made for this port with all haste, and displayed great anxiety to return to England immediately.'

The cynical assumed that she was anxious to find out how much she had been left. The answer was that Baird left everything to his mother and family. Lillie was said to be 'greatly distressed'.

Lillie died aged 75 on 12 February 1929, in Monte Carlo before being returned to be buried in Jersey.

LORD GEORGE BENTINCK

Early reformer

L ord George Bentinck was responsible for introducing into racing many of the features which shaped the sport as it is today. Born in 1802, he died in 1848, but achieved plenty along the way – albeit never his lifelong ambition of owning the Derby winner.

Bentinck it was who, as a prominent Jockey Club member, between 1836 and 1846, set about reforming racing when it was threatening to fall victim to crooks and villains. As early as 1827 his anti-gambling father, the Duke of Portland had established the right of the Jockey Club to warn persons off Newmarket Heath.

Bentinck continued and progressed the reforming work:

- He came up with the idea of dividing racecourse facilities into different priced enclosures.
- He introduced the concept of fining clerks of the course who started races late.
- He introduced the numbering of runners both on the racecard and on a course number-board. He also instigated a draw for numbered places at the start, with jockeys drawing out their allotted place from a bag. There was a £5 fine for starting from the wrong place.
- He insisted on an area for the saddling of runners.
- He introduced pre-race parades in front of the grandstand.
- He did away with the tradition of winning owners presenting the judge with a gift after important races.
- He raised the standards of officiating by judges and demanded greater standards of efficiency for the weighing out and in of riders.
- He reformed the way in which races were started, at a time when the usual method consisted of trying to line

the horses up before shouting 'Go' at them. He banned the use of starters with stutters – most notably one at Goodwood whose impediment often led to lengthy delays. Bentinck introduced a 'flag man' who stood in full view of the riders and dropped the flag when the starter was satisfied that they were in line – the signal for the race to get underway. He would even act as starter himself on occasion.

- He introduced fines for jockeys deliberately 'pulling' their mounts at the start.

A journalist of the time, writing as Sylvanus, was present when Lord Bentinck started the Great Yorkshire Handicap, describing his appearance:

'A tall, high-bred man with an air particularly his own, so distinguished yet so essentially of the country. He had all the eye and complexion of the true Saxon and the indescribable "air noble". His dress added greatly to the charms of his appearance. Dressed in buckskin breeches with exquisitely made boots of the true orthodox length and antique colouring in top; a buff waistcoat of reddish brown, double breasted coat ornamented with the buttons of the Jockey Club; a quiet beaver, placed neither at a right angle nor yet at a left, but in the juste milieu of gentlemanly taste, on a well-formed head of auburn hair, with large whiskers of the same colour.'

Bentinck was involved in the development of Goodwood racecourse and also helped to create a new Derby course at Epsom, enabling much more of the race to be seen from the stands.

A former Army officer not noted for reticence, Bentinck was a heavy gambler – losing £26,000 on the 1826 St Leger, (the year in which he became an MP) which wiped out most of his current assets and forced him to beg reimbursement from his family.

He became an owner a year later although, given his father's dislike of the turf's gamblers, he often hid behind pseudonyms.

He was prone to quarrels, falling out very publicly with a fellow officer, then doing the same with his racing partner – both resulting in acrimonious consequences. A rift with his trainer, John Day, came to a head in the Goodwood Cup of 1845 in which Bentinck beat Day's Weatherbit with his Miss Elis.

Some years previously in 1836, Bentinck had fooled racecourse touts and bookmakers alike when he encouraged them to believe his horse, Elis, would be a non runner in the St Leger because the horse was still at Doncaster shortly before the race with no apparent likelihood of being able to reach Goodwood in time. He cleaned up by taking the lengthening odds, safe in the knowledge that he had arranged to transport his runner in a specially constructed horse-box.

In another highly public incident Bentinck clashed with notorious racing figure of those times, Squire Osbaldeston, to whom he owed £200 from a bet. Bentinck made little effort to settle his debt and the affair resulted in a duel in which the crack shot Osbaldeston was, with difficulty, persuaded to spare Bentinck – firing a bullet through his hat rather than his head.

Bentinck's campaign against turf defaulters won the backing of influential *Bell's Life* – 'Honest men have to thank Lord George Bentinck for this valuable reform of the Turf'. But not everyone supported his efforts, even when he was prominent in the investigation which revealed that the 1844 Derby had been corrupt, with the winner, Running Rein, exposed as a four-year-old 'ringer', Maccabaeus.

'While he is thundering away against poor low-lived rogues for the villainies they have committed, he has been doing the same things which high minded men, like his father, who do not split hairs and make nice distinctions in questions of honour, would think nearly if not quite as discreditable and reprehensible' wrote former racing partner, Charles Greville – a cousin of his.

Bentinck's interest in the turf began to wane as he took on political causes and he sold off his entire stud for just £10,000. Amongst the horses he sold was Surplice. Bentinck's over-riding racing ambition had been to win the Derby, so when Surplice achieved just that in 1848, he was inconsolable. His political friend and subsequent Prime Minister Benjamin Disraeli, famously recalled Bentinck's reaction after Surplice won the big race: 'Bentinck gave a sort of superb groan' recorded Disraeli, "All my life I have been trying for this, and for what have I sacrificed it?"'

Within months Bentinck, whose horses had won seven Classics in all, was dead, from a heart attack.

DESERT ORCHID
Grey days

A combination of ability and an extraordinary equine charisma, set off by his ghostly grey colouring helped Desert Orchid capture the interest and affection even of people for whom horse racing normally barely registered beyond the Grand National. 'Dessie' lived up to his public image for years, even beyond the grave. He boasted his own fan club for 18 years, which was only wound up when co-owner, 'Midge' Burridge explained 'now he's gone it is time to call a halt, there is nothing more to say.'

Foaled on 11 April 1979 when he was initially described as bay in colour, and by Grey Mirage out of Flower Child, and at first given the name Fred, Desert Orchid lived for 27 years – eventually enjoying a longer retirement, during which he was feted and indulged, than even his lengthy racecourse career.

When in December 2005, his trainer David Elsworth left his Whitsbury training stables after quarter of a century, Dessie went along, too, to a new home, Egerton Stables in Newmarket, where Richard Marsh had trained the great 1896 Derby and St Leger winner, Persimmon and 1900 Triple Crown winner, Diamond Jubilee for King Edward VII.

Dessie drew attention to himself very early in his career, when he fell very heavily in a Kempton novice hurdle in 1983, leaving racegoers fearing that he was not going to survive as he stayed down for a lengthy period.

He took a while to come to himself and during 1984/85 was pulled up in the Champion Hurdle and fell on his last appearance of the season. But once he was switched to chasing he began to make his mark and won four races in succession.

In 1986 the Dessie legend really took off when, partnered by Simon Sherwood, and despite starting at 16/1 he bolted away with the King George VI Chase at Kempton by an astonishing 15 lengths from the likes of Wayward Lad, Forgive n' Forget and Combs Ditch.

Few of those present had actually backed the gelding but his front running, bold jumping display caught the eye of everyone watching at home over the Christmas period. He became a standing dish in this race, finishing second the next year, but then winning it in 1988, 1989 and 1990.

His 1989 Cheltenham Gold Cup victory was inevitably achieved in extraordinary circumstances – rain and snow had turned Cheltenham into a heavy going maelstrom – conditions which he just detested. But, as jockey Sherwood reported, 'I've never known a horse so brave. He hated every step of the way in the ground, and dug as deep as he could possibly go.' Fifty-eight thousand at the course, and millions watching on the box, held their breath as Dessie and the almost equally brave Yahoo, slugged it out in the final stages of the gruelling contest with Dessie staying on to win by one and a half lengths. Three cheers rang out for the horse after the race which was later voted the best ever by *Racing Post* readers.

Third in the same race in 1990, behind shock 100/1 winner, Norton's Coin, Dessie bounced back to carry 12st (75kg) to victory in the Irish Grand National, which he won by 12 lengths.

When he won the Agfa Diamond Chase at Sandown on 2 February 1991, you would have got long odds that this would be his final victory. He then finished third in the Gold Cup and ran two more races without winning, before having a final crack at the King George, in which he fell heavily three from home. As the riderless grey got up and ran past the finishing post the cheers were louder than they had been when winner, The Fellow, had passed it earlier. It was all over.

Dessie never ran in the Grand National – connections just felt the left-handed track would not bring out the best in him.

The horse won 34 of his 70 starts and collected over £654,000 in prize money. Retired after the 1991 King George, he survived a life-threatening operation for colic a year later. His presence raised hundreds of thousands for charity at various functions and public appearances – he took part in the pageant for the Queen Mother's 90th birthday – and his fan club added the best part of £50,000 to the total through sales of Dessie-related merchandise.

So popular did the horse become that a Christmas card sent from Australia to 'Desert Orchid, Somewhere in England' was successfully delivered. A rope used to lead him, which Dessie had chewed, was sold at auction for £120.

Dessie was also mentioned in a Budget speech, when Chancellor of the Exchequer Norman Lamont – reacting to a 1990 Gallup Poll which had established that Dessie boasted a national recognition factor of 84 per cent in contrast to his own 77 per cent, declared, 'Desert Orchid and I have a lot in common. We are both greys; vast sums of money are riding on our performance, the Opposition hopes we shall fall at the first fence – and we are both carrying too much weight.'

Dessie died shortly after 6am on 13 November 2006. His ashes were buried at Kempton Park racecourse where a statue pays tribute to him and he is remembered in the running of the Desert Orchid Chase.

There was an unpleasant postscript to the Desert Orchid story in July 2008 when a bronze plaque commemorating the horse was stolen just weeks after being unveiled in Whitsbury, Hampshire, where he spent so much of his life. Former racecourse judge and commentator, Nick Locock, whose idea the plaque was, vowed, 'Fortunately it was insured and as the cast has been retained, it can be replaced. This time we will find a less isolated place for it.' Which does, though, make you wonder why his commemorative plaque should ever have been sited in an isolated place.

Brough Scott penned an appropriate tribute to Dessie in his book *Of Heroes and Horses* – 'He was the warrior who would not weaken, the horse who led the charge under the banner "Fear and Be Slain". That's why we loved and admired him more than any other.'

STEVE DONOGHUE
Come on Steve!

Steve Donoghue learned his trade in France but became the most popular British jockey of his generation. Racing fans were always happy when the cry 'Steve's up' or 'Come on, Steve' was heard, indicating that Donoghue was riding a strong fancy in the next big race.

He was born in Warrington in 1884, the son of an iron worker. He was not the happiest of children, running away from home on more than one occasion, usually to a racing stable – from which he might then swiftly abscond – as he did from tough Middleham handler Matthew Peacock's establishment. He was on his toes again after taking a thrashing when his horse got loose on the gallops and upset the stable star, Flying Fox, at John Porter's Kingsclere Stables. He also had spells with Dobson Peacock and Alfred Sadler junior.

But at the age of 18 he took a post with American trainer Edward Johnson, who was plying his trade in Chantilly, France. He then moved to La Morlaye with George Dodd, thence to Marseilles with John Moore. In 1905, Donoghue finally got off the mark, partnering Hanoi, at Hyeres for M. Trabaud.

But he was hardly competing amongst the big boys, spending most of his saddle time at small, provincial courses. So, in 1907 he moved to Ireland, where he rode for Michael Dawson and Philip Behan, and was married in 1908 to Brigid, a daughter of Behan. Their son, Patrick, later had a brief riding career, winning the 1926 Lincolnshire on King of Clubs. Also in 1908 Donoghue scored his first win in England on Behan's Golden Rod at the Liverpool Spring Meeting.

Donoghue was no puritan, recalled racing writer, Lorin Knight: 'Donoghue and his friends were in the habit of visiting London night clubs as much as three or four times a week, seeking the company of society beauties and chorus girls. He was the Peter Pan of racing – the little boy who never grew up – he was feckless, warm hearted and often irresponsible.'

Donoghue, who 'once rode under NH Rules' according to 1932's *The Turf's Who's Who*, had eventually secured a retainer in Britain for 'Atty' Persse in 1911. Now he began to make headlines as he was partnered with the legendary sprinter, The Tetrarch, known as the 'Rocking Horse' or 'Spotted Wonder' because of his distinctive body markings of grey with what can only be termed white splodges. Many believe, to this day, he was the fastest horse ever to compete on the British turf. He was retired undefeated, albeit after only one season on the racecourse. Steve called the two-year-old, 'The nearest thing to a bullet in animal shape that I ever met. To be on him was like riding a creature that combined the power of an elephant with the speed of a greyhound.'

Donoghue did not let this chance to establish himself pass him by and he won Wartime substitute Derbys on Pommern in 1915 and Gay Crusader in 1917.

On a voyage to South Africa in 1916, he met and fell in love with a Lady Torrington. Wrote Lorin Knight, 'In any case his marriage had already broken down and an undefended divorce action was heard, at which Steve was granted a decree nisi on the grounds of his wife's misconduct with a former jockey.' No scandal ever affected Donoghue's public popularity, however.

In 1919, Donoghue found himself part of a bizarre and unique stewards' inquiry – held in public at Goodwood after Steve had been beaten on favourite Diadem in the King George Stakes when they had been left at the start. Punters were a little miffed with him and the stewards called him in and told him there was to be an inquiry. 'A few minutes afterwards I was making my way to the stewards' room, the proper place for an enquiry to be held when I was astounded to learn that this one was to take place on the open verandah outside, in full view of the public.' It was duly convened, but 'Of course, I was eventually exonerated of any blame.'

After the War he really came into his own and won the 'real' Derby on Humorist in 1921, going to the lengths of 'jocking' himself off of Lord Derby's Glorioso, despite being paid a retainer for first call on his services by that worthy, who was less than pleased with the situation. Minutes before the 'off', Donoghue had been handed a writ for an outstanding debt. Unconcerned, he stuck it into his silks and rode a great race to win on Humorist who, within a couple of weeks, had collapsed and died, suffering from lung disease.

Donoghue won the Derby again on Captain Cuttle in 1922 and Papyrus, 100/15, in 1923, when he again managed to avoid riding the horse his retaining owner – by then, Lord Woolavington – would have preferred.

Donoghue partnered Papyrus on an early celebrated international foray when the Derby hero was taken (along with his pal, the stable cat, Tinker, and five tanks of English water) to the States to challenge US equine champion, Zev, in what was intended to be a series of races over different distances. The dirt tracks over there were far from helpful to Papyrus and the first showdown, a match at Belmont Park, was run for a purse of $100,000 ($20,000 to the runner-up) over one and a half miles on 20 October 1923, after heavy rain, and Papyrus did not have the assistance of US horseshoes to help him get a grip on the slushy ground. That was little excuse, though, as his trainer declined them. Papyrus got first run, but was eventually well beaten by five lengths by the Kentucky Derby winner. The series went no further.

Missing out in 1924, Steve won again in 1925 on Manna. His experience of similarly sharp courses in France had clearly benefited him at Epsom.

He would collect 14 Classic victories in England, together with four Irish Derbys and two Grands Prix de Paris. He dominated the champion jockey title from 1914 until 1923 and in 1920 won 143 races, although in 1917 he won the title with a record low total of 42 winners.

Donoghue and the great stayer Brown Jack won the Queen Alexandra Stakes on six consecutive occasions, from 1929–34.

In 1929 Donoghue married music hall artiste, Miss Ethel Finn – the celebrity pair must have been an early version of the Beckhams! If you doubt that analogy, here is noted racing writer J. Fairfax-Blakeborough in 1932 – 'Even allowing for jockey hero-worship always associated with successful riders, there has probably never been an English jockey who has so captured the imagination and gained the confidence and popularity of racegoers as "Steve".' And in 1923, US magazine, *Time*, had reported that 'Tales are told of subjects literally kissing his feet when he entered a café shortly after winning the Derby.'

He broke his leg when Pamplona fell at Nottingham in 1930 and was out of the saddle for a lengthy spell. Visiting the States at the end of 1931 he was asked to stay over there to partner crack Australian horse, Phar Lap.

When Australian jockey W.R. Johnstone was beaten into third place in the 1934 Derby on 11/8 favourite, Colombo, Donoghue, who had won on the horse as a two-year-old, commented caustically, 'Had I ridden him he would have won on the bit by many lengths. Had any other English jockey who knew the course ridden him, he would have won comfortably.'

In 1937 came his last Classic winner, Exhibitionist in the Oaks, when he was 52, and his last mount came in Manchester's Final Plate that same year.

He was never found guilty by the stewards of an infringement of the Rules. He was a true horseman with a great empathy for the animals he partnered and was excellent on difficult two-year-olds. He suffered his share of dreadful falls – one of them on hard ground during the 1920 Derby. But he picked himself up, having been flung prone into the path of the oncoming field, walked back to the weighing room under his own steam – and rode two winners later that afternoon.

Donoghue was popular with the public, and never got too big for his boots, while his natural charm ensured that he was never short of admirers, some of whom may have been looking for what they could get – indeed, Donoghue was noted for his impulsive generosity which often resulted in his making hand-outs to those who had least deserved them.

He tried breeding and training but, as is so often the case, was nowhere near as successful as in the saddle.

He died suddenly on 23 March 1945, whilst visiting London, yet his name lives on – a Donoghue autograph from 1937 was for sale for £198 from an online memorabilia site in late 2008.

GORDON RICHARDS
Always a trier

Trainer Mark Johnston runs his stable under the proud slogan 'Always trying' – but it is a recycled boast, which originally applied to arguably the greatest of all British jockeys – Sir Gordon Richards, of whom it was quickly automatically stated by the media and his fans: 'Gordon always tries'.

Born in 1904, the son of a miner, he became a greater public idol than any before except Fred Archer, and any after except Lester Piggott. He rode from 1920–54, being greatly helped by the fact that unlike so many other great riders, he had no problems making the weight on his mounts and even aged 50 could do 8st 2lbs (51kg) comfortably.

He got his first mount in public – thanks to a football match. Gordon was a stable lad at Jimmy White's yard in Wiltshire and was playing right back for their soccer side, who were drawing 3-3 with minutes to go, when they were awarded a penalty. White shouted out that if Gordon scored from the spot he'd give him his first ride. Gordon scored, and shortly after, rode Clockwork into fourth place at Lingfield.

Richards, who stood a fraction under 5ft (1.52m) tall, rode 4870 winners from 21,843 mounts, was champion jockey 26 times and won 14 Classics. It was said of him by owner Lord Rosebery that much of his popularity stemmed from the fact that 'the greatness of Gordon Richards lay not in his having won so many races but in having lost so few that he ought to have won.'

Richards made an instant impact in his first full season as a jockey in 1925 when, having won 61 races as an apprentice the year before, he booted home 118 to win the title. In 1926 he had to overcome tuberculosis, which kept him off the track until the next season when he regained his title with 164 victories.

However, he did not ride a Classic winner until 1930 when he took the Oaks on Rose of England and the St Leger on Singapore. He again surrendered the title this season but in a dramatic style not seen again until the dead heat between Seb Sanders and Jamie Spencer in 2007. Richards had come from six down at the start of the final week of the season, to go one up on the last day – until rival Frederick Fox hit back to win the fourth and fifth races of the afternoon, and with them the championship.

It was only loaned to Fox as Richards took it back in 1931 when he became first jockey to Fred Darling's powerful stable at Beckhampton.

In 1933 Richards made history by riding 259 winners – including an amazing run of 12 straight victories. This winning streak began at Nottingham on 3 October when the 29-year-old rode Barnby to score in the final event of the day. Next day at Chepstow, Gordon kicked off by winning the St Andrews Plate on 4/6 favourite, Manner. The Clearwell Selling Plate saw a routine win for even money shot Brush Past, before he won the Bulwark Selling Plate on Miss B and the Severn Stakes on Arcona. Then came a five length cruise for Red Horizon, 7/4 favourite in the Glanely Handicap, setting up the perfect through-the-card six timer as filly Delicia won the Castleford Handicap by a length. The crowd sang, 'Little man you've had a busy day' to him after racing. On a day when Richards had 'thought I would only win one race' he had won the lot without ever having to brandish his whip in anger.

That morning he had even dissuaded assistant trainer Herbert Arnold, who had taken the train to Chepstow with him from backing his six mounts in mixed doubles. Richards later learned that Arnold's boss, Classic winning trainer Frank Hartigan 'had a £5 accumulator on me and won several hundred pounds'

For Richards the afternoon was 'a wonderful experience. I had promised to attend a boxing match at Swindon that night' he recalled, 'and when I turned up they gave me a tremendous reception.'

So, back to Chepstow next day and he opened on The Covenanter at evens, then landed his ninth consecutive winner on Kirrimuir at 4/6, and the tenth on June Rose, 9/4. At this point, revealed Richards in his autobiography, *My Story*, 'even the bookmakers' satchels were being thrown in the air in the general enthusiasm and excitement'. I can only assume bookies were cut from a different cloth in those days! I reckon it's more likely those satchels were being shaken about to try and find some small change hidden there to help with massive payouts. Next, in went Montrose, backed down to 4/7 favourite, and the dynamic dozen was completed by even money chance, Lady Swift.

Would it be unlucky 13? The bookies feared not, and installed Eagle Ray a prohibitive 1/3 favourite, a horse of which Richards said, 'I did not think I could possibly be beaten, as in my view this was the best bet of the whole meeting'. But his luck finally came to an end, and Eagle Ray could only manage third behind the 15-year-old Doug Smith-ridden winner, Lament whose jockey later quaintly remarked 'I had the most collywobbles in my stomach when I realised I had beaten Gordon and stopped his run.'

Racegoers weren't best pleased with Smith, who would later finish runner-up to Gordon seven times for the title, either. After the last race, taking the bus to Wantage to catch his train home, he heard a fellow passenger mutter darkly, 'If I could lay my hands on the little blighter who beat Gordon today I'd kill him.'

It was said that at his peak many bookies were so afraid of financial wipe-out because of the sheer weight of support from small money punters for everything Gordon rode that they refused to offer bigger than 3/1 about any mount he partnered.

Gordon finished second in the 1934 Derby on Easton – his tenth failure to win the Blue Riband. It was beginning to become a matter of comment – and in 1936 he was again second in the great race, rather unluckily, on the hampered Taj Akbar. In this season he rode in over 1000 races. 'I used to book all my rides – no agents in those days – so I'd be on the phone as much as I'd be on a horse.' He was on the favourite in 1937, but Pasch could only manage third. Richards was out of action with a broken leg when, in 1941, his probable mount, Owen Tudor, won the substitute Derby, the Wartime equivalent, run at Newmarket. He was on board odds-on Big Game in 1942 but finished unplaced. In 1944 partly due to the stresses of his job and also of the war, Richards was close to a nervous breakdown and was also suffering bouts of depression. 'Looking back, it seems to me that I nearly went mental.'

After the War, with Gordon in top form again, with 212 winners in 1946, he seemed sure to break the Derby duck in 1947 with 2000 Guineas winner Tudor Minstrel, the 4/7 favourite – but fourth was the best he could manage. The disappointment was eased a little as he set a new record with 269 winners for the campaign.

With Fred Darling now retired, Noel Murless – later Sir Noel – took over the stables but still Gordon couldn't land the Derby.

In 1953 Gordon was knighted for his services to racing shortly before the Derby meeting was run. With characteristic modesty he said, 'I am delighted to receive the honour but I am more delighted at the honour it brings to my profession.'

Murless had no runners in the race, so Gordon was able to take the ride on Sir Victor Sassoon's Pinza. It was his 28th Derby ride. It would be his last. The racing gods smiled on him and, despite the fact that he was beating the new Queen's Aureole into second place, the cheers were immense as Gordon and 5/1 joint favourite Pinza won the race by four lengths.

Gordon was set to partner Her Majesty's Landau in the Derby in 1954 but was injured. He recovered in time for Royal Ascot where he won on Landau, and was third on the same horse in the Eclipse at

Sandown's July meeting. But as he left the paddock on Abergeldie in the next, the filly suddenly reared up and fell backwards, rolling on Sir Gordon and breaking his pelvis and dislocating four ribs in the process. Although he was already planning to retire at the end of the season, the injury prompted him to do so there and then, and he set up as a trainer, with 30 two-year-olds in his charge, sending out his first winner The Saint, for Dorothy Paget, on 9 May 1955.

He trained successfully – albeit without Classic-winning success although he had horses placed in the 2000 Guineas, Derby and St Leger – and retired at the end of the 1969 season, to manage the strings of Mr Sobell and Lady Beaverbrook.

'No shadow, not even one the faintest of grey, ever hung over Gordon Richards' marvelled racing writer Michael Tanner, and that impression was reinforced when he became the first jockey made an honorary member of the Jockey Club. He died in 1986.

ROBERT SIEVIER
Hansom devil

Reputedly born in a London hansom cab in 1860, Robert Standish Sievier was 'an adventurer with very few moral scruples and a great deal of charm' declared the authoritative *Biographical Encyclopaedia of British Flat Racing*.

He was a man quite happy to live on his wits and who would seek to improve his financial position by making money on the racecourse or at the card table. He was also prepared to manipulate the rules to his own advantage wherever possible.

Educated in France, by the age of 16 he found himself in South Africa serving in the Frontier and Armed Mounted Police, having left behind his mother, now a widow. He saw action in South Africa's Zulu Wars, but in his early twenties moved continents again and arrived in Australia where he set himself up as a bookmaker and got involved in high stakes card games; one of which ended in mysterious and tragic circumstances when a man was discovered dead beneath the balcony of Sievier's home – an incident which he seemed unable to explain in any acceptable manner.

Racing journalist Geoffrey Hamlyn, who knew Sievier, recalled, 'Prior to the First World War, Sievier was the most prolific gambler on the turf. He had gone to Australia and revolutionised betting there. Before his arrival most bookmakers bet on the double, usually, "this race and the next". Furthermore, no one ever got paid until settling day.' Sievier set about changing all that: 'When I took up my position on Adelaide Racecourse, I created no little excitement, and when I announced that I would pay on every race immediately and that my transactions would be confined to single and not double events, the bookmaking fraternity looked on me in wonderment, but the public came up smiling and I did a roaring trade. At the end of the first day I showed a profit of £1500, and all the papers next day stated that a prominent English bookmaker had arrived and had paralysed betting in South Australia.'

When Hamlyn met Sievier, he had fallen on hard times, and 'borrowed' a fiver from him – 'but I thought it a great honour to be tapped by such an illustrious figure!' With a failed marriage in Australia behind him, Sievier was back in England by 1888, when he was declared bankrupt. As usual he managed to find a way of emerging relatively unscathed by the situation and within six months he had been discharged and was again to be found at his favourite gambling and racing haunts.

Wife number two arrived in 1893 in the shape of Lady Mabel Brudenell-Bruce, sister to the Marquess of Ailesbury and who had horses with trainer Robert Sherwood, who had won the Derby in 1855, riding Wild Dayrell; then in 1884 sent out St Gatien as a trainer to dead heat in the premier Classic. Sherwood died following a fit in October 1894, and his son, also Robert, took over.

Sievier was running a bookmaking business trading under the name of 'Mr Punch'. Thomas Henry Dey, later to become a well-known bookie in his own right, started his career there and recalled some of Sievier's strokes. Because of his own love of a bet Sievier would frequently raid the coffers for gambling money. 'Unfortunately, Sievier was not satisfied to back only his own horses' remembered Dey, 'But he would back almost any tip that was given to him. Fred Allsopp, the jockey who rode for him, used to wire him his fancies regularly, and it was rarely that Sievier allowed any of them to run unbacked. In addition, he had many counsellors who were tipping to him, and the inevitable result of there being "too many cooks" was that Sievier lost on balance backing horses.'

After 'Mr Punch' ran into difficulties, Sievier changed business names to Field Syndicate, and came up with a cunning way of letting clients think he was fully solvent. He gave Dey 'a fistful of sovereigns, and again another handful, commanding me to throw them loosely into a small drawer in my desk, then to ask claimants in to see me, and nonchalantly offer to offer to pay out of petty cash, at the same time displaying a drawer full of gold.'

Sievier's financial position seemed to improve, perhaps courtesy of his wife, perhaps courtesy of the time he told Dey 'that his pluck in playing up his winnings had won him a quarter of a million'. He placed his horses with up and coming Charles Morton at Wantage, who would send out 11 early 20th century Classic winners.

He won £30,000 when Diamond Jubilee won the 1900 Derby and was £53,000 ahead at the end of that week – 'It was always my practice to play up my winnings' he later wrote, 'What has broken more men on the turf than anything is chasing their losings and buttoning up their winnings.'

In 1901 Morton trained Sievier's two-year-old, Sceptre, purchased as a yearling at the dispersal sale of the late Duke of Westminster's stables, but declined to prepare the horse for the following season's Classics. Sceptre had cost him a hefty 10,000gns, (paid up front, in cash) a record for a yearling at the time, and money which he had acquired from some betting coups – notably Sir Geoffrey winning the Lincoln, The Grafter taking the City & Suburban, and two-year-old Toddington obliging on a couple of occasions when well fancied and backed.

Sievier had bought at the same dispersal sale a horse called after its former owner, Duke of Westminster, and offered to return either that horse or Sceptre to its previous ownership. Vanity got the better of the nobleman, who gratefully accepted back Duke of Westminster, which never won a race.

With Sievier short of a trainer for Sceptre, the owner acquired a stable of his own at Elston House in Shrewton, where he installed and then dispensed with an American handler who turned out not to be up to the task, whereupon Sievier decided to do the job himself.

The filly proved herself to be something special, uniquely winning four of that season's five Classics in Sievier's colours of black, gold facings and sleeves, and red cap. She missed out only in the Derby – for which Sievier had backed her like a good thing, and also crashed to defeat in the Park Hill Stakes. Sievier's wins on her had come at short odds and his financial condition was again parlous as he was struggling to afford the costs of running the stables, which housed other, less successful inmates running in his name. He offered to take on any other horse 'at weight for age and sex for £10,000 over any distance up to 1m' with Sceptre. There were no takers. Sievier, facing bankruptcy again, had no option but to cash in on his main asset and he sold her in 1903 – complete with instructions to 'treat her like a selling plater.' He explained: 'We were compelled to sell Sceptre for reasons we are not ashamed of. We had to meet financial obligations. We sold her to Sir William Bass for £25,000.'

He now launched a sporting paper of his own, *The Winning Post*, which he used to settle scores, engage in feuds and carry on disputes with many and varied turf figures, amongst them wealthy owner J.B. Joel and Epsom trainer Richard Wootton. 'R.S. Sievier's pen has always been as bold as his actions in Turf affairs, milk and water is neither his beverage nor has he used it when writing' said racing historian John Fairfax-Blakeborough.

Sceptre ran 25 races, winning 13, value £38,225, finishing second five times and third three times. The horse died in 1926 and the *Bloodstock Review* eulogised her – 'it is hardly conceivable there was ever a greater racing mare' – and of Sievier it said, 'His career has been one of wildly fluctuating fortune. Within the space of a few months he would be poor, rich, then poor again, but whatever the state of his finances he was invariably optimistic and nonchalant.'

He also found himself in court on a number of occasions fighting various suits. Then in 1904 Sievier was sensationally, mysteriously and almost certainly unjustly warned off. No reason was offered. There was no indication that he had broken any of the Rules of Racing. His enemies had gained revenge on him.

He did, though, have some friends at the Jockey Club and Senior Steward Lord Durham managed to have him reinstated in 1907, the year after his (Sievier's) autobiography was published.

He was by no means intimidated by what had happened, and was soon back to what he did best – pulling off a betting coup, this time with Warlingham, purchased out of a seller at Newbury and then prepared to win the Cesarewitch in 1912. Sievier had bet £2000 at 33/1, and that £66,000 was worth around £3 million in today's values. With it he splashed out and bought Fitzroy House in Newmarket. He was granted a licence to train – but there were still those out there who wanted to rain on his parade, and in 1919 – after he had won the Lincoln with Lady Queensberry's Bucks, his licence was withdrawn – allegedly because as a member of the press he was forbidden from being a trainer.

A racing writer of the time, F.H. Bayles wrote, 'There is nobody who groans less under defeat or displays less outward elation at success. R. Sievier has had full share of animus directed at him. I doubt very much if there is one of his enemies who does not possess all his faults and shortcomings, yet could not boast of a single one of his good qualities.'

His horses were then sent to former jockey Walter Griggs, a man most noteworthy for the fact that he died in Switzerland in 1972 during a game of curling.

Sievier's finances were again in disarray and he went for broke, lining up Monarch for a tilt at the 1922 Victoria Cup and backing it heavily – only to be frustrated when the horse was beaten a short head by The Yellow Dwarf.

A year before his death, Sievier was quoted by the influential *Bloodstock Breeders' Review* as saying, 'In my day, a fellow had to know his business before he trained horses. Nowadays, all a fellow has to do to become a trainer is to walk down St James's Street and buy an umbrella.'

He had never regained his peak financial status, but remained a student of the turf and maintained a regular racecourse presence until attending for the final time on the first day of the Royal Ascot meeting of 1939 and expiring in October of that year.

Sievier once heard that someone had described him as 'a gambler, pure and simple.' 'I may be pure' he snorted, 'But I am not simple.'

CHARLIE SMIRKE
Gentleman Charlie

If a renowned racing character like trainer Clive Brittain declares that a particular jockey is the person with whom he would most like to have a dinner party, you can rest assured that jockey will have something about him which sets him aside from the common herd.

Brittain's dining companion would be Charlie Smirke. 'I only met him towards the end of his career, but 'Gentleman Charlie' was a real boy, always living life to the full,. dressed to the nines and up in London, clubbing.'

He was a popular man – jockey's valet, Fred Dyer, said of him: 'Very few jockeys have been really generous, but Charlie Smirke was one of them. He was a character but a very particular man. If he saw a little piece of cotton on his breeches he'd pick it off straight away'.

Smirke's love of the world outside of racing might well explain why in 1975 Tom E. Webster was moved to comment, 'It's funny that a lot of people when they finish racing, like Charlie Smirke and Harry Carr, never go again'. No odder, though, in all honesty, if you think about it, than a builder not wanting to get into DIY when he retires, or a rock singer recoiling at karaoke.

Smirke's yardstick of success as a jockey was that 'the test of a good jockey isn't the races he should win; it's the ones he wins that he shouldn't win.'

And a man whose own reputation was founded on just that ability, was, for him, extravagant with his praise for Smirke when he attended his funeral on the final day of 1993 'He was certainly the best jockey I've ever seen in my lifetime' said Lester Piggott.

Born a Cockney on 23 September 1906, in Lambeth, London, the son of a boxer, the precocious Charles James William Smirke, who would rack up 11 Classics including four Derbys, rode his first winner on 8 April 1922 when he was 15, partnering an un-named filly to victory in Derby's Highfield Selling Plate. Apprenticed to Epsom-based Stanley Wootton, he had first ridden in public on 27

August 1921, finishing third on King George, which carried a mere 6st 5lbs (40kg), at Gatwick.

Smirke's lengthy association with the Derby began in 1924 – when he still weighed under 7 stone (44kg) – and would end over a third of a century later in 1959. That first ride, on complete outsider, Bucks Yeoman, was dramatic – the horse fell. Incidentally, proof that these were more innocent days – winning jockey, 21-year-old Tommy Weston, celebrated victory with his wife, by jumping aboard a wooden horse on the fairground merry-go-round on the Epsom Downs.

Smirke became retained by the Aga Khan in 1926 – although he didn't get on too well with the Aga's trainer, R.C. Dawson – and continued to ride on and off for that worthy for another 30 years. In March of the same year he wed Miss Alice Marie Hyams, the youngest daughter of Epsom trainer, George – and to demonstrate the status Smirke already enjoyed, they jetted off from Croydon for their honeymoon in Paris.

On 31 August 1928 Smirke was partnering hot favourite Welcome Gift, 4/11, at Gatwick. They were left at the post as the race got under way. Starter, Captain Hubert Allison accused him of having made no effort to start. The Jockey Club held an inquiry and withdrew Smirke's licence, obviously believing that it had been a deliberate act to miss the break. However, it seemed he had been very harshly treated, as Welcome Gift went on to acquire a reputation for dwelling at the start of races.

But Smirke had to earn a living while he couldn't ride – he took menial jobs, but at one point was so hard up that he had to sleep under a tarpaulin on Brighton beach. A useful amateur boxer he also earned cash by sparring with pros.

Every year without fail he applied for his licence to be returned. Every year the appeal was turned down. At one point he was told that he would never be re-considered. It was five years – 26 October 1933 at Newmarket – before he was permitted to ride again.

Returning in 1934 Smirke promptly hit the headlines again as he won the Derby on 15/2 third favourite, Windsor Lad for the marvellously named Maharajah of Rajpipla, which went on to add the St Leger to his record. The Maharajah revealed – 'A few days before the Derby, I was at a private party at which there was a fortune teller. I was persuaded to have my fortune told. "You are going to win